Lecture Notes in Computer Science 6615

Commenced Publication in 1973
Founding and Former Series Editors:
Gerhard Goos, Juris Hartmanis, and Jan van Leeuwen

Bruce Christianson   James A. Malcolm
Vashek Matyas   Michael Roe (Eds.)

Security Protocols XVI

16th International Workshop
Cambridge, UK, April 16-18, 2008
Revised Selected Papers

 Springer

Volume Editors

Bruce Christianson
University of Hertfordshire, Computer Science Department
Hatfield AL10 9AB, UK
E-mail: b.christianson@herts.ac.uk

James A. Malcolm
University of Hertfordshire, Computer Science Department
Hatfield AL10 9AB, UK
E-mail: j.a.malcolm@herts.ac.uk

Vashek Matyas
Masaryk University, Faculty of Informatics
Botanicka 68a, 602 00 Brno, Czech Republic
E-mail: matyas@fi.muni.cz

Michael Roe
University of Hertfordshire, Computer Science Department
Hatfield AL10 9AB, UK
E-mail: mroe@cornstalk.org.uk

ISSN 0302-9743   e-ISSN 1611-3349
ISBN 978-3-642-22136-1   ISBN 978-3-642-22137-8 (eBook)
DOI 10.1007/978-3-642-22137-8
Springer Heidelberg Dordrecht London New York

Library of Congress Control Number: 2011930676

CR Subject Classification (1998): K.6.5, E.3, C.2, D.4.6, H.4, H.3

LNCS Sublibrary: SL 4 – Security and Cryptology

Typesetting: Camera-ready by author, data conversion by Scientific Publishing Services, Chennai, India

Printed on acid-free paper

Springer is part of Springer Science+Business Media (www.springer.com)

Preface

Welcome to the proceedings of the International Security Protocols Workshop. For the 16th workshop in our series we returned to our traditional home in Cambridge. Our theme this year was "Remodelling the Attacker."

We tell our students at the start of a security course that it is very important to model the attacker, but like most advice to the young, this is an oversimplification. Shouldn't the attacker's capability be an output of the design process as well as an input? The papers and discussions in this volume examine the theme from the standpoint of various different applications and adversaries, and we invite you to join in.

People sometimes ask us how we manage to select such an impressive array of contributions to the workshop each year; surely it must take the Programme Committee an impossible amount of time to review all the submissions? Well no, because we don't do it the conventional way. If you make a submission to the workshop[1] it *will* be read by *everyone* on the Programme Committee, but each reader is asked only to return a single score (Win, Draw, or Lose) rather than a detailed review. As with Association Football[2], we award 3 points for a win, and 1 for a draw in the belief that this will reward attacking play. The scores for all the reviewers are simply added. This means that a controversial paper (gaining equal numbers of 3 and 0 scores) will outrank a solid but boring one (which would get just 1 point from each reviewer). Our intention is to select position papers that have potential to spark an interesting discussion, ideally one that will result in the paper being substantially re-written.

The down-side of this is that if your paper is rejected you won't automatically get any feedback. But you do get to hear pretty quickly — the review process takes just over 3 weeks. With this in mind, why not join in? We look forward to receiving your submission and welcoming you to a future workshop.

As usual, our particular thanks to Lori Klimaszewska of the University of Cambridge Computing Service for making the initial transcription of the audio tapes.

January 2011

Bruce Christianson
James Malcolm
Vashek Matyas
Michael Roe

---

[1] Generally advertised in December, at `spw.stca.herts.ac.uk`; let us know if you would like to be alerted by e-mail.

[2] `http://en.wikipedia.org/wiki/Three_points_for_a_win`

Previous Proceedings in This Series

The proceedings of previous International Workshops on Security Protocols have also been published by Springer as *Lecture Notes in Computer Science*, and are occasionally referred to in the text:

15th Workshop (2007), LNCS 5964, ISBN 978-3-642-17772-9
14th Workshop (2006), LNCS 5087, ISBN 978-3-642-04903-3
13th Workshop (2005), LNCS 4631, ISBN 3-540-77155-7
12th Workshop (2004), LNCS 3957, ISBN 3-540-40925-4
11th Workshop (2003), LNCS 3364, ISBN 3-540-28389-7
10th Workshop (2002), LNCS 2845, ISBN 3-540-20830-5
9th Workshop (2001), LNCS 2467, ISBN 3-540-44263-4
8th Workshop (2000), LNCS 2133, ISBN 3-540-42566-7
7th Workshop (1999), LNCS 1796, ISBN 3-540-67381-4
6th Workshop (1998), LNCS 1550, ISBN 3-540-65663-4
5th Workshop (1997), LNCS 1361, ISBN 3-540-64040-1
4th Workshop (1996), LNCS 1189, ISBN 3-540-63494-5

Table of Contents

Remodelling the Attacker
(Transcript of Discussion)

Bruce Christianson

University of Hertfordshire

Welcome to the 16th Security Protocols Workshop, or the XVIth Workshop for those of you still think in Latin, and consequently don't regard IP6 as an advance over IPv1. Our theme this year, the Mornington Crescent of protocol design, is Remodelling the Attacker.

We tell our students at the start of a security course that it's very important to model the attacker, but like most advice to the young, this is at best an oversimplification, and at worst verges on hypocrisy. Even when we know what the attacker is capable of before we start — and we usually don't find this out until after the protocols have been deployed — shouldn't the attacker's capability be an output of the design process rather than an input? Are we modelling the attacker, or are we modelling our knowledge of the attacker? This is a distinction that can become very important when the model changes over long periods of time.

The problems for confidentiality protocols are reasonably obvious. If we have a policy that says, we must not publish these documents until 50 years from now, then when we decide whether or not to use RSA, we are making a judgement about who is going to have a quantum computer at any point in the next 50 years. But when we look at protocols for integrity, it's really not clear how you could ever ensure the integrity of a document that has been in a paperless office for 50 years. For integrity even one-time pad doesn't work. A safe approach is to print a paper copy, and then you just have the problem of how to certify the paper copy. It's really hard to see how to do something equivalent to that certification for a purely electronic artefact.

Do we even have a sufficiently strong notion of identity to distinguish ourselves from the attacker over a period of 50 years? Bear in mind that we are very unlikely to have any personal control over any national identity repository. And in consequence, can we really sustain any practical difference between a vulnerability and a threat?

We have some people who haven't been here before as well as some who have, so I shall just run very quickly through the rules of engagement. This is intended to be a workshop and not a conference, so we expect that what you say should depend on what other people have already said in previous sessions. The talks have been carefully arranged to follow a sequence, and when you present you should try and lead a discussion rather than just delivering a lecture that you prepared before you came. Please reflect on what previous speakers have said, and don't be afraid of taking a risk. If the discussion goes in an unexpected direction, then please let it: don't try and haul it back onto the rails, just ride the wave and see what happens.

B. Christianson et al. (Eds.): Security Protocols 2008, LNCS 6615, pp. 1–2, 2011.

We record the discussions, and those of you who have looked at previous proceedings will see that a transcript of the discussion is published after the revised version of the position paper. Don't panic, you will be able to revise the discussion paper in the light of the discussion, and the transcripts that we publish do not always bear a close resemblance to what was actually said. If we go down a particular line of thought, and it doesn't work, we'll either delete it, or else make it say what should have happened.

Finally, all breakages must be paid for: if you break somebody else's protocol, then you have to try and help them fix it.

We work hard to make this a reasonably secure environment in which to stand up and make a fool of yourself. Here it really is better to speak up and be thought a fool than to remain silent and be mistaken for asleep[1].

---

[1] I actually said "a sheep", but already the transcript has taken on a life of its own.

Fighting the 'Good' Internet War

Dan Cvrček* and George Danezis

[1] University of Cambridge, UK & Brno University of Technology, CZ
[2] Microsoft Research, Cambridge, UK

Abstract. We review the current strategies to counter Internet threats under the light of the classic strategy literature. The literature often advocates proactive action, and dominance of the (virtual, in our case) battlefield, which is the opposite from what we see defenders deploy today. Their actions are instead reactive and exclusively defensive. We propose strategies for defenders to regain the initiative and push security solutions far beyond the reach of current security tools — yet those strategies start mirroring the actions and technologies of the bad guys, and confront us with important technical, legal and moral dilemmas.

> *"He who fights with monsters should be careful lest he thereby become a monster"*
>
> *Friedrich Nietzsche* — Beyond Good and Evil, Chapter IV: Apothegms and Interludes

1 Looking for the Adversary...

Security engineering textbooks [1] teach us that the most prevalent and damaging enemy comes from within an organisation. Yet in the PC and the Internet era not everyone is part or protected by an organisation, or by its system administrators. Huge numbers of home users are left on their own to fend off a number of attackers. They are left exposed to attack by their ignorance of the existing threats, inadequate technical knowledge, the overwhelming dangers stemming from anonymity of Internet, and the huge gap between user interface and correct functionality.

Their vulnerability is not the users' fault, as they cannot be expected to be technical experts, to browse the Internet, send emails, or play games. They make up a huge group of people and machines that without being malicious easily become hostages of real attackers, and a fertile ground from which attacks are launched.

The real Internet enemy are small groups of highly technically skilled people that use innocent and unaware users to carry out their criminal, and usually highly lucrative, activities. Some easily visible signs of their existence include

---

* Dan is partially supported by the Research Plan No. MSM, 0021630528 — Security-Oriented Research in Information Technology.

B. Christianson et al. (Eds.): Security Protocols 2008, LNCS 6615, pp. 3–11, 2011.

the huge quantities of spam, phishing sites or large-scale operations attracting users to anchor on pages packed with malware, to turn their machines into bots.

These all are observable signs of the enemy's existence but still, the enemy itself is well hidden. Our goal, in this paper, is to suggest strategies and tactics to uncover them.

2   Waging War — History Lessons and Internet Warfare

Humanity has a long history of military conflicts, from which we can learn. This section picks some interesting ideas from several famous military strategists, namely Carl von Clausewitz [CvC] [2], Antoine-Henri Jomini [AHJ] [4], Sun Tzu [ST] [6], Mao Ce-Tung [MCT] [5], and Maurice's Strategikon [MS] [3]. Ideas that we find useful for even a warfare in a digital environment — it shows that some military principles go way above military actions.

2.1   Military Strength

Some key elements of strength are outlined from Carl von Clausewitz's [CvC] work:

- Strength of forces is not only defined by numerical strength and their organisation, but also with their relationship to "country and terrain", *i.e.* they should take the environment into account. The relative strength of the forces can be improved by advanced guards and outposts, proper lines of communication, and the command of heights [CvC].
- The defence is built around several types of elements: militia (armed population that can be effectively used to defend enemy), fortresses (strongholds that offer protection but also gain influence), the people, and allies. [CvC]
- The defence in physical sense comprises of: defensive position (it cannot be bypassed), flank position (can be bypassed by the enemy, but it holds), defence of special types of terrain (swamps, flooded areas, forests, . . .). [CvC]

Internet. Attackers are well aware of the importance of terrain: they overtake weakly defended machines, to use them as a multiplier of their strength. Hiding behind those hosts also makes them invulnerable to direct technical or legal attacks. This behaviour, and the logical extension to [CvC] suggestion is the foundation of *guerilla warfare*, the study of which is of some importance in the context of Internet conflict.

The fortresses can be viewed as security vendors and their services offering protection mechanisms — probably a common view today. Their infrastructure, be it incident handling, virus reverse-engineering, signature updating, or monitoring should be strengthened against attempts to disable it.

The militia are the security aware Internet users, that deploy security software, sometimes aid in the monitoring of threats or debugging of applications, as well as apply security patches. Their role is not offensive, it is rather to make it difficult for the adversary to gain more ground from which it can launch attacks. Their coordination can happen through security vendors, as well as on a peer-to-peer level.

2.2   Initiative

Clearly, the side that is more active is also able to enforce the rules of the warfare. This is important for any type of warfare and also extensively covered.

- Aggressive action will deprive enemy of time. It will make him do quick decisions and increase the chance of strategic errors [ST].
- All the resources must be engaged, and the purpose of the engagement is one of: destruction of enemy, conquest of locality, conquest of object [CvC].

Internet. Every action on the digital battlefield must be carefully prepared, because the actions will be instantaneous, responses automated, and the fight very short. Aggressive action may force the enemy to alter their tools and procedures, omit some precautions, to become nervous. The goal will be to create pressure on speedy actions that are not routine and require manual interventions.

What are the goals of our fight? It will differ from time to time. Probably, we will want to conquest an object — a botnet operated by the enemy. We may want to clean users' machines, but we would then be forced to defend an area, which would require a lot of resources. We want to hit heads and cut them from the rest of the enemy's army (botnets). Finally we may want to destroy the enemy — find the operator of the bot net, and who they work for, and secure a conviction against them.

2.3   Tactics

We believe that tactics used to combat malicious parties on the Internet are always a step behind and a strategy does not really exist. However, Jomini stated several centuries back that the key to warfare is strategy. Let us start with several notes from history.

- There is an asymmetrical relationship between attack and defence. One should try to reverse the asymmetry whenever possible. Attacks have several decisive advantages of attack: surprise, benefit of terrain, concentric attack, popular support, and moral factors [CvC].
- Divide and conquer, a particular tactics that further developed *e.g.* by Matyas Rakosi for Hungarian Communist Party in the late 1940s as salami tactics, uses alliances to increase political power [AHJ].
- If you use a common sense, you are inevitably doing a bad strategy choice [ST].
- Inner line of operations, *i.e.* operations inside the enemy's army will allow for fighting separate parts of the enemy's forces [ST].
- Divide forces to arouse the masses, concentrate forces to deal with the enemy. Red Army fights by conducting propaganda among the masses, organising them, arming them, and helping them to establish ... power [MCT].
- Mobilisation of the whole nation forces the enemy to "defend the area" and we can pick the right time and the right place to fight battles [MCT].
- Ambushes are of the greatest value in warfare. The most powerful is an ambush from both sides and the timing should be precise to maximise the effect [MS].

Internet. We believe that we can make use of most of the tactics used above. The most proper seem to be Mao Ce-Tung's principles.

Yet the most neglected advice when it comes to Internet conflict, is the focus on offence. Defenders make no attempt to 'reverse the asymmetry' and instead believe that security shall come by digging deeper trenches around the few secured hosts. This gives the adversary full strategic advantage to attack when, where and how she wishes.

2.4   The Power of Information

Many commanders have quickly realised the power of information and careful planning. Interestingly, there are more rules related to concealment of own actions and strengths.

- Hiding real purpose of actions is an important element in strategy [CvC].
- Conceal your plans, or plan for several steps ahead [ST].
- One should not engage enemy in combat or show their strength before learning the enemy's intentions [MS].
- One should prevent hostile reconnaissance and thereby conceal the second line of their forces [MS].

Internet. There is a warfare already and so we can learn a bit about our enemy and study their behaviour. We can design new tools and use them in the war but no-one is really doing any plans. We are fighting isolated battles and loosing the war.

The plans are very easy to read if anyone bothered to do that, as the threat posed by them is very small.

The organisation of the enemy consists of a head, support groups (organise specific crimes), and working units. The working units will cover the following activities: vulnerability discovery, exploit design, spam management, managing DNS records, coding, web site building and managing, managing botnets, sales agents.

The most activities are offline and the enemy goes on-line only the manage the botnets and web sites, and sales agents). It is also possible to detect the on-line malicious activities — the actual attacks. We can learn from the way the bot-nets are commanded and organised, but our tools must be equally stealthy so they cannot become easy targets in the wars of bot-nets.

3   Battleground

The battleground is already set by the enemy — organised crime groups. We cannot change it and we do not want to change it, in fact. It is formed by users that are most vulnerable. These are not actively trying to get rid of the negative effects the enemy's activity has on their machines, but they could be easily persuaded to join the warfare by providing their computing resources.

3.1 Enemy

The organised groups use a very flexible structure and hide their on-line activities among unaware Internet users.

- Heads of operations — they are on-line only for short periods of time, and there are no limits regarding the place of their Internet connections.
- Information gathering servers — must be on-line for considerable amount of time (at least hours) but they can be physically moved around. The connection is provided via updated DNS records.
- Bots — users' machines that are taken over by the group and used for various types of hostile activities. These are not directed against owner of the machine, thus decreasing incentives for the owner to deal with the situation.

It is very hard to find the heads or the servers gathering information. The only chance is to find the machines forming the botnets. So what is the goal of the war?

3.2 Current Tactics and Strategy

The good guys are so far reasonably predictable and the organised crime groups made provisions against them. We can see two basic approaches the good guys use:

1. Develop and sell security mechanisms
2. Identify dangerous websites and provide the information to interested users

Obviously, neither approach is trying to fight the enemy directly. They only protect those users who are vigilant and aware of security threats. When we take into account the size of this niche security market and compare it with the total number of the Internet users, we can see that it does not hurt the enemy the least. The basic problem of the above mentioned approaches is that they target different subset of users from those targeted by bad guys. What is the structure of the enemy's army?

The approach for an effective fight would be similar to the Mao Ce-Tung approach — to use "the people" and to create the "militia". First of all, however, we have to learn and find the enemy.

3.3 Reaching the Battleground

The key problem for securing systems today is to reach the digital battleground and to encounter the enemy at all. Current defence strategies are reactive: poorly fortified systems are lame ducks, to attacks launched from behind the crowd of innocent yet compromised machines. While feeling the full might of the adversary, our only reaction is to mend our shields in the hope they will resist the next round of offensive technology innovation. No one is surprised when in the long run they break!

The main problem is the communication channels the good guys employ. Security vendors expect customers to fly to them and pay good money to be afforded any protection. Unfortunately most home users not only do not seek those products but are definitely not ready to pay for them, even in the rare cases they are aware they exist.

The adversary, on the other side, is targeting exactly those users that security vendors fail to attract. Using spam or search engines as their communication channel, they attract security unaware users and turn their machines into part of the digital battleground.

Defenders will never effectively fight the enemy until they are able to reach, one way or the other, those users. This will involve distributing security software in innovative ways to meet the adversary.

- The most obvious way to reach users who follow-up links and get infected through spam is to *use spam*. Some may object to this tactic, by arguing that it might train users to click on spam even more. We do not advocate running an advertisement or awareness campaign promoting the of untrusted software. At the same time we have to recognise that the only way to reach users that have not been moved by campaigns with the opposite message is through this channel.

- A second vector of infection are unpatched machines running services with known vulnerabilities that are waiting to, or are already, infected with malware. It is only a question of time until those are turned to weapons against third party systems. Clearly the most forward way of reaching those machines is exploiting the vulnerability to install software.

  Again, many objections can be raised including legal and technical ones. The first objection is that overtaking an unpatched machine may lead to financial damage or may affect its stability. This is undoubtedly true, and only a matter of time until this damage is caused by a malicious user taking over the machine for nefarious purposes. It is all good keeping our hands clear, and arguing that at least the damage was not caused through our actions; yet on the utilitarian balance sheet we have let a greater evil take place: the machine being infected and the computer being used for further mischief.

- Similar strategies can be deployed using any infection or propagation vector that malware utilises, as well as vulnerabilities in the malware itself, that is often not of the highest quality. Web-pages serving infected files, search engine poisoning, phishing sites, *etc.*

  Those strategies can also be deployed against networking equipment that stands unpatched and vulnerable, such as cable modems or wireless routers that are misconfigured or buggy.

A common objection to the *efficacy* (leaving aside the numerous objections as to the *morality* of the matter) of this deployment strategy is that intrusion detection systems, anti-virus software or security services will detect and neutralise our deployment attempts. Hosts that deploy those counter-measure should be deemed safe, and would not the least benefit from the active attempts to block the adversary described above. Yet if those protection systems would be universally deployed and effective we would not be witnessing the levels of compromises we do today — the day they are the proposed deployment approach would be unneeded, at the safe time it stops being effective.

3.4 Identifying the Enemy

Once we have found means to deploy software on the digital battleground that is comprised by infected machines, the battle is just starting. It may be tempting to be too earnest at this point, patch a single security vulnerability and vacate the ground. This strategy is naive, since a vulnerability is probably indicative of a pattern of security neglect typical of a user and a machine, rather than a one-off incident.

Instead of doing a quick cleaning job the position represented by the machine should be fortified and the defenders should be ready to hold their ground. This means deploying effective tools to allow us to carry out tactical decisions and plans. The tools should implement tasks within the main strategic plan: reconnaissance, analysis of information, elimination of the enemy's activity, as well as trace the enemy.

The reconnaissance activity should be able to retrieve as much useful information as possible. At the same time, the tools used on the battleground must be hard to detect and circumvent — it's necessary to use stealthy and polymorphic technologies, as well as hard to detect communication channels. The adversary who owns the compromised territory acts as a defender that might have deployed sophisticated systems to prevent us from reaching it and freeing it.

One could envisage the following components being needed:

- Monitoring capabilities being deployed reporting and aggregating information on lists of processes, start-up processes, outbound and inbound network connections and their details, or unusual system activity. Defenders can use these to detect out breaks, vulnerable services, as well as track attackers.
- Since the adversary will attempt to disrupt communications a robust, and DoS resistant networking infrastructure has to be constructed. This involves allowing the defensive software to create a peer-to-peer mesh and use it for robustness as well as hiding the command and control centres of the defensive operation.
- The deployed software itself should be hardened against any detection mechanisms the adversary might have deployed on compromised hosts. This mandates the use of polymorphic code, stealthy root-kits as well as obfuscated binaries.
- Finally the back-end system — databases for storing important data, analysing observations from robots, and issuing commands — have to be hardened against attacks, or even better hidden using covert communications.

It is obvious that if one is serious about conquering back the infected ground that the adversary controls, they cannot limit themselves to conventional

technologies. They have to be ready to put on their offensive hat, to defeat a
well motivated and security aware defender — in this case the adversary.

Yet no strategy deployed should be at the detriment of prudent security practices. The offensive deployment strategies described here should gracefully fold
back in case the user installs proper protective software or a serious patching
regime is followed. It is not acceptable to try to disrupt those, merely to allow
for offensive propagation to still be possible — this is *a key moral distinction*
between those that offensively deploy software as a self-defence strategy versus
the adversary that does it for malicious purposes.

4   The Permanent War Economy

No conflict is ever settled for good. Any resolution is based on political strategy
that depends hugely on economic interests and the relative power of all parties.
(No one will negotiate as long as they think they can unconditionally win.)

The cost of law enforcement has to always be compared to the significance of
the crime. This significance from the social point of view is different from the
profitability of the crime that would be limited. Economic tools can be used to
model equilibriums but it is unlikely that crime can be completely eliminated so
long as there is an economic incentive for it. Hence it is unlikely that defenders
will ever stop their activities, and there is a need to find sustainable ways to
finance the perpetual defence effort.

The money for waging the war should not be received from the "battleground", from users allowing us to use their machines. Although it is probably
possible to differentiate offered services to attract some reward: monitoring a
machine can be for free, but a fee can be charged for the removal of malware.

A secondary source of revenue may be entities interested in data about the
state of Internet threats to assess overall potential dangers. We could inform
potential targets of *e.g.* DDoS attacks about the danger and negotiate a price
of further services if they find the information valuable. Or if an attack cannot
be blocked, we may be able to identify the source of the attack and allow thus
future crime prosecutions.

The general idea would be to build the business model on the revenues from
big players and potentially services for common users (Robin Hood strategy).

Acknowledgements

We thank the research institutions that employ us and that in no way share the
views expressed in this paper.

References

1. Anderson, R.: Security Engineering: A Guide to Building Dependable Distributed
   Systems, p. 640. Wiley, Chichester (2001)
2. von Clausewitz, C.: Principles of war, London, John Lane, p. 64 (1943)

3. Maurice, emperor of the East. Maurice's Strategikon: handbook of Byzantine military strategy / translated by George T. Dennis, p. 178. University of Pennsylvania Press, Philadelphia (1984)
4. Jomini, A.-H.: The art of war. Greenhill Books, Presidio Press, London, Calif (1992)
5. Paret, P., Craig, G.A., Gilbert, F.: Makers of modern strategy: from Machiavelli to the nuclear age, p. 941. Princeton University Press, Princeton (1986)
6. Tzu, S.: The Art of War (2008), http://www.sonshi.com

Security Protocol Deployment Risk

Simon N. Foley[1], Giampaolo Bella[2,3], and Stefano Bistarelli[4,5]

[1] Department of Computer Science, University College Cork, Ireland
[2] SAP Research, Mougins, France
[3] Dipartimento di Matematica e Informatica, Università di Catania, Italy
[4] Dipartimento di Scienze, Universitá degli Studi "G. D'Annunzio", Pescara, Italy
[5] Istituto di Informatica e Telematica, CNR, Pisa, Italy

Abstract. Security protocol participants are software and/or hardware agents that are — as with any system — potentially vulnerable to failure. Protocol analysis should extend not just to an analysis of the protocol specification, but also to its implementation and configuration in its target environment. However, an in-depth formal analysis that considers the behaviour and interaction of all components in their environment is not feasible in practice.

This paper considers the analysis of protocol deployment rather than implementation. Instead of concentrating on detailed semantics and formal verification of the protocol and implementation, we are concerned more with with the ability to trace, at a practical level of abstraction, how the protocol deployment, that is, the configuration of the protocol components, relate to each other and the overall protocol goals. We believe that a complete security verification of a system is not currently achievable in practice and seek some degree of useful feedback from an analysis that a particular protocol deployment is reasonable.

1 Vulnerabilities in Deployed Protocols

The deployment of a protocol is a collection of interacting software/ hardware components that collectively implement the protocol in its environment. Components range from agents that fully implement a protocol principal, for example, an authentication server running on a bastion host, to entities that partially support the principal, for example, a hardware token authenticator. These components may suffer a variety of vulnerabilities.

Design Vulnerabilities are errors in the underlying design of the protocol whereby it fails to achieve its intended security goals. For example, a replay attack on the protocol that enables a principal to masquerade as a different principal [2,5].

Implementation Vulnerabilities. The software that implements the protocol may be vulnerable to attack. For example, a component with a buffer-overflow vulnerability may be vulnerable to a stack-smashing attack from another principal that could lead to, for example, disclosure of keys, replay attack, *etc.* Improper

B. Christianson et al. (Eds.): Security Protocols 2008, LNCS 6615, pp. 12–20, 2011.
© Springer-Verlag Berlin Heidelberg 2011

implementation of a client may also facilitate an attack, for example, a Kerberos client that does not discard the user-password (long-term key) once the ticket-granting ticket/key is obtained from the authentication server.

Configuration Vulnerabilities are a consequence of any improper configuration of the component that might lead to its compromise. For example, an authentication server that stores long-term cleartext keys in a file that is accessible by all users. An authentication client that incorporates a hardware token authenticator might be considered less vulnerable than a client that relied on a fixed password for its long-term secret.

System Vulnerabilities. The platform that hosts a component may itself be vulnerable to attack. For example, deploying an authentication server on a system alongside a web-server would be considered a poor choice. Similarly, hosting an authentication server on a hardened bastion host managed by a competent administrator might be considered less vulnerable to attack than hosting it on an out-of-the-box workstation that has outstanding software patches.

There are many further vulnerabilities that could be considered, for example, cryptographic API vulnerabilities, vulnerabilities in weak cryptographic operations, and so forth. We do not intend to analyse or model vulnerabilities per-se, but instead reflect vulnerability and threat in terms of an abstract degree of *confidence* that we have in a component's secure and proper operation. The degree of confidence of a component can be based on evidence (a 'correct' protocol running on a bastion host) and/or subjective views (the administrator of this system is considered to be incompetent). We do not intend to only consider the deployment of components for which we have complete competence: we are interested in determining whether protocols that are deployed as combinations of good, bad and indifferent components are good enough.

2   Protocol Deployment Risk

Degree of confidence [6] is defined in terms of the set C of confidence levels that is ordered under $\leq$. This is interpreted as: given $a, b \in C$ then $a \leq b$ means that we have no less confidence in a component with confidence level b than a component with confidence level a. For example, we might define confidence levels lo $<$ med $<$ hi, with the obvious interpretation, for example, we have lo confidence in a component executing on an open-access workstation and have hi confidence in an authentication server executing on a bastion host. In this paper a c-semiring [3] is used to represent degree of confidence. This provides a variety of measures for confidence, ranging from simple orderings such as lo $<$ med $<$ hi to numeric measures such as fuzzy and numeric weightings.

We consider confidence in the context of the cryptographic keys that the protocol components are expected to manage. For example, we might have a high degree of confidence that an authentication server component, with few known vulnerabilities, properly secures the keys that it manages; this might reflect a confidence that it will not leak keys to the public channel.

Another ordering $\leq$ is defined over the class of cryptographic keys referenced in the protocol to reflect the degree to which they require protection [1]. For example, a long-term password would be considered more critical than a short-term session key, since compromise of the latter is a once-off threat, while compromise of the former may lead to repeated attacks. The set $\mathcal{K}$ of key classifications forms a lattice under $\leq$ with a lower bound element public that represents the public channel.

Example 1. An authentication and key distribution server Trent manages long term and session keys. Trent shares long term keys with principals Alice and Bob, and issues short-term session keys. The following Needham-Schroder style protocol is followed to achieve key exchange. For the moment we do not consider the components that Alice, Bob or Trent might comprise.

$$\text{Msg } 1 : A \to T : A, B, N_A$$
$$\text{Msg } 2 : T \to A : \{\!|K_{AB}, A, B, N_A, T_T|\!\}_{K_A}, \{\!|K_{AB}, A, B, T_T|\!\}_{K_B}$$
$$\text{Msg } 3 : A \to B : \{\!|K_{AB}, A, B, T_T|\!\}_{K_B}$$

Three symmetric keys K_A, K_B and K_{AB} are used in this protocol, and we define corresponding key classes levels Ka, Kb and Kab; class public corresponds to the public channel.

Figure 1 defines the class ordering $(\mathcal{K}, \leq)$. Long-term keys are used to transfer session keys and, therefore, we have Kab < Ka and Kab < Kb where Ka and Kb are disjoint (cannot deduce one from the other), and $\top$ defines the universal upper bound on the ordering. This reflects an assumption in the protocol that long-term keys are considered more security-critical than session keys: in the absence of ephemeral keys, loss of the long-term key implies loss of the short-term keys (but not vice-versa). $\triangle$

The key classification ordering defines the flow constraints between keys, for example, long term key Ka information should not be permitted to flow to session key Kab information. Rather than relying on a binary interpretation of how key related information may/ may not flow, we take a qualitative-based approach that is similar to the notion of assurance in [9,7]. Define

$$minConf : \mathcal{K} \times \mathcal{K} \to \mathcal{C}$$

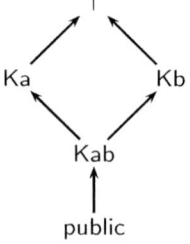

Fig. 1. Key classification ordering $(\mathcal{K}, \leq)$

where $minConf(k, k')$ defines the minimum confidence required across the protocol deployment that a key of class k does not flow to class k'. The lower bound $\perp$ in the confidence c-semiring is interpreted as no flow restriction and thus, if $k \leq k'$, then $minConf(k, k') = \perp$ in the confidence c-semiring, since, in this case, the flow is permitted.

Example 2. Consider the set $(\mathcal{C}, \leq)$ of confidence ratings nil $<$ lo $<$ med $<$ hi, where nil is the lower bound and corresponds to no flow restriction. Given the protocol in Example 1 then there are no flow restrictions on public as a source, that is, $minConf(\text{public}, x) = \text{nil}$ for any $x \in \mathcal{K}$. By reflexivity of $(\mathcal{K}, \leq)$ we also have $minConf(x, x) = \text{nil}$ for $x \in \mathcal{K}$.

Key class $\top$ represents the most security-critical key (aggregate of the long-term keys) and we define:

$$minConf([\top, \text{public}]) = \text{hi} \qquad minConf([\top, \text{Kab}]) = \text{hi}$$
$$minConf([\top, \text{Ka}]) = \text{med} \qquad minConf([\top, \text{Kb}]) = \text{med}$$

An authorization server that manages both long-term keys and the session key (interval $[\text{Kab}, \top]$ requires greater confidence (hi) in its protection than its clients (confidence med) that manage one long-term key and session key; in the former, we require greater confidence that the keys cannot be leaked. We have:

$$minConf([\text{Ka}, \text{Kab}]) = \text{med} \qquad minConf([\text{Ka}, \text{Kb}]) = \text{hi}$$
$$minConf([\text{Ka}, \text{public}]) = \text{med} \qquad minConf([\text{Ka}, \top]) = \text{nil}$$

with a similar definition for Kb. Protecting only a session key requires less confidence:

$$minConf([\text{Kab}, \text{public}]) = \text{lo} \qquad minConf([\text{Kab}, \text{Ka}]) = \text{nil}$$
$$minConf([\text{Kab}, \text{Kb}]) = \text{nil} \qquad minConf([\text{Kab}, \top]) = \text{nil}$$

$\triangle$

Each protocol component can be regarded as managing a number of different kinds of keys. The authentication server in Example 1 manages Ka, Kb and Kab key and the client manages Kab and Ka keys. Every component c, is bound to an interval of the key classification lattice, where $int(c) = [l, h] \in \mathcal{K} \times \mathcal{K}$, and $l \leq h$ is interpreted as follows:

- l is the lowest classification key that the component encrypts messages with. Here encrypt is like 'send' in terms of information flow between key classifications.
- h is the highest classification key that the component decrypts messages with. Here decrypt is like 'receive' in terms of information flow between key classifications.

We also write $int(c) = [int_\perp(c), int_\top(c)]$.

Each protocol component c also has a confidence rating given as $rating(c)$ that also reflects the minimum effort that would be required by an attacker to compromise component c. For example, we might have high confidence in the authentication service in Example 1 that is deployed on a hardened SELinux server, but have low confidence in the client component implemented as freeware and running on an open-access workstation. In the case of the authentication server we are confident that keys will not be leaked nor messages encrypted/decrypted in a way that does not follow the protocol specification. This confidence comes from a belief that the protocol is properly implemented and that it is unlikely that the hosting server can be compromised. On the other hand, and in the absence of further information, our degree of confidence that an open-access workstation running freeware follows the protocol and/or cannot be compromised, is low as it may be subject to a variety of attacks ranging from Trojan Horses in the protocol implementation to vulnerabilities such as buffer overflows in the underlying system.

Example 3. The components in Example 1 are defined with the following intervals.

c	$int(c)$	$rating(c)$
A	[public, Ka]	med
B	[Kab, Kb]	med
T	[Kab, $\top$]	hi

Principal A manages keys in the range [public, Ka], because it sends/encrypts data on the public channel and decrypts/receives up to Ka class information. Note that in this deployment we assume that principals B and T do *not* write to the public channel.

The table also provides sample confidence *rating* for principals. We have medium confidence that principal B properly protects its key information in the range [Kab, Kb] — this assumes that B does not access to the public channel — perhaps B is known to be confined to a protection domain which does not give it direct access to the public channel. In practice, the rating of a component should depend on the keys it protects: we might have a high degree of confidence that B does not write Kb information to the public channel while have a medium degree of confidence that it does not write Kb to Kab. For the sake of simplicity in this paper we restrict ourselves to the interpretation of the *rating* function as a property of the component that is independent of the keys it manages. $\triangle$

Definition 1. Each protocol component must meet the minimum required confidence, that is, for every component c then

$$\forall x, y : \mathcal{K} \mid int_\perp(c) \le x \le int_\top(c) \land int_\perp(c) \le y \le int_\top(c)$$
$$\Rightarrow minConf(x, y) \le rating(c)$$

that is, the component achieves the required degree of confidence for every pair of keys that it manages. $\triangle$

When a deployed protocol executes, there is a resulting flow of messages between components. Let $A_x \rightsquigarrow B_y$ represent a flow of a message encrypted using an x-level key by A and decrypted using a y-level key by B.

Definition 2. A protocol configuration is *classification-safe* if for all components A and B then,

$$A_x \rightsquigarrow B_y \Rightarrow x \leq y \wedge int_\perp(A) \leq x \leq int_\top(A) \wedge int_\perp(B) \leq y \leq int_\top(B)$$

$\triangle$

Example 4. The protocol in Example 1 has three direct flows: $A_{\text{public}} \rightsquigarrow T_{\text{public}}$, $T_{\text{Ka}} \rightsquigarrow A_{\text{Ka}}$ and $T_{\text{Kb}} \rightsquigarrow B_{\text{Kb}}$, and is classification-safe. We expect that the analysis in protocol entailment, described in [1], can be adapted to provide a semantics for the $\rightsquigarrow$ relation. $\triangle$

3   Cascading Risks in Protocols

The *cascade vulnerability problem* [9,8] is concerned with secure interoperation, and considers the *assurance risk* of composing multilevel secure systems that are evaluated to different levels of assurance according to the criteria specified in [9]. The transitivity of the multilevel security policy upheld across all secure systems ensures that their multilevel composition is secure; however, interoperability and data sharing between systems may increase the risk of compromise beyond that accepted by the assurance level. For example, it may be an acceptable risk to store only secret and top-secret data on a medium assurance system, and only classified and secret data on another medium assurance system; classified and top-secret data may be stored simultaneously only on 'high' assurance systems. However, if these medium assurance systems interoperate at classification secret, then the acceptable risk of compromise is no longer adequate as there is an unacceptable cascading risk from top-secret across the network to classified. Similar cascading risks can be demonstrated in a security protocol.

Example 5. We extend the protocol in Example 1 to include mutual authentication using the session key K_{AB}.

$$\text{Msg4 } B \rightarrow A \ \{\!|A, B, T_T|\!\}_{K_{AB}}$$
$$\text{Msg5 } A \rightarrow B \ \{\!|A, B, T_T - 1|\!\}_{K_{AB}}$$

As a consequence of these additional protocol steps we have additional explicit flows between A and B involving the key K_{AB} in the protocol. These flows ($A_{\text{Kab}} \rightsquigarrow B_{\text{Kab}}$ and $B_{\text{Kab}} \rightsquigarrow A_{\text{Kab}}$) represent the encryption-sending and receiving-decryption using K_{AB} by both A and B. Since A and B are trusted to manage this classification of session key, these flows are classification-safe.

The confidence rules require a minimum confidence level of hi for a component to be considered trusted to manage both Ka and Kb keys. Having a confidence of hi, component T is considered trusted to manage both Ka and Kb keys. Confidence can be considered to represent the degree of confidence that one can have that a component cannot be compromised. In this case, the effort required by an attacker corresponds to the effort required to compromise the hi-rated T, and, for example, reveal K_A to B using the following (modified) message run.

$$\alpha \text{Msg 2: } T \rightarrow A \ \{\!|K_{AB}, A, B, N_A, T_T|\!\}_{K_A}, \{\!|K_{AB}, A, B, K_A|\!\}_{K_B}$$

As long as the effort required to compromise T is at least hi, then the risk of this attack is considered acceptable.

Consider an attacker that compromises component A. In this case the effort required by the attacker corresponds to the effort to compromise a med rated component A, and, for example, embed a Ka classified key in a message encrypted by session key with classification Kab, and send it to B; this effectively copies a Ka key into a Kb key.

$$\beta \text{Msg 4 : } B \rightarrow A \ \{\!|A, B, T_T|\!\}_{K_{AB}}$$
$$\beta \text{Msg 4 : } A \rightarrow B \ \{\!|A, B, K_A|\!\}_{K_{AB}}$$

However, the confidence requirement is that in order to copy Ka to Kb requires at least the effort to compromise a level hi rated entity, while the above attack is achieved by compromising med-rated components.

The protocol contains a cascade vulnerability. Individual components meet the minimum ratings based on the $minConf$ confidence rule defined above, however, the interoperation of A and B due to the mutual authentication step in the protocol does not. There is a cascading path from a Ka key managed by component A to a Kb key managed by component B, via session key K_{AB}. △

Example 6. The previous example assumes that the components A and B are trusted to properly manage both long-term and session keys and that these keys are continuously available. However, in practice, both keys are typically not continuously available to the component. For example, a Kerberos login client discards its long term key (user passwords) once a ticket/session key has been obtained; if one-time passwords are used, the client does not have any access to the underlying long term secret.

In order to better reflect this situation we model each protocol client (A, B) in terms of two separate component entities: a login/connection manager and a session manager. These are intended to correspond to the software components that implement the component. The login manager is responsible for properly using the client's long- term key to obtain the session key and then handing this key off to the client's session manager.

We extend the protocol description to include these components, where A^{conn} and A^{sess} correspond to the connection and session managers that represent A, and similarly for B.

$$
\begin{array}{lll}
\text{Msg 1:} & A^{conn} \rightarrow T & A, B, N_A \\
\text{Msg 2:} & T \rightarrow A^{conn} & \{\!|K_{AB}, A, B, N_A, T_T|\!\}_{K_A}, \{\!|K_{AB}, A, B, T_T|\!\}_{K_B} \\
\text{Msg 2i:} & A^{conn} \Rightarrow A^{sess} & K_{AB}, A, B, N_A, T_T \\
\text{Msg 3:} & A^{conn} \rightarrow B^{conn} & \{\!|K_{AB}, A, B, T_T|\!\}_{K_B} \\
\text{Msg 3i:} & B^{conn} \Rightarrow B^{sess} & K_{AB}, A, B, T_T \\
\text{Msg4:} & B^{sess} \rightarrow A^{sess} & \{\!|A, B, T_T|\!\}_{K_{AB}} \\
\text{Msg5:} & A^{sess} \rightarrow B^{sess} & \{\!|A, B, T_T - 1|\!\}_{K_{AB}}
\end{array}
$$

c	$int(c)$	$rating(c)$
A^{conn}	[Kab, Ka]	hi
A^{sess}	[Kab, Kab]	med
B^{conn}	[Kab, Kb]	conn
B^{sess}	[Kab, Kab]	med
T	[Kab, ⊤]	hi

Fig. 2. Component intervals and ratings for the extended protocol

In this protocol, $P \Rightarrow Q : M$ represents the sending of a message M over an internal/private software channel from P to Q that is assumed secure. In practice this could be implemented as message passing or API calls within the platform that implements the clients.

Figure 2 provides revised interval and ratings for the components of this revised protocol. Note that we assume high confidence for the connection managers on the basis that we have high confidence in the proper operation of the login client and that long-term keys are not available once session keys are issued. The session managers in the example are rated as med but can be safely rated as lo given the minimum requirement $minConf[\mathsf{Kab}, \mathsf{Kab}] = \mathsf{lo}$.

The protocol generates the following flows between its components.

$$T_{\mathsf{Ka}} \rightsquigarrow A^{conn}_{\mathsf{Ka}}; \ A^{conn}_{\mathsf{Kab}} \rightsquigarrow A^{sess}_{\mathsf{Kab}}; \ A^{sess}_{\mathsf{Kab}} \rightsquigarrow B^{sess}_{\mathsf{Kab}};$$
$$T_{\mathsf{Kb}} \rightsquigarrow B^{conn}_{\mathsf{Kb}}; \ B^{conn}_{\mathsf{Kab}} \rightsquigarrow B^{sess}_{\mathsf{Kab}}; \ B^{sess}_{\mathsf{Kab}} \rightsquigarrow A^{sess}_{\mathsf{Kab}}$$

Based on the ratings in Figure 2, it follows that the flows between these components are individually classification-safe. △

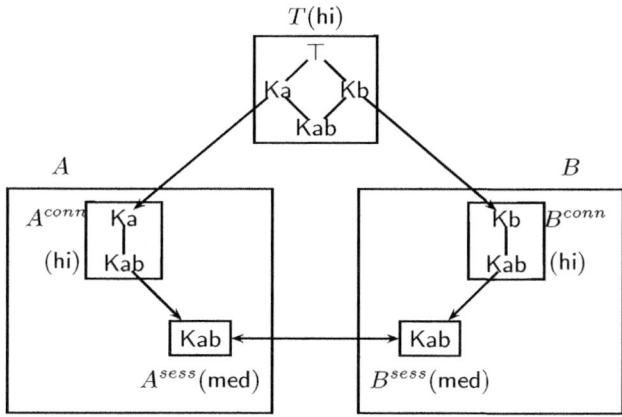

Fig. 3. Cascade-free configuration for the Kerberos-style protocol

4 Discussion

In this paper we considered a quantitative-based approach to evaluating the deployment of security protocols. The approach focuses on how confidence in protocol components can be traced across the deployment; it does not analyse vulnerabilities in the underlying behaviour of the components (for example API attacks [4]) or their interaction (for example protocol analysis [5,2]), though such techniques could be used to inform the degree of confidence measure.

A Needham-Schoeder style protocol deployment was analysed in this framework. For reasons of space and ease of exposition, the deployment was deliberately simplistic. Nevertheless it was possible to demonstrate a variation of the channel cascade problem in the deployment. It would be interesting to explore a richer deployment that included, for example, authenticator token components and components that are dynamically selected during the initial protocol parameter negotiation phase that is typical of practical protocols.

References

1. Bella, G., Bistarelli, S.: Soft constraint programming to analysing security protocols. Theory and Practice of Logic Programming 4(5), 1–28 (2004)
2. Bella, G.: Formal Correctness of Security Protocols. In: Information Security and Cryptography. Springer, Heidelberg (2007)
3. Bistarelli, S.: Semirings for Soft Constraint Solving and Programming. LNCS, vol. 2962. Springer, Heidelberg (2004)
4. Bond, M., Anderson, R.: API-level attacks on embedded systems. Computer 34(10), 67–75 (2001)
5. Dolev, D., Yao, A.C.: On the security of public key protocols. IEEE Transactions on Information Theory 29(2), 198–208 (1983)
6. Foley, S.N.: Conduit cascades and secure synchronization. In: Proceedings of ACM New Security Paradigms Workshop (2000)
7. Foley, S.N., Bistarelli, S., O'Sullivan, B., Herbert, J., Swart, G.: Multilevel security and the quality of protection. In: Proceedings of First Workshop on Quality of Protection. LNCS, Como, Italy. Springer, Heidelberg (2005)
8. Millen, J.K., Schwartz, M.W.: The cascading problem for interconnected networks. In: 4th Aerospace Computer Security Applications Conference. IEEE CS Press, Los Alamitos (1988)
9. TNI. Trusted computer system evaluation criteria: Trusted network interpretation. Technical report, National Computer Security Center (1987) (Red Book)

Security Protocol Deployment Risk
(Transcript of Discussion)

Bruce Christianson
(for Simon Foley)*

University of Hertfordshire

The level of confidence you need in the secrecy of the key you are using to upload your initials to the high score on Tour of Duty is probably different to the confidence you need to do a multi-million pound transaction. So the basic idea of this model is to classify cryptographic key sensitivity in terms of some sort of partial order: authentication master keys are more sensitive than the keys that they're used to protect; and generally a session key that is encrypted under a long term key is less sensitive than the long term key that's being used to encrypt it. If you've got the higher one, then it's possible to obtain the lower one, simply by looking at what's gone through the protocol. For example, if your protocol has got a message like that in it, then this key is below this one in the partial order.

Here is a Needham-Schroeder style protocol. We can think of the keys as corresponding to communication channels between the principals who share them. For the moment we'll just think of the components as corresponding to the principals, we're going to think of each principal as one blob, and within each principal there's a little lattice which consists of the keys that that principal, that component, can get access to.

And we trust (when we say trust, think: hostage) the components to adhere to the protocol, because otherwise we can't prove anything. Trust is never as good as knowledge, it's a substitute for it. So we trust the components to adhere to the protocol: servers don't broadcast their master keys on channels to individual users, clients don't reveal user passwords on shared key sessions.

Now, the level of confidence you have depends on who you are. Client A may have a great deal more trust in Client A than Client B does. If you know the authentication server is on a host with particular properties, that might influence your assessment of how likely they are to publish their key. So we're going to have another ordered set that corresponds to the confidence levels, in this very baby example there are three confidence levels, none, medium and high, and they're in a linear order. You don't need that restriction, you can have a partial order, you can have a semi-lattice more generally, where you have some way of aggregating confidence levels together, and the aggregation operation respects the partial order.

George Danezis: It's not a semi-lattice in general, because the combination operator need not be the minimum. Probably you actually start juggling with individual cases.

---

* Simon Foley was unable to attend, and his position paper was presented at short notice by Bruce Christianson.

B. Christianson et al. (Eds.): Security Protocols 2008, LNCS 6615, pp. 21–24, 2011.
© Springer-Verlag Berlin Heidelberg 2011

Reply: I'm going to try and duck your question by saying, for the moment let's assume that it's the minimum, the meet operation in the semi-lattice. I agree that that is a conservative approach.

We also have a view about what sort of confidence level we require: we've got a view about how happy we would be if a particular leak occurred. This is the confidence that we have that K_b doesn't get leaked on the channel K_{ab}, and we're happy with a medium level of confidence for that. We're going to get very upset if the authentication server's master secret key that it uses to secure all its secrets gets leaked on a channel controlled by a session key. If we can agree a session key, and as a result of that the authentication server leaks its master secret, we're very upset about that. If all that's happening is that we're leaking a key that a particular client shares with an authentication server, on a channel that the client agreed using that authentication server, we're not so upset.

Frank Stajano: When you say, we will be very upset, is "we" A, B, or Eve?

Reply: Yes, good point. Everybody will have their own version of this table. Each party who has an interest in this system, A, B, Eve, the government, Lucifer, and so forth, will have their own version of this table. Let's assume for the moment that this is A's table, and that B might have a different table.

What I'm describing here is a particular technique, lots of different people might use this technique for different purposes. Protocol designers might use it to make sure protocols have nice properties. Users might use it to make sure the protocol meets their needs. Attackers might use it to make sure the protocol is vulnerable to attack before they invest their effort on it. But for the moment the ground rule is that everybody has their own version of this table that describes what they want from the protocol. And the interesting question is, how can you use this table?

There are certain default entries: if you know that K^- leaks K, then your confidence in keeping K a secret, given that you know K^-, is zero, the bottom element in the order. Then we specify a level of confidence (from the elements in the lattice) that each component adheres to in the protocol as published. For example, B knows this is running on some pretty wizzy hardware operated by some people who are reasonably competent and who have a reputation for being honest; whereas B has moderate confidence that A is going to be honest, and moderate confidence in his own competence.

Tuomas Aura: If you think about this specific situation, then A is going to really depend on B, so in that case it makes sense that the confidence that A has in B is high, if A has no confidence in B then the protocol won't work anyway.

Reply: Yes, that is exactly right, the level of confidence that we're assigning here is compliant with the desired outcomes.

Virgil Gligor: So the lattice that you refer to is really the lattice that Kerberos uses?

Reply: Yes. The three element lattice is now nearly powerful enough, for this example.

Virgil Gligor: The reason why you have to minimise the confidence is because you've got to have a hand-off, so if the session keys are compromised, you want to ensure that the damage is limited. The master keys, that are used to encrypt the long-term keys, are not used for any other purpose. The lattice is pretty much intended to capture that. We are trying to make sure that A does not attack B the other way around, for example A gets information, encrypts it, and B has some interesting way of masking the keys.

Reply: That is exactly what these two entries are doing here, that's a very good point.

Virgil Gligor: Potentially you have to do that because otherwise A could mount the attack.

Reply: Yes, here we treat key leakage as an atomic event. That is a gross oversimplification, but it's something that this model doesn't attempt to capture. At the moment, we are presenting a plain vanilla version of the idea, so we're assuming that the protocol explicitly represents all the material that's available, we assume that the attacker, and the analyser, and the parties, all have access to the same idealised messages, so we're making the same questionable assumptions that a lot of other people do.

George Danezis: The situation is different when a key happens to be shared with an application server. So the fact that you have the same type of protection on A and B is not symmetrical.

Reply: No, there's no reason why the lattice has to be symmetrical. That's interesting when you start sticking protocols together in the way that Virgil is alluding to.

We've specified a level of confidence that each component adheres to the protocol, we've built up a table about our desired outcomes, and we observe that each component meets the minimum confidence requirement for what we get out. (Because obviously, if you've got a component that's less secure than the desired outcome, no amount of security protocol design in the world is going to help you.)

So now we add a mutual authentication step to the protocol, which is what usually happens next. We agree a session key, not because computers get bored and want something to do, but because we're going to use the session key to do something else. Usually the first thing that we use the session key for is authentication, and we use some dreadful protocol like this to do it, which we can think of as using K_{ab} to correspond to this channel here. And sure enough, you can see exactly what happens, we now have only medium confidence that K_a is not leaked to B. This is exactly the point that Virgil made earlier, we were absolutely fine, we had a wonderful protocol, it passed all the tests, it respected the lattice, but as soon as we compounded it with an authentication protocol, we now have a route by which B can learn A's long-term key, which as Virgil said, may have been exactly B's agenda in trying to get A to use Needham-Schroeder in the first place.

So, the counter-measure is to re-model the principals. Instead of treating each principal as corresponding to one component, we separate out, within the principal, different components (corresponding to different parts of the protocol) to different elements of the lattice. Now we have a proper handoff, we agree the session key by Needham-Schroeder, then there is internally a handoff protocol that moves the session key to another component, and then we do the authentication protocol between those components. And now we discover that the level of confidence is high that the master key is not leaked, because we've re-modelled the protocol.

Those of you familiar with multi-level security will be feeling *déja vu*, it's a similar problem, raising similar questions, and this is where we get back to a covert channel kind of analysis. Is there a cascade in a particular configuration, and how do we eliminate those in a reasonably efficient manner? Everything is much as you'd expect, you can determine cascade freedom in polynomial time, eliminating cascades optimally is really, really hard, but there are perfectly good polynomial algorithms for fairly nearly optimal elimination orders that are no worse than protocols that people already use.

To recapitulate briefly: protocol deployment, heterogeneous components, degrees of confidence; everybody does their own reasoning, we're all agreed about what the protocol is, but we don't have to agree about what we think the odds of compliance are, or even the particular order of the keys. We may have different views about which key is leaked to which other key, because I might know about a cryptographic attack that you don't. The degree of confidence could be based on empirical evidence, or you might be a Bayesian. You can do it at the initial configuration, or when the protocol is designed, or even after you've initiated the connection, but before you do anything irrevocable with it.

Here is the lattice more or less corresponding to Kerberos, we've got the tickets granting service to the various principals, and as you see, the lattice is not symmetrical here, I think this is an essential observation. What's interesting is that in order to disentangle the cascades you have to split the client into three separate components, and you have to manage the handoff protocols internally, they could be done over a LAN or a non-trivial IPC.

Virgil Gligor: So, the client has a specific reason to remove any possibility that the long-term secret might be attacked, and the reason why they did that decomposition was because they thought, and rightly so, that if they placed a long-term password with a short-term ticket granting service . . .

Reply: Yes, essentially the client is breaking the cascade. All we've really done with this particular example is to show that Kerberos got it right: so if someone said, oh Kerberos is needlessly complicated, this model gives you a way to get a knock-down proof that it's exactly as complicated as it needs to be.

But when you have a situation that is a bit like Kerberos, and you want to know whether it's OK to use a particular combination of protocols without having to spend three weeks thinking about it, you can use a tool like this to find out quickly whether your principal structure is adequate for the protocols you are using.

Do Not Model the Attacker

Jan Meier

Security in Distributed Applications, Hamburg University of Technology, Germany
j.meier@tu-harburg.de

Abstract. We identify attacker modelling as major obstacle when
searching for ways to defeat security protocols. For protocols verified to
be secure, attacks are discovered. Since this problem is not limited to the
Dolev-Yao attacker but applies to all modelled attackers, we propose a
new approach. We argue that formal verification methods should be used
to show the impact of analyst provided actions have on protocols. This
approach frees verification tools from having to know all the actions an
attacker could perform. We show the benefits of having both the security
proof and an explicit list of considered actions. Implementers can easily determine if the protocol is suited for their application. Additionally,
developers understand the requirements an implementation has to fulfil.
Lastly, our approach allows proofs to be adapted to new environments
without changing the verification tool.

1 Introduction

Analysing the security of a given protocol with a particular attacker in mind
puts us in a bad position. We discard all results that a different attacker might
achieve from the analysis. Consequently, from such an analysis we only learn
if this one attacker considered can breach security. Since we do not know the
actual attacker who attacks the protocol, we have to assume how the attacker
behaves. From successful attacks in the past we learnt that malicious users never
behave as expected.

For successful attacks, attackers have to perform at least one action left unsecured by the designer. Buffer overflows [1, chap. 14] or format string vulnerabilities [2] are two possibilities to accomplish code injection. Exploiting these
vulnerabilities requires the attacker to provide malicious input to a program in
order to overwrite stack managing data.

When the conditions change in which a protocol is used, the attacker can
acquire more actions to defeat the protocol. An example of additional actions
due to technology change surfaced in the domain of Bluetooth enabled mobile
phones. With an attack called "BlueSnarfing" the attacker was able to read
private information from popular mobiles used in 2005 [3]. The problem resulted
from the use of the Object Exchange (OBEX) protocol [4]. This protocol was
initially designed for the use of infra-red as transmission medium. By switching
to the radio based Bluetooth technology, the attacker was able to overcome
the restrictions of an infra-red connection. Therefore, the attacker could send

B. Christianson et al. (Eds.): Security Protocols 2008, LNCS 6615, pp. 25–35, 2011.
© Springer-Verlag Berlin Heidelberg 2011

requests to the mobile and was able to receive corresponding information from the phone without being noticed by the victim.

Implementation bugs and broadcasting messages are only two examples how attackers break security. In both examples, attacker are able to perform unconsidered actions. The security community learnt this lesson many times the hard way. So we should not expect to model an attacker in such a way that this model represents a real attacker.

After deploying a protocol, fixing a security vulnerability based on design flaws becomes a challenging task. Resolving the vulnerability requires to alter at least one message of the protocol. Thus, every system relying on the flawed protocol has to be updated. Formal methods are therefore used to systematically analyse every possible protocol run to make sure that security vulnerabilities do not materialize once the system is deployed. For example, we want to be sure that an attacker could never learn a session key established by legitimate protocol participants. Basically, verification tools utilize search strategies. A model checker [5, chap. 3] searches a state space to find states with defined properties. These properties typically define protocol stages we do not want to occur. We denote the state the protocol is in and the knowledge of every protocol participants as stage. Here, we do not distinguish between legitimate and illegitimate participants. Protocol stages and broadcasted messages are unconnected. Thus, stages comprise knowledge beyond the information contained in sent messages.

Analysing security properties by proving a theorem [5, chap. 4] is another option. Depending on the level of automation, the prover searches for the correct deduction rule itself. Only when the prover cannot make a reasonable choice, it asks the user.

Since protocol stages comprise both protocol state and participants' knowledge, we can categorize them into wanted and unwanted stages. In all unwanted protocol stages, the security has been breached. A verification tool, therefore, tries to arrive in an unwanted stage. If the tool cannot find a way to any unwanted protocol stages, the protocol passes the verification check. Verification tools, however, do not build a path to such unwanted stages on their own. Thus, the modelling task of an analyst is twofold. First, she has to model the protocol itself. Secondly, the user has to model potential progress indicating how one could advance from one stage to another as well. These progressions are essential in discovering attacks. If the analyst forgets to model a progression, possible attacks might go undetected. The potential progressions, however, are not modelled directly but are derived from the used attacker model. For the following discussion it is unimportant how these progressions are built into formal methods. In the domain of model checking the progressions are explicit. Theorem provers express the progressions through deduction rules.

The idea behind using formal methods, however, is to gain a general understanding of a system. We seek for invariant properties. When introducing an attacker model to our formal methods, we lose such invariants since the validity of properties may change between different attacker models. Therefore, we defeat the main benefit of using formal methods.

Ideally, we want to know if a certain security property holds for every protocol stage any protocol participant could create. This goal is extremely hard to achieve. On the protocol design level, there is too few information about the actual implementation. These implementation details for example might enable the attacker to guess a nonce. We, however, are interested in an more abstract view. What kind of building blocks are essential for protocol security and what properties must these building blocks fulfil. This shifts the question formal methods answer slightly. We do not answer whether an attacker could break protocol security. Rather, we answer the question what an attacker could achieve given she can perform defined actions.

In this paper, instead of focusing on explicit attacker modelling, we focus on assumptions. However, we do not examine every conceivable assumption but limit ourselves to actions. In order to reach it goal, every cryptographic protocol assumes certain actions to be infeasible. Our goal is to show the benefit of using analyst generated actions instead of a fixed attacker model. Section 2 describes the importance of actions when the authenticity is evaluated. Section 3 describes how to avoid the modelling of domain knowledge. Related work is discussed in section 4. Finally, section 5 concludes the paper.

2   Actions in Protocols

Creating, receiving, and understanding protocol messages involve actions of various kinds. In essence, we can divide such actions into two groups. The first group consists of necessary actions to complete a protocol run. Depending on the protocol, required actions include but are not limited to encryption, decryption, basic arithmetic, comparing and combining numerical or character strings. The second group comprises optional actions an attacker can accomplish. Examples for these actions include capturing and replaying of messages, guessing of nonces or keys, and systematically testing every possibility of a given search space. Actions belonging to the second group are important when we want to determine the set of protocol participants able to reach the protocol goal.

The underlying assumption of every security protocol deals with the feasibility of actions. Ideally, unwanted actions from the second group mentioned above should not be of any help when an attacker tries to reach the protocol goal. A participant of a protocol run judges the authenticity of received messages by the feasibility of creating this message. Suppose a legitimate participant A shares a key with another entity T. A did not distribute the key any further. She trusts T to keep the key secret either. Whenever A receives a message encrypted under this key, she attributes T as the creator for this message. A believes that creating a valid message always requires the encryption key. Furthermore, she believes the key is undisclosed. If a malicious protocol participant is able to disprove A's believe, A is deceived.

While a protocol run advances, the number of legitimate and rogue participants being able to create valid messages decreases. The protocol successfully reaches its goal if only the anticipated participant is able to construct the expected message finishing the protocol run. Assume two participants are able to send a message fulfilling the senders requirements. Typically, participants do not consider this situation. Rather, the participant has one distinct candidate in mind. However, if another participant has the possibility to create the response, she could act as an attacker and make the receiver believe that she is a legitimate participant.

Unfortunately, successful attacks are not limited to one particular abstraction layer. Attackers could exploit a design flaw, implementation weaknesses, bugs, and everything lying in between to successfully defeat the protocol. Implementation details, however, are beyond the abstraction layer dealing with messages sent back and forth only. In these messages, assumptions are hidden. An implementation has to consider these assumptions in order to be secure. With the help of actions, we try to distil assumptions. The goal is to find not only assumptions the designer was aware of but also assumptions the designer confused as facts. We utilize the Needham-Schroeder protocol [6] described at the message abstraction layer. We demonstrate several actions endangering the security of the Needham-Schroeder protocol. The list of malicious action is certainly not complete. With the example we rather want to show how difficult it is to think of all action in advance. Substituting an attacker model for a set of actions, therefore, does not solve the problem.

A participant, legitimate or rogue, *Alice* starts the protocol by sending the message A, B, N_A to the server requesting a session key for a conversation with the participant *Bob*. This message has no protection. However, the nonce creation is very important for reaching the protocol goal reliably. *Alice* must ensure that the nonce N_A was never used before. If Alice's nonce generation fails to deliver these requirements, an attacker might acquire more actions to successfully attack the Needham-Schroeder protocol. When Alice uses a nonce twice, an attacker could replay a previous captured message, tricking Alice into using an old key. The impact of the predictability of N_A, however, cannot that easily be answered. To evaluate the impact, further actions have to be factored in.

In reply to the first message, a participant acting as a trusted third party (TTP) creates a session key for the participants *Alice* and *Bob*. A badly chosen session key opens up more actions an attacker could carry out to successfully defeat the protocol. The session key, therefore, must not have been used before and has to be unpredictable for an attacker. The server sends the message $\{N_A, B, K_{ses}, \{K_{ses}, A\}_{K_B}\}_{K_A}$ back to *Alice*. At this point, we are assuming that *Alice* is a legitimate participant because she shares a key with the server. This, however, does not have to be alway true. Lowe described for the public key version of the Needham-Schroeder protocol in [7,8] a situation where a malicious protocol participant has an authentic public key pair. This knowledge allows the malicious participant to arrive in an unwanted protocol stage.

Alice determines the authenticity of the second message by comparing the two nonces from this message and the previous one she sent to the TTP. In order to conclude authenticity of the message from the correct nonce, *Alice* must believe in the secrecy of the communication key K_A shared only between *Alice* and the server. Thus, all actions disclosing the key must be prevented in order to reach the protocol goal. Again, such actions may not prevented by the protocol itself. An attacker could for example compromise the server to learn the key. Furthermore, the attacker could search the entire key space in order to find the correct key. The protocol only defines the messages that are sent back and forth. It does not specify what kind of protection measures have to be used in order to securely store the encryption key. Rogue participant's possible actions do not solely depend on the key storage but also on the used encryption algorithm. Suppose the protocol implementer chose a block cipher in electronic codebook mode [9]. If each message fragment fits into one block, an attacker could create a new message out of messages from previous messages and protocol runs. Basing on this observation, Pereira and Quisquater show in [10] how to delude *Alice*. Attackers are able to disguise the publicly known nonce N_A as the session key K_{ses}. Protocol implementers, therefore, must choose a different cipher mode, linking various parts of the message together.

For the third message, *Alice* forwards $\{K_{ses}, A\}_{K_B}$ which was included in the second message sent by the server. Participant *Bob* judges the authenticity by recognizing the communication partner indicated in this message. When the decryption of the message results in a meaningful communication partner, *Bob* is assured that the message of encrypted under the key he shares with the TTP. Regarding this message, an attacker could carry out the same malicious actions as she could in conjunction with the second message. Now, however, the attacker could in addition replay an old message [11].

This attack is important since it exploits a flaw in the protocol design. *Bob* has no means of checking if this message belongs to a recent protocol run. Eavesdropping, storing, and injecting are required actions to mount this attack. With this attack, an attacker could trick *Bob* into using an old key. This might be a key the attacker has already compromised. Here, the attacker could impersonate *Alice*.

Upon receiving the third message, *Bob* creates a new nonce and sends it decrypted under the session key to *Alice*. Using this nonce, *Bob* checks if *Alice* uses the same key and therefore was the one who initiated the protocol run. This time, the nonce N_B is encrypted. If a new session key is used every time, an attacker cannot recognize that *Bob* used a nonce twice. In addition, *Alice* would get a wrong result when she tries to decrypt the nonce with a key different than K_{ses} from this recent protocol run. When *Alice* receives the message $\{N_B\}_{K_{ses}}$, there is no cryptographic means in order to check if the message was indeed sent by *Bob*. After *Alice* has decrypted the nonce, she subtracts one from the nonce and encrypts the result with the session key K_{ses}. Lastly, *Bob* compares if the value sent by *Alice* matches his result of subtracting one of the nonce he generated for the forth message.

It is very easy for an attacker to create a fake fourth message. Since *Alice* has no expectations of the nonce she dutifully receives every message, decrypts it, and does the arithmetic operation. After encrypting the message, *Alice* sends the message back to *Bob*. At this point, *Alice* believes that *Bob* agreed to communicate with her using the key K_{ses}. The attacker, however, is not capable of communicating meaningfully with *Alice* since she lacks the session key. The impact of the fraudulent message, therefore, depends on the scenario after the protocol completion.

The list of possible actions does not make any statement about the security of the Needham-Schroeder protocol. Rather, these possible actions emphasize the importance of the protocol environment. Constrained devices like smart phones are likely unable to prevent all mentioned malicious actions when running the Needham-Schroeder protocol. The Java 2 Micro Edition (J2ME) was designed for mobile devices like smart phones. The pseudo random number generator used in J2ME, however, is insecure [12]. The reference implementation for the Secure Socket Layer (SSL) made by Sun for mobile systems was shown to be insecure as well [13]. Modelling possible exploits, however, has the same disadvantages like modelling the attacker. We lose generality. As technology advances, new and therefore unregarded attacks may surface. For that reason, finding all possible actions is not realistic either. Therefore, the modelling of actions does not lead to more general verification results.

3   Domain Knowledge

Since proofs answer questions with either "yes" or "no" only, it is important to understand how these results were generated. Especially, when verification tools produce proofs stating that the protocol is secure. In this case, the attacker model used by the verification tool must be understood.

In general, any attacker model strives to represent the most powerful but still realistic attacker. Today, for example, we do not know an efficient algorithm to factorize a large integer composed of two equally sized primes [9]. Empowering attackers to solve factorization of large integers, therefore, does not reflect reality. Furthermore, such attacker models do not help comparing the security of different protocols. Every protocol based on the RSA cryptosystem [14] would be classified as insecure. RSA implementations were broken, but not because the problem of factorizing large integers was solved. Instead, successful attacks against the RSA cryptosystem benefit from weak usages of the RSA cryptosystem [15].

Without any additional information about implementation details, the Dolev-Yao attacker model [16] is a very powerful attacker. This model empowers any attacker to decrypt every message she possesses the key for. If Dolev-Yao attackers learn a key later, they still are able to decrypt already sent messages. Dolev-Yao attackers are unable to understand messages encrypted with a key they do not know. Knowing the cryptographic key, these attackers are able to encrypt their own messages as well. Besides cryptographic operations, Dolev-Yao attackers are allowed to have great influences on transportation of messages. They can eavesdrop, suppress, and replay any message. To mount successful attacks, Dolev-Yao attackers can use any information they learnt in the past.

As powerful as Dolev-Yao attackers are, they cannot detect weak implementations or bugs. This inability reveals the first difficulty which arises when attacker models are used to analyse security properties. Generic attacker models are fixed to one particular abstraction layer. The Dolev-Yao attacker model, for example, abstracts from implementation details. For example, it does not need any knowledge about the encryption algorithm and the programming language used. Dolev-Yao attackers concentrate on the input and output of various protocol participants only. This layer is best-suited to detect design flaws since it does not feature unnecessary detail. A flawless design is a prerequisite for protocol security. The analysis, however, should go beyond the message layer. At this layer, assumptions about the impracticability of actions could easily be confused as facts. Often, once attackers are able to violate assumptions, they are able to break the protocol as well. Thus domain knowledge is needed to evaluate whether the stated assumptions hold.

Another downside of attacker models are their lack of flexibility. When the environment changes, attacker models have to be redesigned to capture all possibilities the environmental change creates. If the change is not fundamental, there are applications where the old attacker model still is applicable. For different needs, different attacker models are needed since their is not an attacker model suiting all applications. Anderson *et al.* argue for the use of different attacker models when analysing the security of sensor networks [17]. Depending on the application, attackers should lack the ability to monitor the whole network traffic in the deployment phase. With such a weakened attacker lightweight protocols can be analysed since they are not instantly broken as it would be the case when a Dolev-Yao attacker model is used.

Attacker models also are not flexible enough to detect new attack schemes since developing new attacks requires creativity. This needed creativity is not built into attacker models. Even if it would be possible to build a creative attacker, still the aforementioned domain knowledge is required. Therefore, verification tools using today's attacker models will not invent unknown attack patterns to break the security of protocols. The result of verification proofs is further weakened. Besides considering only one out of many possible attackers, the verification examines only known attacks. This missing creativity, however, is not unique to attacker models and is a fundamental problem which we do not attempt to solve in this paper.

Ultimate protocol security is not obtainable since protocol security relies on environmental properties being beyond the protocol's control. Thus, we do not only need a weakened attacker but also a stronger attacker reflecting the possibilities the application environment offers. Postulating the adaption of attacker models for every protocol and its intended use, results in a multitude of different attacker models. Having multiple attacker models requires the selection of the best fitting attacker model. Verification tools, however, cannot make this selection since it requires domain knowledge. When multiple attacker models exist, the best fitting model must be selected. This selection requires domain knowledge. Therefore, verification tools cannot select a model and have to delegate this task to the users of the tools. Besides domain knowledge, analysts need security expertise to choose the best fitting attacker model.

Since domain knowledge and security expertise are needed to analyse protocol security in a realistic setting, we can abandon attacker models altogether. Instead, we propose to analyse protocols in the presence of analyst provided actions. This approach makes the actions considered during the verification process explicit. Thereby, security proofs loose their unconditionality.

Proofs only hold for these environments the analyst had in mind, when carrying out those proofs. Changing the environment also invalidates the proof. Stating considered actions determine the circumstances under which security proofs hold. Deciding if the proved protocol fits the intended application, therefore, becomes much easier. Application designers are able to identify what the prover had in mind when she carried out the proof.

This approach, however, does not save us from missing crucial actions. Verification tools cannot detect whether an analyst forgot an action. To enable tools to observe forgotten actions, we would have to provide tools a complete list of action. In section 2 we argued that providing a list complete under any circumstance cannot be given. Due to the same reasons, verification tools cannot decide if the set of provided actions is maximal.

Another approach is to state actions having the potential to break the protocol. We refer to these actions as forbidden actions. The goal of this approach is not to design protocols secure against all imaginable malicious actions. However, a list of forbidden actions allows application designers to check against such actions. Unfortunately, verification tools cannot ensure the completeness of the stated forbidden actions. Actions breaching protocol security, therefore, can go undetected.

Suppose a given protocol $\mathcal{P}$ and a set of actions $\mathbb{F}$ breaching the security of $\mathcal{P}$. A protocol is unsuited for a given environment, if this environment does not prevent all actions from $\mathbb{F}$. Application designers have to alter the environment so that no action from $\mathbb{F}$ can be performed in order to use $\mathcal{P}$ securely. Environments allowing forbidden actions not stated in $\mathbb{F}$ are not considered. Thus, it might still be possible to breach protocol security.

In contrast to verification results generated with the help of attacker models, action driven verification results do not only depend on the protocol modelling. To judge the quality of action driven verification results, one has to evaluate actions fed into the verification tool. In order to be beneficial for many different environments, the sets of allowed and forbidden actions should be as big as possible. The set of appropriate environments can be further shaped if allowed and forbidden actions are used together.

4   Related Work

In the area of cryptographic protocol analysis, the work of Dolev and Yao [16] is influential. Their attacker model can be emulated using the action driven approach. Eavesdropping, suppressing, replaying, encrypting, and decrypting messages are actions in themselves. However, the capability of using every information learnt from messages sent previously must be divided into two separate actions. First, an action representing the storage of every message is required.

To use stored information, a second action in form of a database look up has to be performed.

Dolev and Yao's as well as the action driven approach both describe what kind of actions attackers are able to carry out. In this setting, we want to prove that no sequence of these actions violates protocol security. The action driven approach additionally allows the protocol analyst to specify her own set of actions. Besides detecting successful attacks, this approach could also be used to extract assumptions the protocol security is based on.

While the Dolev-Yao attacker model is the most widespread, other attacker models exist. In this paper, we already mentioned a weakened attacker introduced in [17]. The strength of this attacker is time-dependent. When deploying a sensor network, the attacker is not able to eavesdrop the whole network. After the network detection, however, the authors assume that the attacker will have the ability to eavesdrop every message. In this paper, we did not investigate the possibility of actions over time.

Bellare et al. coined the expression "concrete security" [18,19]. The goal of concrete security is to provide a security notion for cryptographic algorithms in practice. In [18] the authors investigated if a cipher block chaining message authentication code (CBC-MAC) [1, chap. 11] can be broken with fewer resources required to break the underlying encryption algorithm.

While Doley and Yao explicitly list the actions attackers are able to perform, Bellare et al. specify what attackers cannot do. They introduce "concrete bounds" for cryptographic algorithms and show that no attacker can solve this problem more efficient than this bound. Parameterizing the attacker's resources, allows Bellare et al. to determine the security of cryptographic algorithms.

5   Conclusion

We identified attacker models as a major obstacle when protocols are analysed. The modelling is both inflexible and obscured deep in the model or the verification tool. Furthermore, models with an attacker consider only attacks the designer of the verification tool knew about. Whenever a new attack pattern is discovered, previous proofs have to be revisited.

Instead of looking for all possible actions one could think of, the protocol designer knows which actions have the potential to breach security. By augmenting protocol descriptions with actions the designer thought to be infeasible, we can check if these actions indeed are impossible to carry out. In the case of the Needham-Schroeder protocol, recombining encrypted messages must be an infeasible action in order to reach the protocol goal securely. Furthermore, we can add details to the protocol specification and check if the actions still are infeasible. For example, using the electronic codebook mode renders the recombination of encrypted messages feasible under certain circumstances. If the target environment does not prevent all forbidden actions, we know that we cannot use this protocol securely.

The action driven approach certainly does not solve every problem. Analysts using this approach need security expertise to specify actions attackers are able to perform. In order to obtain meaningful verification results, analysts have to find the balance between action being to powerful and being to weak. No protocol seems to fit the application scenario, if too powerful actions are assumed. Furthermore, assuming too powerful actions might result in a protocol design which protects against unrealistic threats. A protocol with practical vulnerabilities like denial-of-service attacks could be the result. A verification result based on too weak actions would indicate a secure protocol when in fact there are practical attacks.

It remains future work to support the analyst in evaluating possible actions systematically. Time dependency of actions is another direction to expand the action driven approach. For the purpose of comparison, a verification tool using the action driven approach has to be built as well.

Acknowledgement

I would like to thank Dieter Gollmann for his inspiring comments leading to a number of improvements to this paper.

References

1. Gollmann, D.: Computer Security, 2nd edn. John Wiley & Sons Ltd., Chichester (2006)
2. Howard, M., Leblanc, D.: Public Enemy #1: The Buffer Overrun. In: Writing Secure Code. Microsoft Press, Redmond (2003)
3. Heredia González, K.M.: Demonstration of "BlueSnarf" Vulnerability in Bluetooth Telephones. Project Work (2005)
4. Infrared Data Association: IrDA Object Exchange (OBEX) Protocol (2003)
5. Huth, M., Ryan, M.: Logic in Computer Science: Modelling and Reasoning About Systems, 2nd edn. Cambridge University Press, Cambridge (2004)
6. Needham, R.M., Schroeder, M.D.: Using Encryption for Authentication in Large Networks of Computers. Communications of the ACM 21(12), 993–999 (1978)
7. Lowe, G.: An Attack on the Needham-Schroeder Public-Key Authentication Protocol. Information Processing Letters 56(3), 131–133 (1995)
8. Lowe, G.: Breaking and Fixing the Needham-Schroeder Public-Key Protocol Using FDR. In: Margaria, T., Steffen, B. (eds.) TACAS 1996. LNCS, vol. 1055, pp. 147–166. Springer, Heidelberg (1996)
9. Menezes, A.J., van Oorschot, P.C., Vanstone, S.A.: Handbook of Applied Cryptography. CRC Press, Boca Raton (2001)
10. Pereira, O., Quisquater, J.J.: On the Perfect Encryption Assumption. In: Degano, P. (ed.) Proceedings of the Workshop on Issues in the Theory of Security (WITS 2000), pp. 42–45 (2000)
11. Denning, D.E., Sacco, G.M.: Timestamps in key distribution protocols. Commun. ACM 24(8), 533–536 (1981)
12. Klingsheim, A.N., Moen, V., Hole, K.J.: Challenges in Securing Networked J2ME Applications. Computer 40(2), 24–30 (2007)
13. Simonsen, K.I.F., Moen, V., Hole, K.J.: Attack on Sun's MIDP Reference Implementation of SSL. In: 10th Nordic Workshop on Secure IT-systems (Nordsec 2005), pp. 96–103 (2005)

14. Rivest, R.L., Shamir, A., Adleman, L.M.: A Method for Obtaining Digital Signatures and Public-Key Cryptosystems. Communications of the ACM 21(2), 120–126 (1978)
15. Boneh, D.: Twenty Years of Attacks on the RSA Cryptosystem. Notices of the American Mathematical Society (AMS) 46(2), 203–213 (1999)
16. Dolev, D., Yao, A.C.: On the Security of Public Key Protocols. IEEE Transactions on Information Theory 29(2), 198–208 (1983)
17. Anderson, R., Chan, H., Perrig, A.: Key Infection: Smart Trust for Smart Dust. In: Proceedings of the 12th IEEE International Conference on Network Protocols, ICNP 2004, pp. 206–215 (2004)
18. Bellare, M., Kilian, J., Rogaway, P.: The Security of the Cipher Block Chaining Message Authentication Code. Journal of Computer and System Sciences 61(3), 362–399 (2000)
19. Bellare, M., Desai, A., Jokipii, E., Rogaway, P.: A Concrete Security Treatment of Symmetric Encryption. In: 38th Annual Symposium on Foundations of Computer Science, pp. 394–403 (1997)

Do Not Model the Attacker
(Transcript of Discussion)

Jan Meier

Hamburg University of Technology

Tuomas Aura: You criticised the fact that tools have built in assumptions, but this depends on the tool user. If you think of things such as program-defining tools, or program checkers, something that you want someone to use over and over again, they should do things automatically, and get it right most of the time. In that case you don't want the user to start to model the assumptions, or the security protocols, but you instead want these to be built in, in all possible combinations.

Reply: Yes. Maybe as a compromise you could think of basic environments, for which you could come up with a set of actions, and then the user could select these sets of actions. This would solve the problem that the user has to model these actions all over again, but also would allow him to use a more tailored set. Again, you would have the problem that you maybe don't quite have the right set, so the user could make a mistake, but this could be a way to have a set of actions depending on the environment.

Virgil Gligor: Picking up on Tuomas' point, I think tools have limited capabilities, for example the protocol verification tools could not implement verification based on Dolev-Yao, in particular because they couldn't model operations very well anyway. So if you want to use it as a tool, know the limitations of the capability of the tool. It doesn't mean that embedding another side of modelling is the wrong thing to do, you just have to know the limitations.

Reply: Do you mean the one who extends the model has to know the limitations?

Virgil Gligor: No, everyone.

Reply: Does the guy on the street really use a protocol because you give him the proof this protocol is secure?

Virgil Gligor: The man in the street couldn't care less about our proofs, but people who care about these proofs need to know. For example, look at this tool, here are the Dolev-Yao capabilities, and here are the assumptions and the proofs, you can go and check them, you know exactly what the other side can do. Is that enough? We don't know, but at least we know their capabilities, that doesn't mean that the model has done something wrong.

Reply: No, I don't want to say it's wrong, and as you said, it's built in. But I'm not quite sure if we are really interested in whether a Dolev-Yao attacker is able to break the security of the protocol. For me, a proof has always some generality, it's always true.

Virgil Gligor: Is the objection that these proofs are unique in the sense that you have to do the proof again from scratch for each protocol?

B. Christianson et al. (Eds.): Security Protocols 2008, LNCS 6615, pp. 36–37, 2011.
© Springer-Verlag Berlin Heidelberg 2011

Reply: No, I meant that when you do a proof that the pipe is hot, then the pipe is hot for all time, but when we prove what we have in the attacker model here, this proof is only true for this particular attacker model. But don't we want to strive for something more general? I'm really not sure we need a model of the adversaries.

Virgil Gligor: I think we have to distinguish between definitions and models. Whether we model the attacker in some abstract way is secondary, but we have to have a precise definition of the adversary. If we don't have that, we don't have a security problem to solve, period. So whether we model the adversary, or define it in some other way, explicitly by action, as you suggest, or by something else, is a secondary matter, but we need a definition. Security problems don't exist without an adversary.

Reply: Yes, and my point is that you really want to have weak assumptions that it is very hard for an attacker to go around. So I'm really not interested if the Dolev-Yao attacker can or cannot break a protocol, I want to know what kind of assumptions the attacker has to go around to break the protocol.

Bruce Christianson: I'm not sure it's quite true to say that attackers aren't interested in proofs, because a proof that A implies B is also a proof that not B implies not A, so of course the proof shows the attacker where to look. And real attackers have an ability which the Dolev-Yao attacker does not have, which is the ability to move between levels of abstraction. I think this is actually a very good point that you're making, that modern proofs are not good at writing down the assumptions in a form related to the bit budget. If you use a 128-bit nonce the cost of attacking is different to a shorter one. Sometimes you want to say, is there an attack which costs Eve less than a certain amount, where the things she might be spending money on are essentially the cost of breaking assumptions, for instance, to give Eve information she shouldn't have, or making Alice believe something that isn't true.

Tuomas Aura: Sometimes it might be useful if you have a tool that proves the security of a protocol, and you hide your models, and afterwards the tool could list the assumptions that we have made in the proof.

Virgil Gligor: And you know exactly what is going on.

Reply: Yes, but everyone has to know the assumptions.

Michael Roe: You are agreeing violently. The problem I had is with protocols that alter the assumptions. For example, Mobile IPv6 return routability: the tools erroneously conclude it isn't secure because the tools assume Dolev-Yao whereas the protocol assumes a weaker attacker. The problem is getting the tools to model that, because you just give them the protocol and they don't let you say say, well the attacker has limited resources, like for example, he can break a network at one point but he can't tap it locally. It is a real problem trying to model that.

Virgil Gligor: So I think a better title might be, Be Careful of Your Model, or Be Explicit about what your Model is, or better yet, Define the Adversary but Forget Abstractions.

Generating Random Numbers in Hostile Environments

Jan Krhovjak, Andriy Stetsko, and Vashek Matyas

Masaryk University, Faculty of Informatics
{xkrhovj,xstetsko,matyas}@fi.muni.cz

Abstract. This paper discusses basic security aspects of distributed random number generation in potentially hostile environments. The goal is to outline and discuss a distributed approach, which comes to question in the case of attacker being able to target one or several mobile devices. We define communication paths and attacker models instead of providing technical details of local generation. This paper also includes a discussion of several issues of such distributed approach.

1 Introduction

Since mobile devices typically use a wireless channel for communication, the security of transmitted data plays a very important role for many applications — consider, *e.g.*, mobile banking. High-quality and unpredictable cryptographic keys, padding values, or per-message secrets are critical to securing communication by modern cryptographic techniques. Their generation thus requires a good generator of truly random and pseudo-random numbers.

The difference between truly random and pseudo-random numbers is given by the process of their generation. Truly random numbers are typically obtained by sampling of some physical phenomenon (*e.g.*, thermal noise) while pseudo-random numbers are computed by a faster deterministic algorithm. The classical cryptographic pseudo-random number generators use truly random data only as an initial input (seed) to the algorithm.

The security of local generation of truly random (and also pseudo-random) data relies primarily on the quality of used sources of randomness. The mobile phones typically provide some good sources of randomness — *e.g.*, noise present in audio and video input — that we analysed in [1]. However, the possibility to predict and/or influence such sources of randomness implies a possibility to predict generated data.

The security of pseudo-random number generation relies on the design of particular cryptographic pseudo-random number generator and its resistance to cryptanalysis. In addition to that, modern *hybrid generators* periodically use truly random data during the whole generation process — this improves the generator security by increasing resistance against state compromise attacks at the expense of higher demands on truly random data.

B. Christianson et al. (Eds.): Security Protocols 2008, LNCS 6615, pp. 38–50, 2011.

Since mobile devices or their sources of randomness can be under attack — consider, *e.g.*, malware or influencing video input by changing ambient light intensity — we can involve several cooperating mobile devices in the generation process. These devices can perform generation at the beginning of (or during ongoing) communication with other devices. This distributed approach can support better random or pseudo-random number generation in case of attackers being able to target only some (but not all) of the mobile devices.

Local generation, from the attacker point of view, is obviously strongly dependent on the attacker possibilities to control a mobile device and to influence or predict used sources of randomness. The situation is quite different when we consider distributed random data generation. In this case, the attacker possibilities depend also on the communication model and methods for secure gathering and using remotely generated data.

The rest of this paper is organized as follows: In the next section, we define attacker models for local random number generation. Section 3 focuses on definition of basic communication paths and describes several problems that we encountered. Section 4 sketches possible mechanisms for gathering random data in hostile environments and discusses problems that should be considered.

2   Attacker Model for Standalone Mobile Devices

Recall that random data for cryptography purposes must have good statistical properties and must be unpredictable. These two conditions are jointly satisfied only if the truly random data are generated with utilization of a good physical source of randomness and post-processed by a cryptographic pseudo-random number generator.

A successful attacking (*i.e.*, unobservable influencing) of such sources can result in non-uniform random data or in completely predictable (or even worse constant) data that is not random. Utilizing several sources of randomness and combining their outputs is a common practice to avoid a prediction of a generator output in the case when the attacker influences some (but not all) sources of randomness. Better statistical quality and faster generation (without increasing of entropy) is accomplished by utilizing digital post-processing, *e.g.*, by cryptographic pseudo-random number generator. Hybrid generators then also allows to increase the inner state entropy by periodical reseeding and continual accumulation (pooling) of truly random data.

We often assume that the attacker has no access to the generating device — in this case the post-processing can hide many statistical defects or even influence the source of randomness that results in generation of constant data without entropy. The situation is more difficult if an attacker somehow obtains an inner state of pseudo-random number generator — *e.g.*, due design flaw, implementation error, or by readout of the memory content. In this case, the attacker can also easily predict all pseudo-random data before next reseeding. Potential simultaneous influence of the randomness source then allows to predict pseudo-random outputs even after reseeding.

Currently, all mobile phones that want to access mobile network are equipped by the subscriber identity module (SIM). It is a smartcard that provides secure storage, secure computational environment, and it also contains physical truly random generator — typically based on sampling of several free running oscillators. However, SIM cards are under control of the mobile network operator and there are very limited possibilities of their usage by common users — often restricted only to the secure storage of contacts or short text messages (SMS).

The future technical progress may result in mobile phones with second smartcard that will be under full user control. In this case, all cryptographical operations, including generation of random numbers, could be performed inside the card similarly as in classical SIM Toolkit applications, and the external sources of randomness can only serve as an additional (but non-reliable) input.

The main problem of mobile devices is that their computational environment is not secure. Such devices can contain malware (malicious software as viruses, Trojan horses, etc.) and all generated random data could be easily replaced by non-random data before they reach the appropriate application (located in mobile device or inside SIM card). One possibility to prevent unwanted malicious software or even firmware installation lies in the introduction of a trusted platform module (TPM).

All this implies that the real attacker model for standalone mobile device is strongly dependent on the attacker possibilities to control the device or used sources of randomness. We define four classes of attacker for standalone mobile devices:

Type I (weak outsider) – the attacker had temporary read access to the mobile device and knows the internal state of device — including pool — before beginning of the generation. He has no possibility to access to the mobile device again, but he has access to the information about the environment of victim (he can stay in the proximity of victim, he can record audio/video of the victim to the camera, etc.) and he has also a limited capability to influence this environment (e.g., disturbing the signal, overexposure the lens of digital camera, etc.).

Type II (strong outsider) – the attacker has in addition to the weak outsider almost all detail information about victims environment and he is capable fully influencing this environment. The term "almost" reflects uncertainty arising from interactions between user, device, and environment (several physical effects, errors in measurement, etc.).

Type III (weak insider) – extends the capabilities of previous strong outsider by adding a full control over the mobile network operator SIM card with the possibility of remote reading from or writing to the SIM card.

Type IV (strong insider) – in addition to previous scenario, the attacker has a temporal write access to the mobile device. Therefore, he can also compromise the firmware/software of the mobile phone (e.g., by rewriting flash, installing malware) and hence he has a full control over the phone (including interprocess communication) with a possibility to remote access to the mobile device again.

Clearly, a digital post-processing by cryptographic pseudo-random number generator causes that an attacker always needs to know the device internal state. Hoverer, as we discussed in the introduction, a careful user should always expect that sources of randomness in a standalone generating devices can be under attack. A successful attack (performed by weak or strong outsider) and the knowledge of internal state always results in a predictable data output.

It is extremely difficult to guarantee that the external source of randomness is not under an ongoing attack. Several online statistical tests can be performed, but they can probabilistically detect only a basic (and limited) set of statistical defects. An additional and more convenient way how to secure a pseudo-random output is to prevent attacker from copying the internal state by utilizing secure storage inside the SIM card. This works only until the mobile network operator starts to act as/with an attacker, being capable to read/write content of SIM card that is in his ownership.

Preventing attacker with full access to the device is the most difficult task that can be meaningfully accomplished only by introducing a trusted platform module. Since we want to keep our discussions realistic, we expect a type four attacker being able to target several (but not all) remote devices. However, we assume the local devices (including SIM card) behave always correctly. This guarantees (in terms of probability) that a trustworthy local device obtains at least some random data from remote parties and thus is resistant against first three types of attackers. The clarification of this strict assumption is described below.

3   Communication Model

Since we are interested in random data generation in mobile environments, we will distinguish between *consuming mobile device* that requests random data and *generating mobile device* that (*e.g.*, upon a request) generates random data. Sometimes we consider a *generation computer* located in the Internet or GSM network that (*e.g.*, upon a request) also generates random data.

In the basic scenario we expect that the owner of a trustworthy consuming device always selects trusted remote users to generate random data. Particular generating device replies with a message that includes requested random data and declaration about the amount of entropy in this data. Based on the user reputation the consuming device makes a decision about the amount of claimed entropy of the obtained random data. This reputation can be predefined by the consuming device owner and we call it static reputation.

Unfortunately, there is no way how to assess the statistical quality of obtained sample of random data and how to validate the amount of entropy in such data. Even a device of a user with good reputation could become the victim of the malicious code (viruses, Trojan horse, *etc.*) that can produce only pseudo-random data with no entropy. This prevents also using all dynamic reputation system that automatically recalculates reputation. The only meaningful solution of this problem is using random data from several devices where at least one device is expected to be honest and the communication between devices is well secured.

In this section we focus on the communication issues and we restrict ourselves to the situation when both communicating devices behaves correctly.

3.1   Communication Paths

For a precise definition of attacker models in the distributed environment, it is essential to know the communication model that includes network topology, used security mechanisms and their fundamental vulnerabilities. All these communication properties are briefly discussed in Appendix A and a detailed description of these issues can be found, *e.g.*, in [2] or [3].

We define several path types that are used in definitions of attacker models. The device at the beginning of path is always a consuming mobile device; the device at the end of the path is the generating mobile device or computer. The path can also lead through the Internet and the first computer that provides Internet connection to that devices on end-points of the path is denoted as a *gateway*.

Type 1 – the simplest local path can be established between two mobile devices or a between mobile device and a computer. These paths can be point-to-point (via, *e.g.*, IR or USB interface) or point-to-multipoint (via, *e.g.*, Bluetooth or WiFi). Paths between two mobile devices can lead over one or several intermediate devices. For example, in the case of Bluetooth the path can lead over one superior/master device. Another example is a large WiFi network where two mobile devices can be connected to different access points. Therefore, communication path between these mobile devices can lead through several access points.

Type 2 – the GSM communication path established between two mobile devices can lead over several GSM networks. These paths can be created by standard GSM technologies (*e.g.*, SMS or MMS). Moreover, the mobile network operator has a capability to improve his network by additional special GSM services that can extend network functionality (*e.g.*, servers that provide on demand random data). In this case the communication is established between mobile device and such GSM service server.

Type 3 – mobile device can communicate with other mobile devices or computers through the Internet. The access to the Internet can be established through a gateway, which could be personal computer or wireless access point. The path between consuming mobile device and gateway (and between gateway and generating mobile device) is covered by the simplest paths of "type one". Internet or similar packet oriented network (based on TCP/IP, X.25, *etc.*) is either used between gateways or between a gateway and the generation computer.

Type 4 – hybrid paths through the Internet where one or two gateways on the path are in fact GPRS support nodes of different GSM networks. The path between consuming mobile device and gateway (and between gateway and generating mobile device) is covered by the paths of "type one" and "type two". For example, consumer mobile device can request random data from the generation computer or the generating mobile device connected to the Internet through the gateway — another computer or access point. Moreover, the gateway for the generating mobile device can also be a GPRS support node.

Note that leased lines can be used to interconnect different GSM networks. The description of mechanisms that secure data flow in such lines is not publicly available. The lack of this information implies that the leased lines should not be trusted even when the mobile network operator (or its employees) behaves honestly.

3.2   Attacker Model for Distributed Systems

Since the attacker is able to eavesdrop some communication links, they have to be secured in terms of authenticity, confidentiality and integrity. In order to design secure systems, which support distributed random number generation, we should take into consideration the communication paths and the corresponding attacker models. (We enclose the attacker models in Appendix B.)

We define four different attacker types according to the communication paths described above. However, as we are not able to detect potential modification or observation of the transferred data, we assume that each particular communication link in the path must be secured. This can be done either by the owner of the infrastructure (*e.g.*, GSM network operator) or by end-point mobile device (by means of end-to-end security). This implies that our attacker models degrade and all types of attackers can be prevented by securing the whole communication path.

In the next section, we consider the cryptographic protocols that allow two or more distributed parties to establish a shared secret key and contribute to the process of its generation. The authenticated protocols are designed to work in hostile environment and to provide end-to-end security, and can be used to prevent all attacker types.

4   Gathering of Random Data in Hostile Environments

As was mentioned above, the local random data generation can be performed in a hostile environment and the mobile devices and their sources of randomness can be under ongoing attacks. Therefore, we suggest to involve more parties (mobile devices) in the process of random data generation. Such mobile devices can be considered as independent (remote) sources of randomness[1]. In general, the more generating mobile devices are used, the less probability to attack all of them is — due to usage of different devices, environment, and to certain point also a communication paths.

Consuming device can obtain random data from generating devices either per explicit request or as a secondary product of ongoing communication (*e.g.*, audio/video conference). In the former case the user sends the request for random data to one or several generating mobile devices. In the latter case the random

---

[1] The remote mobile device can provide both raw and post-processed random data.

data are transferred during communication. This functionality can be supported either by a mobile network operator service or by a third party application, which in turn uses existing network services (*e.g.*, SMS, MMS).

In the distributed environment we can also distinguish between two methods of obtaining the random data per explicit request — direct or indirect. In both methods the consuming mobile device requests another device to provide random data. Direct method means that the response is sent directly back to the consuming device. Indirect method, on the other hand, means that the response is sent through another mobile devices (can be predefined by user), which add their own random data. The last device sends the accumulated random data back to the consuming device. It is an open question whether such method brings some significant advantages (*e.g.*, for ad-hoc networks) and so would be more effective than the direct one.

Technology improvement (*e.g.*, 3G/4G networks) introduces the possibility of audio/video conferences. To assure confidentiality in such conferences, the participants typically have to agree upon a shared secret key, which is used to encrypt the ongoing communication. This scenario requires all participants to contribute the random data to the shared key. This fact benefits particularly the consuming devices which are locally influenced by the attacker (type one or two). The shared key could be treated as a random data generated in the distribution manner.

The disadvantage of this method is that all participants share the same random data that are predictable (with no entropy) for an adversary inside the group. Therefore, we propose to keep a distinct pool of random data for each communication group. The random data stored in a pool associated with a particular group can be used to secure communication only within this group.

4.1   Distributed Contribution Protocols

In this section, we discuss (multi-party) cryptographic protocols that can be used for distributed random data generation. These protocols enable each user to accumulate random data from multiple participants — therefore, we call them *distributed contribution protocols*.

We consider the group key agreement (GKA) protocols as possible candidates that can be utilized for distributed generation of random data. A brief description of several basic GKA protocols can be found in [4]. These protocols are typically based on Diffie-Hellman key establishment and work in several rounds. Each participant of protocol generates new (or modifies obtained) Diffie-Hellman value(s) and sends it/them back to the initiator (or to the next member) of the group. The detailed messaging is dependent on particular logical topology of a protocol, however the modification of exchanged values always involves the usage of randomly generated data.

These protocols provide either no authentication or many-to-many/many-to-one authentication (typically based on secret key/password of remote party). The many-to-one authentication scheme assumes that all participants authenticate themselves only to one participant (*e.g.*, initiator of the communication) and they have no direct assurance who are the group members. The non-authenticated protocol could be easily transformed to the authenticated one — for example, by the means of digital signatures.

More sophisticated versions of protocol are designed to fit to concrete physical topology (*e.g.*, GSM network), but the advantage here is only in more effective messaging or in offloading of complex computations from resources-restricted mobile devices [8]. Another class — fault-tolerant GKAs — allows to detect parties that do not follow the protocol [7]. However, since the underlying Diffie-Hellman problem is considered as hard, all exchanged values can be always without any harm observed by an attacker.

Note that classical authentication protocols often rely on shared secrets that are typically stored inside the device and this fact implies only the device authentication. More sophisticated password-based authentication protocols (*e.g.*, password-based GKA) provide better user authentication, but also often requires more random data. Several innovative methods allows perform user post-authentication by audio-visual means, which requires even less random data then classical authentication. This kind of authentication relies on the ability to recognize the user face/voice and other behavioural characteristics [5]. Another scenario utilize visual checking of exchanged Diffie-Hellman values that can be for easier verification transformed to usual language words [6].

4.2   Chicken-and-Egg Problem

The distributed approach to random data generation has one significant drawback. As we mentioned above, the transfer of random numbers must be secured. However, common mechanisms for ensuring authenticity, confidentiality and integrity (but also, *e.g.*, anonymity or information hiding) are based on classical cryptography, which in turn is dependent on random data as secret keys, padding values, *etc.* This implies a classical chicken-and-egg problem and breaking this circle seems to be impossible — from both information-theoretic and complexity-theoretic points of view.

The main reason is that encryption of high-entropy data behaves similarly as a pseudo-random number generator. The maximal entropy that can be obtained from encrypted data is limited by the entropy of the secret encryption key. We cannot count on more entropy then the entropy of the encryption key, because the adversary has a possibility to attack the secret key. The solution could be reestablishing a shared key for each request for random data, however, this process requires that all involved parties have a reliable source of random data.

Despite this drawback, we propose to use both raw and post-processed random data obtained from remote parties as an independent additional input for next digital post-processing — *e.g.*, by a hybrid pseudo-random number generator or a non-deterministic entropy extractor. Such secure non-deterministic transformation is the only way how to solve the problem that the whole group shares the same random data, usage of which then has to be restricted to this group. We are aware that both techniques require some amount of truly random data and the entropy outside the group will be restricted to the entropy of that truly random data. The main benefit here is that we obtain more secure and reliable method of generation (regardless of entropy) in the presence of attacker type one or two.

As we have mentioned, the direct usage of random data obtained from remote parties can be done only for securing communication within a particular group. Due to the entropy issues, we recommend its usage only for short-term encryption keys or other secrets that are intended for applications where the data to be protected are sensitive only for limited time period — e.g., daily stock price forecasting or common day-to-day audio/video conferences. Other direct usage without digital post-processing is not recommended. Note that this holds also for local generation in the presence of attacker type one or two, especially in the case when we want use local random data for first key agreement or establishment.

The only way to completely avoid usage of digital post-processing is utilizing the SIM card at least to establish a secure communication channel. In this case is also recommended to use the secure storage of the SIM card to protect seed files and all randomness pools.

5 Conclusion

Since a mobile device (or its sources of randomness) could be influenced by an attacker, there will be scenarios where one should consider extending a local random number generation to the distributed one, with several mobile devices involved.

We examined various communication paths that can be used to interconnect mobile devices (e.g., Bluetooth, GSM, Internet, etc.). Any proposed secure system has to be designed under a defined attacker model. Therefore, we looked closely at different attacker types according to the communication paths involved. Further, we discussed multi-party cryptographic protocols that could be used for distributed random data generation. We considered one class in more detail — the group key agreement protocols, where the shared secret key could be treated as random data generated in a distributed manner.

Our aim was to point out distributed random number generation as a possible way to obtain high quality random data. Obviously, even the distributed approach has its advantages and disadvantages. We presented some possible solutions and we hope to encourage a further discussion of this approach.

Acknowledgment

We acknowledge the support of the research project of Czech Science Foundation No. 102/06/0711.

References

1. Krhovják, J., Švenda, P., Matyáš, V.: The Sources of Randomness in Mobile Devices. In: Proceeding of the 12th Nordic Workshop on Secure IT System, Reykjavik University, pp. 73–84 (2007); ISBN 978-9979948346

2. Eberspaecher, J., Voegel, H.-J., Bettstetter, C.: GSM Switching, Services, and Protocols. Wiley, Chichester (2001); ISBN: 978-0471499039
3. Xiao, Y.: Link Layer Security in Wireless LANs, Wireless PANs, and Wireless MANs. Springer, Heidelberg (2007); ISBN: 978-0387263274
4. Boyd, C., Mathuria, A.: Protocols for Authentication and Key Establishment. Springer, Heidelberg (2003); ISBN: 978-3540431077
5. Laur, S., Pasini, S.: SAS-Based Group Authentication and Key Agreement Protocols. In: Cramer, R. (ed.) PKC 2008. LNCS, vol. 4939, pp. 197–213. Springer, Heidelberg (2008)
6. Čagalj, M., Hubau, J.-P.: Key agreement over a radio link. EPFL-IC Technical Report, No. IC/2004/16 (2004)
7. Tseng, Y.-M.: An Improved Conference-Key Agreement Protocol with Forward Secrecy. Informatica 16(2), 275–284 (2005)
8. Bresson, E., Chevassut, O., Essiari, A., Pointcheval, D.: Mutual Authentication and Group Key Agreement for Low-Power Mobile Devices. In: The Fifth IFIP–TC6 International Conference on Mobile and Wireless Communications Networks, pp. 59–62 (2004)

Appendix A — Basic Communication Properties

In the following text we briefly summarize basic information about GSM network architecture and communication techniques of mobile devices.

GSM Network Architecture

The GSM (Global System for Mobile Communication) network topology typically consists from two or three main subsystems. The first is *base station subsystem* that consists of mobile phones, base transceiver stations (BTS), and base station controller (BSC). Mobile phones are in fact generic devices that are personalized by subscriber identification module (SIM) card. BTSs are responsible for wireless connection with mobile phones and BSCs manages multiple BTSs and performs spectrum allocation as well as handoffs.

The second is *network and switching subsystem* that consists of mobile switching center (MSC) and several registers and databases. MSC manages multiple BSCs and provides connection to wired telephony network. Registers and databases are necessary for authentication, network management, storing information about (roaming) subscribers, *etc.*

The last subsystem called *GPRS core network* is used to for support general packet radio services (GPRS). It consists of several centralized GPRS support nodes (GSN) that allows connection and data transmissions to Internet. The most important GSNs are serving GPRS support node (SGSN) that is responsible for delivering data packets, and gateway GPRS support node (GGSN) that is gateway between GPRS and external packet data networks.

GSM security mechanisms are authentication (challenge-response protocol), confidentiality (encryption by symmetric cipher), and anonymity (temporary identities). However, only the user must be authenticated to the network and confidentiality of data (voice, signaling information, *etc.*) is preserved only on the radio path. The exception is GPRS core network because all data transmissions over GPRS are encrypted on the path between mobile phone and SGSN.

These security features imply obvious properties and vulnerabilities of GSM networks — *e.g.*, using false BTS station that can force mobile phone to disable encryption, interception of communication on remaining part of the network, lawful interception, *etc.*

Communication Techniques of Mobile Devices

In the previous section we restricted ourselves to discussion of GSM/GPRS architecture and its security issues. We shall consider all mobile devices capable to connect GSM networks (including PDA phones, notebooks with GSM PCMCIA cards, *etc.*) because many of them have own O/S and support various applications that may require well-secured communication. We shall also summarize and keep on mind all possible methods of communication that can be established by these devices and thus can be a subject of various attacks. Note that we use GSM/GPRS as our reference mobile network, but similar discussion can be done, *e.g.*, for UMTS/HSDPA or other 3G/4G networks.

The most versatile mobile devices are, from our point of view, PDA phones. These devices have own operating system, can run various applications, and support a lot of communication techniques:

1. Infrared (IR) – short-range wireless link that requires direct visibility of communicating parties. IR link is unprotected and uses no authentication or encryption.
2. Bluetooth (BT) – short-range wireless radio link. Direct visibility is not required and thus password-based authentication techniques are used. First successful authentication (so-called BT pairing) allows paired devices to communicate without further authentications. The communication is protected by stream cipher E0.
3. Wireless access point (WiFi AP) – medium-range wireless radio link that supports optional unilateral user authentication and encryption (*e.g.*, WEP or WPA).
4. GSM/GPRS network – radio link between mobile device and BTS is protected by A5 algorithm but particular mobile operator knows all secret keys in his network. Transmissions in wired part of network (with exception of GPRS) are typically unencrypted.
5. USB interface – unprotected wired link typically between mobile device and computer that can share connection to the Internet.

The communication between mobile devices or between mobile device and some (semi)trusted server always utilizes some of these techniques.

Appendix B — Attacker Model for Distributed Systems

The attacker models are divided into the four different types according to the communication paths described above. Note that we always expect that consuming device is trusted and cannot contain malicious software as viruses, Trojan horses, *etc.*

Attacker type 1 can exploit weak points of communication path type 1.

The USB and IR point-to-point communication link use neither authentication nor encryption mechanisms. That fact implies that an attacker can eavesdrop all the communication and impersonate any device. For example, the attacker taps the USB cable. However, such attacks are not easy to be done due to the physical characteristics of the USB and IR links. Both of them provide short-distance communication, but USB cable is under control of its owner and IR requires direct visibility between communication devices.

The WiFi and Bluetooth communication link use authentication and encryption mechanisms. WiFi authentication is unilateral — only end-point devices have to authenticate themselves to access point (in infrastructure mode) but not vice-versa. That leads to the fact that an adversary can act as legitimate access point. Bluetooth authentication is based on the knowledge of the shared password and is bilateral. In case of three or more parties involved into communication path Bluetooth and WiFi have the same security flaw. Man-in-the-middle attack is always possible, because secure protocols are always performed only between the master/AP and slave/end-point devices and never between two slave/end-point devices.

The link could be secured using encryption. However, Bluetooth encryption algorithm E0 is considered to be weak. WEP used for securing WiFi has problems with key management and initialization vectors set-up. Several access points can be connected by either wired or wireless links that also could be attacked by an adversary.

Attacker type 2 can exploit weak points of communication path type 2.

GSM network requires mobile device authentication (algorithm A3/A8 also called COMP128), but GSM network does not authenticate itself to the mobile device. That fact gives the attacker the possibility to create fake BTS, which acts as an original one. Such attacker can perform man-in-the-middle attacks or can disable A5 encryption between mobile devices and BTS. Moreover, A5 algorithm is not public and some previous versions were broken.

A more disturbing attack scenario involves untrusted mobile network operator (including its employees) or/and lawful interception performed by the government.

Attacker type 3 can exploit weak points of communication path type 3.

Communication path type 3 extends communication path type 1, therefore, it contains all path 1 weaknesses. Since the communication path type 3 goes trough the Internet or similar packet oriented network it also suffer from vulnerabilities typical for this type of networks.

Attacker type 4 can exploit weak points of communication path type 4.

Communication path type 4 extends communication path type 3, therefore, it contains all path 3 weaknesses. Since the communication path type 4 goes trough the GSM network it also suffer from vulnerabilities typical for that type of network.

Generating Random Numbers in Hostile Environments
(Transcript of Discussion)

Jan Krhovjak

Masaryk University

Tuomas Aura: In what kind of situations would you request random data from other devices, or what devices have core operations on random numbers?

Reply: For example, you can have audio/video conferences. If you are in a hostile environment, then you expect to be under attack. Typically in mobile devices there are not many sources of randomness, and if you want to have better random data, you must combine it with some random data from someone else.

Tuomas Aura: So you use the application data as a source of randomness. Do you explicitly send random bits from one device to another, or do you use the application data as a source of randomness?

Reply: I will be talking about that shortly. You can send random data generated by some kind of random number generator, or possibly by two random generators, but you can also use random data from, for example, a video stream, from video contents. I will be talking later about when it is necessary to secure this communication, because if the data can be observed then there will be no entropy in such randomness, I am not talking only about the communication issues.

We have a little bit of a problem of entropy definition, as, in the case of audio/video conference, or these group key agreement protocols, keys are typically shared among more parties. There is a problem with the unpredictability because the key can contain a lot of entropy, but if someone sees the key, then from his point of view there is no more entropy, so if the attacker is inside the group, we will say that there is no entropy until later. And we propose a mechanism such as group entropy for some video conferences, we propose to maintain distinct pools for each communication group. There is also an interesting question regarding the audio and video streams, because since all recipients of these streams see these streams, there is zero entropy in the data, so it would be nice to define or propose some secure transformation into different streams.

From a practical point of view it is quite easy because I can have a random number generator on each device, or some encryption function with different cryptographic keys, and I can process those things. If I have a 128-bit key, and receive a 128 kilobyte picture, there is probably this amount of entropy in it. But if I get the next picture, will there be another 128 bits of entropy? It's hard to assess such practical things from this point of view. In this case we typically expected that we sent the request and some device sent us directly a response, however it can be done another way: we send a request for random data, the

B. Christianson et al. (Eds.): Security Protocols 2008, LNCS 6615, pp. 51–53, 2011.

device that the request was sent to generates some random data, then the request is sent on to the next device, the next device also generates random data, but using its own entropy, and this hop-by-hop technique can be used. However, we currently don't know if there is any practical usability, because it can be always replaced by this direct request. If you know how to deal with the problem of entropy, all ideas are welcome.

Tuomas Aura: I think this is enormous trouble to generate random numbers, how many random numbers do you need in that thing, apart from a couple of nonces in the beginning?

Reply: I think it's dependent on the application. If you have long-term or short-term keys you probably won't want much randomness, but if you use encryption, and padding values, initialisation vectors, and if your connection is quite fast, then you ...

Tuomas Aura: But you can use pseudo random numbers for those.

Reply: Yes, but that is limited. When you look at the problem from this point of view, the entropy from some random numbers is limited by the entropy of the seed you use. When I can influence the source of your random data, or disable your random number generator, the source of the random number generator is important.

Caspar Bowden: There's a more fundamental question, is the remote source of entropy the source of entropy?

Reply: If nobody sees it, then yes.

Caspar Bowden: Well that's OK if the remote source of entropy knows these states. But if you have a remote new source of entropy, with a permission, then someone else knows what the random number generator is in the remote source?

Reply: Yes.

Virgil Gligor: One of the apparent problems here is that what the adversary does is not well-defined. If we define an adversary so that we can never generate any secure random numbers, then you don't have a source of entropy. So the point is to define your adversary precisely enough and say, look, even in the face of this adversary I can still generate sufficient entropy for my application. If the adversary is not well-defined then it's not clear what solution we have.

Reply: We can do the definition well in the case of the local device, but when we try to define the other side, based on the communication paths, we always found that we need end-to-end security. You have the same data, and if one piece of the data was seen by an attacker, it's not secure.

Virgil Gligor: You're absolutely right. So then we have a security problem, because for security you need entropy, and for entropy we need security.

Reply: Yes, and many of our discussions end with this.

Virgil Gligor: So do you have any way to break this vicious cycle?

Reply: We found that if you use many generating devices and collect from many sources, for example, mobile devices and unlimited networks, the attacker can influence this, but if he doesn't know for whom the data actually is, he has to select the victim.

Virgil Gligor: So you do have an adversary model, so the adversary can only attack a fraction of the communication links?

Reply: Yes.

Virgil Gligor: And consequently if you collect entropy from all the communication links, and perhaps you have some local way to pick somewhat randomly, then the adversary would not have a high chance of getting to the entropy.

Caspar Bowden: I read about a gadget a few years ago where you point an antenna at a quasar, and you pick up white noise from a particular spot in the sky. That's how you authenticate a quasar.

Reply: But how do we agree what the quasar sent?

Bruce Christianson: Well that's easy enough, you can exchange the error correcting bits in the open. There are similar proposals for using purpose-built satellites, and one for using fibre optics at this very workshop a couple of years ago[1]. It's fairly easy to have a beacon service that will spray random numbers at you, and you can pseudo-randomly choose a very small subset of them. Often the hard part is knowing that you're connected to a source of authentic random numbers, rather than one that's controlled by an attacker.

Reply: I think the quasar was a bit of a gimmick, but the satellite thing is more closely related to this workshop. The original proposal by Michael Rabin was based on truly secure cryptography where the storage capacity of the attacker was bounded[2].

Michael Roe: It's a scheme that sounded very promising, but then he went off to describe a system where you have lots of nodes generating this data and sharing it between themselves, rather than using a lot of broadcasts, and I was unconvinced by his suggestions that the attackers wouldn't be able to specifically target people.

Bruce Christianson: But in the context of this talk, you need something like that. To lever your secrets up, you need some sort of scrambling, because otherwise it doesn't matter how much entropy you're collecting from remote services, that is only as secure as the key that it's encrypted under.

---

[1] See LNCS 5087, pp 261–275: Vintage Bit Cryptography.
[2] Maurer, 1992, Journal of Cryptology, vol. 5, no. 1, pp 53–66.

Cyberdice: Peer-to-Peer Gambling in the Presence of Cheaters

Frank Stajano and Richard Clayton

University of Cambridge Computer Laboratory
15 JJ Thomson Avenue, Cambridge, CB3 0FD, United Kingdom

Abstract. We describe a simple gambling game in which n participants each put down a fixed amount of money and one of them, selected at random, wins and takes it all. We describe how this game can be operated in cyberspace, without knowing anything about the other participants except for the bit strings they transmit. We show how the genuine winner can convert the bit strings back into money, without any other gambler or eavesdropper being able to do so before her. We also show that it is possible to have confidence in the fair running of the game even if all the other participants, including the dealer, are crooked and are prepared to manipulate the protocol to their advantage. The paper initially develops a naïve protocol for running the game, and shows various ways in which a gambler can cheat by ceasing to send messages once it is clear that she is losing. We incrementally build this up into a protocol that resists drop-outs, collusion and dishonesty from all players, by relying on the honest behaviour of some non-gambling 'issuers' whose role is to convert currency into bit strings and vice versa.

1 Introduction

Five people sit around a table and throw dice in turn: whoever gets the highest score is the winner[1]. This is a simple game of chance that designates a winner out of a group of people.

Now consider bringing this game to cyberspace. Participants can't see each other throwing the dice: all they know about each other is that they send and receive bit strings. They may be strongly motivated to cheat: imagine they are playing for money, with each gambler paying a fixed fee to play, and winner take all. You never see their faces: they could be spam lords, phishing operators or other remorseless online criminals, so assume that they will definitely cheat if given the chance — simply asking participants to publish the outputs of their individual random number generators won't do.

The problem to be solved is twofold: firstly, we seek a protocol that allows a group of adversarial players to determine a winner fairly, even in the presence of cheaters and even if they know nothing about each other except the bit strings

---

[1] Yes, there might be *ex-aequo* winners. For the moment, imagine dice with 2^{32} sides so that this occurrence is unlikely. We shall properly fix this problem later.

B. Christianson et al. (Eds.): Security Protocols 2008, LNCS 6615, pp. 54–70, 2011.
© Springer-Verlag Berlin Heidelberg 2011

they exchange. Secondly, we need a protocol and a digital payment system that will ensure that the winner gets paid by the losers, even if the losers are dishonest and have no intention of honouring their debts.

This paper offers three main contributions to security research. The first is Cyberdice, a peer-to-peer gambling protocol that satisfies the above requirements for a game. The second is a sub-protocol that addresses the digital payment issue: how to 'put money on the table' in the form of a bit string while ensuring that only the winner (unknown at that point) will be able to redeem it. The third contribution, at a more general level, is the discussion of a class of protocol attacks in which malicious principals choose at each step whether to continue following the prescribed protocol or not.

The paper starts by setting out our requirements for the protocol (Section 2) and by introducing our approach (Section 3). In Section 4 we present 'Cyberdice 0.1', a naïve version of the protocol that fails to prevent cheating if players choose not to follow the protocol to its conclusion. In Section 5 we change our requirements to address this type of cheating and discuss the true difficulty of the problem we have posed. In Section 6 we present 'Cyberdice 0.9', a modified version of Cyberdice 0.1 resistant to players dropping out. However this protocol can still be simplified and enhanced, so in Section 7 we present the full detail of 'Cyberdice 1.0', which meets all our extended requirements and, as part of it, we present the sub-protocol for ensuring that the winner gets paid (Section 7.4). We finish by discussing related work in Section 8 and offer some concluding thoughts in Section 9. For convenience, an appendix offers a one-page reference to the sequence of messages exchanged during the protocol.

2   Why Is Peer-to-Peer Online Gambling Hard?

Gambling in cyberspace is hard, because it very difficult to know who you are playing with, or whether you can locate them in the future to hold them to account for their past actions. No player will be prepared to trust any other player sufficiently that they would let them 'run' the game; for the same reason, the protocol cannot rely on a trusted third party to select the winner, because that trust might be misplaced.

If any third parties such as banks are involved in supplying digital currency, we do not want to rely on such third parties to act as trusted casino operators — firstly because we assumed that the players would not trust anyone to roll dice fairly; secondly because we do not want those pseudo-banks to be tainted by the stigma of the gambling act. Their only responsibility must be to issue bit strings that can be used as currency and then exchange them back into currency according to a previously agreed deterministic criterion for accepting or rejecting the claim. It must be possible for the currency-issuing third party to convince an external auditor that they acted appropriately and in strict agreement with that stated deterministic criterion.

The protocol must be fair, in the sense of selecting a winner with equal probability from amongst all the participants, regardless of whether any or all of them misbehave. It must still be possible for any player to win even if all of the other players collude, and for that matter to win with exactly the same odds as if everyone played honestly.

It must be possible to play over an insecure communication medium such as, say, Usenet News: we assume that any message may be overheard by any player (or third party) and that players or third parties may act as Dolev-Yao adversaries capable of intercepting, deleting and rewriting any messages.

However, to have some chance of constructing a solution, we assume that the nodes are capable of running strong cryptographic algorithms that the adversaries cannot break, and that the internal actions and secrets of the nodes cannot be observed.

Finally, it must be possible for anyone, including third parties as well as the participants themselves, to reach the same conclusion about who won the game by observing all the messages sent and received by the players.

Cyberdice honours all of the above constraints.

3   Cyberdice: The Core Ideas

3.1   Handling Money in Cyberspace

In order to take part in the game, gamblers first need to put their money on the table. Doing so in cyberspace is not trivial: if a bit string can be converted into currency by any beneficiary, then, as soon as a player publishes it, any other dishonest player (or eavesdropper) can grab the digital cash string and spend it. On the other hand it is not possible for the player to 'put on the table' a digital cheque written out to a specific beneficiary, because at that stage the winner of the game is yet to be decided.

In Cyberdice, the idea is to pay a trusted third party (acting more as an escrow agent than as a bank) to issue a bit string that can only be redeemed for currency (minus a small handling fee) by the winner of a designated game. Such third party is called an *issuer*. Anyone who overhears the string can bring it to the originating issuer agent for payment; but the issuer will only pay after being presented with indisputable evidence that the bearer won the game mentioned in the string itself.

There are therefore three kinds of participants: issuers, dealer and gamblers (the latter two also referred to collectively as 'players'), whose roles and functions are described in greater detail below.

3.2   The Issuers

The Cyberdice protocol does not require an issuer to overlook or run the game in any way: in fact it even allows each gambler to use a different issuer. The issuers merely act as 'transducers' between the world of currency and that of bit strings: their only job is to accept money in escrow, publish signed strings and redeem bit strings with certain properties against deposited money, after verifying the credentials of the redeemer. The winner collects their takings from the relevant issuer(s) in turn, by presenting the necessary evidence. By staying outside the game itself, the issuers cannot lose money — indeed we expect them to charge a fee for each conversion operation they perform. In essence, the main requirement is that the chosen issuers be 'well known' and trusted by their customers to honour their contracts. We also assume that issuers are robust against Denial Of Service (DOS) attacks and therefore that they will always be contactable within a reasonable time (which we will not presume is true for the players, whose cyber-existence is ephemeral).

3.3   The Players

Unlike the issuers, the players — both the dealer and the gamblers — are not trusted by anyone. Hence they are required to put their money into escrow before the real action starts. Dealers[2] collect a fee from anyone wishing to gamble at their game and therefore compete against each other on fees, as well as on the reputation of the issuers they choose to work with.

Ignoring dealer and issuer fees, the type of gambling game we discuss essentially consists of collecting s currency units from each of n gamblers and then handing over the whole $s \times n$ amount as prize money to the designated winner, chosen randomly from the n gamblers with uniform probability. This would be a game in which the dealer never makes a profit or a loss. Instead, since there are fees, it is a game in which the dealer is guaranteed to make a small profit at each game run, regardless of who wins — as opposed to a game such as roulette where the dealer has an advantage in the long term but may lose out on individual game runs.

One may wonder why any rational gambler would ever take part in such a game, since the expected return is always less (because of dealer and issuer fees) than the payment required to play. Just so that you can follow the paper without worrying about this point, we refer you to the classic work by Markowitz [8] that explains such chance-taking behaviour through the non-linearity of the function linking wealth to its utility: when we can't afford to lose, we prefer $1,000,000 with certainty instead of a 1-in-10 chance to win $10,000,000; but, for much smaller amounts, we may prefer one chance in 10 to win $10 rather than $1 with certainty.

4   Cyberdice Version 0.1

We now present an initial (flawed) attempt at the Cyberdice protocol; and then discuss how it can be attacked by players who do not follow the rules.

The game starts with the dealer announcing that a game will take place and setting out the rules, the costs, the allowed number of gamblers and the time-scale for the various protocol steps (so that everyone always knows whether they should still wait for someone else's response or not).

---

[2] There is only one dealer per game; but the plural reflects the fact that there may be several independent games.

This first message, in common with all messages in the protocol, is signed by its sender (in this case the dealer), contains a unique randomly chosen nonce and clearly identifies message type and source/destination. These precautions will ensure that messages from another game or another protocol stage cannot cause any confusion. Viz: we assume throughout this paper that all the usual hygiene precautions are in place, and so we need not worry about replay attacks, duplication of messages, or the use of one message in place of another. Our only concern is attacks upon the high-level design of the protocol.

The gamblers who wish to take part then correspond with an issuer of their choice[3] to purchase a bit-string that represents their game joining fee. This bit string is tied to the particular game and represents an irrevocable commitment by the issuer to pay the fee to the game's winner (or, if it can be shown that the game did not proceed, to reimburse the gambler who deposited that fee). The gamblers send these bit-strings to the dealer asking to take part in the game, along with a commitment to the random number for their dice roll (*e.g.*: they publish $h(r||x)$, a cryptographic hash of their random dice roll number r concatenated with a nonce x).

The dealer then selects the gamblers for the game, using any criteria she wishes (she may not trust particular issuers to pay up, or she may refuse particular gamblers for personal reasons). Having made the selection, she publishes the list of gamblers who will take part in the game. Since the random numbers chosen by the gamblers are not known to the dealer (they were only committed to), the dealer cannot predict the result of the game as a function of the subset of gamblers she chooses.

The gamblers who were not selected can now recover their money from their respective issuers (by showing the selection message that indicates they will not play in the game). If the dealer fails to make a selection by a given time (which was specified in the original announcement of the game) then all of the gamblers will be entitled to get their money back[4].

The gamblers now reveal their random numbers (to which they committed earlier) and these values are combined to determine the winner. Just picking the highest value would clearly not work, as dishonest players would choose the highest possible value instead of a random one. We might, if they were all unsigned 32-bit values, add them together modulo 2^{32} and designate as winner the highest number smaller than the total. Alternatively, we might hash each gambler's random number concatenated with the total, and then pick the highest result. The winner will be able to collect her winnings by visiting each issuer in turn, with the relevant signed messages as proof of her success[5].

---

[3] Nothing prevents several gamblers from choosing the same issuer. In other words there is a one-to-one mapping from the set of players to the set of issuers, but this mapping is not invertible in general.

[4] We will need to describe the mechanism by which we prove this negative, but since this protocol still has much more significant flaws, we will fix those first and come back to this point later.

[5] Note that at this stage we have not yet provided a mechanism to guarantee that the winner will be unique. See Section 7 for that.

4.1 Timing Attacks on Cyberdice 0.1

When the gamblers reveal their random values in turn, the last gambler to reveal will know whether she won or lost before she makes her announcement. If she won, fine; but, if she lost, then there is little incentive — apart from her honesty and sense of fair play — for her to bother announcing the random value, and the game will be incomplete.

The DOS problem can be fixed by adding a further time-out, pre-set in the initial game announcement message. If a gambler does not reveal their random value within the appropriate time, then she is excluded, and the total (or the hash value) is calculated without her contribution playing any part.

Unfortunately, if gamblers collude, there is still an advantage to be gained from failing to reveal one's random values. For simplicity we will just consider the case where two dishonest gamblers collude, and they both arrange to play 'last'; but the attack is trivially extended to a collusion among the last k gamblers. If they both fail to reveal their random values then they lose; but they now have the choice of revealing one or the other value, or both — and if one of these three alternatives makes one of them the winner they will share the spoils; in other words, they cannot *guarantee* a win, but they can materially improve their chances.

The collusion might not even be pre-arranged. The last gambler can calculate which of two other gamblers will win depending on whether she sends the final message or not. Either or both of these gamblers can be contacted (quickly, as the time-out approaches) with an offer to split the proceeds by guaranteeing a win.

5 Why Is Online Gambling Really, Really Hard?

We can now see that the difficulty with our protocol is that we need to construct a random result from the random contributions of all the gamblers; but if gamblers collude they can have some influence over the result by choosing whether or not to reveal what their contribution was.

We cannot easily fix this problem by fining the gamblers for disrupting the game. The only way to ensure that a gambler does not withhold their random value would be to ensure that they would lose more than they could possibly win — viz: they would have to escrow an amount equal to the total amount being wagered. This might be an acceptable solution where four people were wagering a tenner each, but would make it impossible to run games where a million gamblers were wagering a dollar each — even millionaires might not be prepared to risk their money when an unexpected network outage could see them fined.

We cannot fix this problem by having the gamblers announce their random values instead of merely making a commitment — the dealer could then rig the game at the point at which the selection of gamblers is made by picking a combination that meant a particularly favoured gambler was the winner.

We could perhaps have the gamblers announce the values encrypted with a 40-bit-key cipher or some other easy-to-break encryption. If they fail to reveal the values then the other gamblers mount a brute-force attack to discover the encryption key. This is not especially elegant, and it would be unwise to play against the NSA — who might be able to decrypt the values at an early enough stage for them to mount a collusion attack. It would be good to have access to a 'nobody will be able to decrypt this message before time t' primitive, but this is known to be a hard problem if one cannot resort to trusted third parties or tamper-resistant hardware.

6   Cyberdice 0.9

Let's skip a few more vulnerable revisions of the protocol and jump forward to one that provides the properties we need. Some readers may feel that our solution is a little bit like cheating: we shall make the assumption that the issuers who provide digital currency for the game are honest. We shall use them indirectly to provide a final randomised stirring of the pool of random values, so as to designate a winner fairly.

We run the protocol exactly as in Cyberdice 0.1 presented above, up until the point at which the gamblers reveal their random values. At this stage, the dealer constructs and signs a message which contains these random values[6]. The signed message is then submitted to each of the issuers used by the gamblers, and they also sign it[7]. The random pool which will be used to decide the winner is created from the values of the signatures which the issuers make.

The game can be seen to be fair, in that it is well-known (albeit possibly hard to prove) that signatures made with high quality cryptographic primitives are random. If this isn't believed to be true of signatures in general, then placing their values into a canonical order and then calculating a cryptographic hash of this concatenation will provide an 'even more random' value.

Essentially, we have finessed away the 'last gamblers can quit when they see that they are losing' problem by asserting that the need of the issuers to preserve their reputation prevents them from reneging on their obligation (paid for in the fees they charge for their bit strings) to provide a signature. Now the last gambler can't yet *see* whether she will win or lose when she is still in a position to quit, and the last issuer (who can see it) is bound not to quit for the reasons above.

We have already given issuers special properties that we do not ascribe to gamblers: we assume that they will act honestly when presented with proof of a win; we assume that messages to or from them can never be blocked; we assume that they keep an indelible record of the message they have signed; and so on. Assuming that no issuer is so beholden to a gambler that they will withhold their signature does not seem all that unreasonable a stretch. However, we will return to the honesty of issuers in Section 8.

---

[6] For hygiene reasons, the message might include all previous messages as well, in a canonical order, so as to be sure that no relevant state is being omitted.

[7] This operation is linear in the number of issuers involved, which is bounded by the number of players.

7 Cyberdice 1.0

Now that we have effectively chosen to use the signatures of the issuers as a source of randomness within the game, we can simplify the protocol by eliminating the gamblers' dice rolls. Doing so also finally guarantees the uniqueness of the winner. We present this latest refinement pretty much from scratch (so that it can be read and attacked independently of what led to it) and in somewhat greater detail than we have bothered with so far.

7.1 The Principals

The principals taking part in each game are a *dealer* (who neither wins nor loses, but always makes a profit by collecting a fee from the gamblers, independent of the outcome), several *gamblers* (who may win or lose; always pay fees to the dealer and to their chosen issuer in order to play, whether they win or lose) and several *issuers* (who don't take part in the gambling process; they hold money in escrow for a fee and turn it into bit strings that can be later redeemed by presenting other, related bit strings with certain properties). Issuers will also sign messages upon request, under certain conditions.

The main security aim of the protocol is to ensure that, if issuers are honest, a gambler will win or lose with the same probability regardless of whether the other gamblers and the dealer play honestly or dishonestly (they might even all collude against one honest participant).

The protocol is not resistant to dishonest behaviour by issuers; it tries however to offer some robustness by allowing participants the freedom to choose issuers they trust: the dealer specifies up front which issuers are acceptable for the gamblers to use, while the gamblers can see both this list of allowed issuers and the dealer's own choice of issuer before deciding whether to participate.

A gambler pays her chosen issuer a sum consisting of three components: stake s, dealer's fee f_d, gambler's issuer's fee f_{gi}. If she wins, she redeems the prize of $n \times s$ from the dealer's issuer, where n is the number of players who played. The dealer pays her chosen issuer a sum consisting of two components: the maximum possible prize money, that is $n_{max} \times s$, where n_{max} is the maximum number of players that the dealer will admit to the game, and the dealer's issuer's fee f_{di}. At the end of the game, the dealer collects the leftover money $(n_{max} - n) \times s$ from her issuer and, separately, the stakes of all the gamblers from the gamblers' own issuers.

A gambler cannot be cheated by any combination of the other players (gamblers and dealer) if issuers are honest, but could be cheated if issuers are dishonest[8]. Similarly the dealer cannot be cheated by any combination of the gamblers

---

[8] Issuers must be honest not just about handling money (as is obviously the case for the dealer's issuer, who could refuse to pay out the prize, and the player's own issuer, who could pocket the stake money and not blog (*q.v.*) the gambler's stake), but also about honouring their contract in terms of signing follow-up messages by a given deadline as agreed. Failing that, it is also possible for a gambler to be defrauded by the action or inaction of another gambler's issuer.

if issuers are honest, but can be cheated if issuers are dishonest. An issuer, instead, cannot be cheated by any other participant[9], whether issuer, dealer or gambler.

Issuers all provide the same service, so they compete against each other on reputation and fees: those who have a good reputation can afford to charge a higher fee. Each issuer has what we shall call a blog — a facility that lets her publish timestamped and signed messages on her web site to an append-only, integrity-protected log. Issuers cannot 'rewrite history' because they must sign the messages they post on their own blog. If an issuer altered and re-signed an earlier post, any reader who kept a copy of the previous version of that post could expose the issuer's tampering, causing a loss of reputation for the issuer and therefore an indirect financial loss[10]. We assume that issuers are sufficiently powerful that communication channels to and from them cannot be cut off by denial of service attacks; in other words it is always possible for anyone to talk to an issuer and to read the blog of an issuer.

7.2   Starting a Game

To start a game, the dealer prepares a message of type M_0 ('invitation') that describes the game parameters[11]. These parameters are: the dealer's fee f_d (the 'tax' that the dealer collects from each admitted gambler, forming the dealer's profit), the stake s (the amount that each gambler 'puts on the table' to form the prize money that the winner will eventually receive), the identity of the dealer's issuer (the issuer who will hold the prize money deposited by the dealer and who will pay it out to the winner), the maximum number of gamblers n_{max}, the list of acceptable issuers for the gamblers to use, the deadline t_2 by which would-be gamblers must gamble, the deadline t_5 by which the dealer promises to publish the 'game seal' message M_5, as well as some more deadlines necessary to ensure completion of the final payback phase in a finite time (see appendix). The M_0 message also contains the ephemeral public key of the dealer[12], which doubles as a unique identifier for this game.

The dealer sends this message to her chosen issuer, together with the dealer's issuer's fee f_{di} and enough currency to cover the maximum prize that the game

---

[9] Under the obvious baseline assumptions that signatures can't be forged *etc.*

[10] Conversely, an attacker who were capable of forging the issuer's signature could also frame the issuer by pretending she tampered with her own blog — although an adversary with the ability to forge the issuer's signature, which is outside our threat model, could probably use it for much more profitable attacks.

[11] We continue to assume, as we have done elsewhere in the paper, that all appropriate hygiene precautions are taken to ensure that messages are labelled, and contain appropriate randomly chosen nonces, typically in the form of the ephemeral public keys of the players, so that the protocol is immune from low-level attacks such as replays and the introduction of messages from other runs of the protocol. We also assume that participants always perform all the applicable consistency checks (including verification of signatures) on any messages that they receive, so that simple forgeries will be immediately detected.

[12] A new key pair is chosen by each player for each game.

might award: that is to say $n_{max} \times s$. The dealer's issuer, having accepted the payment, timestamps and signs the message (yielding M_1, 'certified invitation') and publishes it on her blog.

Potential gamblers see the certified invitation. In order to play, a gambler must choose an issuer among the ones deemed acceptable by the dealer and send to that issuer, together with an amount of money equal to the issuer's fee f_{gi} plus the dealer's fee f_d plus the game stake s, a message of type M_2 ('stake') containing the following fields: the M_1 to which the gambler is responding, the ephemeral public key of the gambler and the gambler's signature.

The gambler's issuer timestamps, signs and blogs the gambler's message, yielding M_3 ('certified stake').

Then the gambler's issuer also forwards this M_3 to the dealer's issuer. The dealer's issuer in turn timestamps, signs and blogs M_3 to yield an M_4 (a 'doubly certified stake').

Missing deadlines. Whenever the dealer misses a deadline, evidence for which is available in the dealer's issuer's blog, all the players get fully reimbursed, fees included, and all the issuers get back (out of the money that was originally left in escrow by the dealer) the fees that they had to refund to the players — so that neither gamblers nor issuers lose out if the dealer fails to perform. The remainder of the money put in escrow by the dealer is then returned to the dealer. So long as the stake s exceeds the gambler's issuer's fee f_{gi}, the money left in escrow by the dealer $(n_{max} \times s + f_{di})$ will clearly be sufficient to reimburse all the issuers, in reason of one f_{gi} per bet; whereas, to reimburse the gamblers, the issuers simply return the same money that the gamblers originally paid, namely $s + f_d + f_{gi}$ per bet.

Meaning of signatures. What is the meaning of an issuer's signature on a message? Does it imply that the issuer performed all possible sanity checks on it (*e.g.*: 'the M_3 refers to a game for which I published the certified invitation M_1 in my blog, there is a good signature on it from some issuer, the issuer was cited as acceptable in the M_0 invitation', *etc...*)? Possibly, but not necessarily; a minimalistic and equally valid alternative would be for the issuer to perform essentially no checks and for the signature to mean simply 'I got paid to notarize that I received this string so here is my timestamped certification of it, but I didn't even read it — it could be dirty jokes in ancient Babylonian for all I care' and leave all responsibility for the correctness of the string to the entity who brings the message for signing. There is a trade-off between the two goals of detecting malformed or fraudulent messages as early as possible vs. involving the issuers in as few aspects as possible of the gambling game.

7.3 Deciding on the Winner

The dealer monitors the blog of her own issuer for any M_4 that refers to her M_1. She accumulates them in a list until she reaches the stated maximum number of gamblers or, in any case, until she (almost) reaches the t_5 deadline. She then chooses the participants who will take part in the game, using whatever criteria she wishes. She forms a message of type M_5 ('game seal') by signing the concatenation of M_1 with the list of the M_4 of all the chosen participants in order of time-stamp. She then submits M_5 to her issuer, who timestamps, signs and blogs it as M_6 ('certified game seal'). If the dealer fails to send her M_5 to her issuer before t_5, the issuer still signs and blogs an 'empty' M_6 containing the relevant M_1 and a flag signalling that no M_5 was received for that game by the deadline. In such a case the game defined by that M_1 is declared void: all gamblers who have an M_4 listed in the dealer's issuer's blog are entitled to get a refund of their stake and of their fees from their own issuer[13]. If instead the dealer sends an M_5 by t_5, then the game proceeds. All the gamblers who submitted an M_2 but are not selected in the M_6 are entitled to a refund of their stake (but not their fee) from their issuer: there is no difficulty for a rejected gambler in proving this entitlement to her issuer, merely by exhibiting both the M_3 and the M_6.

At this point, assuming that the game is proceeding, the M_6 is passed around all the participating gamblers' issuers in turn, in the order in which they were listed in the M_0, and each one of them signs and blogs the bundle consisting of the M_6 with all the signatures collected so far[14]. Once all the issuers involved have signed it (just once each), the bundle comes back to the dealer's issuer as M_7 ('multi-signed game seal'). The reason for this round of signatures will be explained after we describe how the winner is selected.

Anyone with access to M_7 can now determine the winner by processing it with the following deterministic algorithm. If n is the number of M_4 messages in M_7, we hash the M_7 and let $i = h(M_7) \mod n$. This index $i \in 0 \ldots n-1$ points at one of the M_4 messages in the order in which they are listed in M_7, and the gambler who submitted that message is the winner.

The dealer's issuer executes this algorithm, appends the computed i of the winner to the M_7, and then signs and blogs the lot as M_8 ('winner announcement'). The outcome of the game is thereby published and anyone can verify that the selection of the winner happened fairly, according to the prescribed rules.

Why do we require all the issuers to sign the bundle in turn? Imagine if none of them signed it, and the message to be hashed were the M_5 supplied by the dealer. Then the dealer could privately try various subsets of gamblers to accept, checking each time who comes out as the winner, and eventually committing to the selection that favoured specific colluding players (or even 'sock-puppets', i.e. fake identities, of the dealer herself). In a previous version of the protocol we blocked this by computing the hash on M_6, i.e. on the version of M_5 signed by the

---

[13] The money escrowed by the defaulting dealer and held by the dealer's issuer is divided among all the gambler's issuers involved, proportionally to the number of M_3 issued by each, to cover the loss of fees. If any is left over after reimbursing all of the gamblers' issuers' fees, which depends on the number of players who chose to gamble, then it may be collected by the dealer.

[14] Note that we are not assigning a message number to the intermediate versions of the bundle. Doing so would only add gratuitous complication since the number of signers varies from game to game.

dealer's issuer; but this set-up is still subject to the same fraud if dealer and issuer collude. Since the dealer himself could be a sock-puppet of the issuer (!), this is not satisfactory, especially as the fraud is undetectable by someone observing the logs and therefore would not be reflected in the issuer's reputation. By requesting the signatures of all issuers involved, in a predetermined order, this fraud is eliminated unless *all issuers* collude — in which case anyone playing might as well go home.

We further specify that the underlying signature scheme must be completely deterministic, in the sense that once the public key is fixed there is only one possible valid signature for any given message. Failing that, it might be possible for the last signer to fiddle with the signature until the hash pointed at the desired winner.

7.4   Delivering the Money

To claim her prize, the winning gambler goes to the dealer's issuer and requests the money by exhibiting an M_{10} ('prize claim'). Logically, this M_{10} need only contain a *reference* to the game, since everything necessary is blogged at the dealer's issuer, but for good measure we'll instead also include in it the whole M_8.

Given M_8, the dealer's issuer (like everyone else) can read out who the winner is; so she must now make sure that she is handing over the prize money to the actual winner. The gambler proves that she is the winner by signing with her secret key a challenge supplied by the dealer's issuer. The 'prize challenge' M_{11} can be seen as a receipt for the prize amount, which the dealer is asking the winner to sign. If the gambler returns it with a good signature (M_{12}, 'prize response'), then the dealer's issuer hands over the prize money. Note that the submission of the prize claim M_{10} must happen within another deadline, t_{10} that was also mentioned in the original M_0. The dealer's issuer in turn timestamps, signs and blogs the winner's response as M_{13} ('prize receipt'), to let everyone know that the winner confirmed that she received the money (or, alternatively, that nobody came forward to claim the prize).

We emphasize that it would be possible for the dealer's issuer to defraud the winner here (the winner's prize response, which is in effect later treated as proof that the winner was paid, is signed by the winner just *before* the money is handed over), which is why the issuer is 'trusted' — using Morris's definition of a trusted entity as one that can violate your security policy. If either the payment or the receipt has to happen first, in the window between the two events the party who moved first is exposed if the other quits. We trust the issuer more than the player so we put the heavier burden on the player, but we highlight the importance of the requirement of atomicity for any 'transducer' subprotocol between an issuer and a player in which a conversion between money and a bit string takes place: this happens now, at the end of the game between winner and dealer's issuer, but also between dealer and issuers, and also at the start of the game when dealer and gamblers escrow their money. In all these cases atomicity is required, and in all these cases we give the advantage to the issuer. All these 'transducer' subprotocols are marked with an 'atomic' bracket in the appendix.

For subprotocols where an issuer pays a player rather than vice versa (M_{10}–M_{13}, M_{20}–M_{23} and M_{30}–M_{33}, collectively referred to as $M_{?0}$–$M_{?3}$), we require the issuer to include low-level evidence of the payment having taken place (think of some kind of bank transfer reference) in the blogged 'receipt' message $M_{?3}$. That way, if a dishonest issuer obtains a signed $M_{?2}$ from the player but fraudulently doesn't pay her, then evidence of such non-payment is accessible to all in that issuer's blog.

Finally, within yet another deadline t_{20}, the dealer must visit her own issuer and claim any leftover money (*e.g.* if she deposited money for a 20 person game but only 14 played) and also visit each of the gamblers' issuers to collect the gamblers' game stakes, using a challenge-response subprotocol very similar to the one used above by the winner to prove that she was the dealer and exhibiting M_{13} as evidence that the game concluded properly and the legitimate winner got paid.

As an aside, the full game definition should also include clear rules about who gets to keep the escrowed money if those entitled to it fail to claim it by the deadline.

7.5   Discussion

Assuming that all issuers are honest, the protocol ensures that neither the dealer nor any gambler can defraud the other players. Crucially, this is achieved without specifically involving the issuers in the gambling process: the issuers only honour their pre-agreed contracts about issuing bit strings for money and later converting other bit strings back into money (provided that those bit strings verify certain pre-agreed properties). Conceivably, the issuers could offer this same service for other purposes than allowing their customers to play Cyberdice, which makes their role independent of the gambling aspect and, therefore, potentially legitimate even in jurisdictions where gambling might be illegal. This, in turn, leaves — in theory — some scope for official regulation of issuers and statutory protection of customers against misbehaviour by an issuer.

If some issuers are dishonest, players are vulnerable. If a gambler left money in escrow with a dishonest issuer, the dealer risks not receiving that money (which legitimately belongs to her, since it repays an equivalent amount she deposited with her own issuer to be given out as prize money). Similarly, if the dealer chose a dishonest issuer, the winner risks not receiving her legitimately earned prize. At least in both of these cases it is easy to convince any third party, including an arbitrator, that the issuer misbehaved, simply by exhibiting the messages signed by the various parties. This can be used to accumulate reputation credits (both positive and negative) for the issuers. Since we explicitly allow gamblers and dealer to accept or refuse to take part in a Cyberdice game on the basis of the issuers involved, we at least have a mechanism to protect players against known-bad issuers. Although it would be possible for an issuer to suddenly turn bad despite an unblemished reputation history, our framework tries to prevent this from being advantageous for the issuer: while players are essentially anonymous and short-lived (they all use ephemeral keys), issuers by contrast are long-lived and owe all their business (potentially including business not related to Cyberdice) to their good reputation. So long as cheating by an issuer is detectable and worth much less than the rest of the business that a reputable issuer might legitimately obtain, then incentives are properly aligned to deter issuers from cheating.

Much more worrying is the possibility of issuers committing frauds that the protocol cannot detect, such as the one mentioned above when we explained what might happen if we didn't ask all issuers to sign the M_6. Even though it is hard to defend against frauds by entities we are forced to trust, as the Morris quote cited earlier reminds us, we would like the protocol to at least allow *detection* of frauds perpetrated by a single crooked issuer in presence of other honest ones[15]. We consider it acceptable to be vulnerable to undetectable frauds in the case where all issuers collude against the players, especially given all the subtle issues related to time-stamping that we are not examining for lack of space[16].

8   Related Work

The game of Cyberdice is essentially a secure multi-party computation, a problem for which there is a rich literature, dating back at least to the Byzantine generals problem [7]. However, many of the published protocols implicitly assume that the participants comply with the rules and will send all of the messages required of them. For example, in Yao's solution [10] to the Millionaire Problem (compute the Boolean value 'x greater than y', knowing x and without learning y) his Alice learns the result the computation first and must send the final message to Bob to allow him to obtain the same information.

The game portion of Cyberdice, excluding the crucial payment issues, is the multi-party computation of a random number, clearly connected to the widely studied problem of distributed coin flipping [1,2].

In multi-party computation the requirement that it be hard to construct a commitment knowing other players' commitments (but not the values) is known as *non-malleability*, a term put forward by Dolev *et al.* [3]. Combining this with a robustness requirement (that players cannot give up in the middle of the protocol) gives a property called *independence*. Various protocols [6,9] for solving the problem have been proposed but they require $\mathcal{O}(N)$ messages and $\mathcal{O}(N^2)$ computations and they assume that only a proportion (typically at most $1/2$ or $1/3$) of the players are cheating. In Gennaro's scheme [6], verifiable secret sharing (VSS) is used by each participant to make their commitments. A (t, n) threshold scheme is used to verify (in a zero-knowledge manner) that there is no

---

[15] This suggests that players should not all use the same issuer, otherwise it would be too easy for 'all issuers' (*i.e.* just the one) to collude against the players. There is robustness in diversification.

[16] The authoritative clock for the Cyberdice timestamps ought to be, for consistency, that of the dealer's issuer. What attacks could a malicious dealer's issuer perform by fraudulently manipulating that clock? Could we build any defences around the hypothesis that at least some of the other issuers may have the correct time throughout? *Etc.*

cheating at this stage. If at a second, reveal, stage any participant fails to take part then the holder of the shares of their secret can reconstruct their key and reveal the value they committed to.

Faust *et al.* have improved this in *v*-SimCast [5] by using Gennaro's scheme for commitment combined with Rabin's idea of backing up secret keys using VSS [9]. The scheme does not require any zero-knowledge proofs and is particularly efficient when multiple rounds occur with the same participants, because the VSS operation need only be performed once. The scheme is secure provided that half or more of the participants are honest.

Faust's scheme is therefore inappropriate for our threat model for cheating players, in that we have a constantly changing population (so the efficiency of running multiple rounds is absent) and because we wish to enable one honest gambler to take part even if everyone else is crooked. However, it is much more appropriate for solving the issues we raise in Sections 7.3 and 7.4 to enable us to deal with a small proportion of issuers failing to live up to their responsibilities.

Finally, the fear that in cyberspace everyone else may be out to get you has clear parallels with Douceur's description of the Sybil Attack [4] — where an attacker attempts to control a peer-to-peer system by pretending to be multiple independent identities which we previously referred to as 'sock-puppets'. Douceur shows that, apart from making unrealistic assumptions about resource parity and coordination, the only way that such attacks can be prevented is by introducing a centralized certifying authority that attests to the uniqueness of the participants. Although Cyberdice is much more permissive and does not preclude players (including dealers) controlling multiple identities, Douceur's principle has some resonance with our need to rely upon the good behaviour of the issuers.

9   Conclusions

We presented a mechanism to allow gamblers safely to 'put money on the table' in cyberspace, based on issuers holding money in escrow in exchange for bit strings that can later be redeemed when certain conditions are met. Interestingly, issuers offer a legitimate service that is totally independent of the gambling game.

We presented a protocol that selects a winner fairly (*i.e.* randomly) even if all the gamblers and the dealer are dishonest, and even if all players but one collude against the remaining one.

Although this result might at first appear to exceed the theoretical boundaries established in the literature for secure multi-party computation, in that it reaches a fair outcome even if *none* of the players is honest, it does so by relying on external entities, the issuers, whom the players must to some extent trust. We have strived to keep the issuers as far away as possible from the gambling process and to ensure that their behaviour can be audited but it is still possible for them to defraud the players undetectably if they all collude.

We consider this work an interesting exploration of the issues surrounding a completely adversarial multi-party computation, in which principals not only might send forged messages but might even stop playing altogether as soon as they notice that they are losing.

Acknowledgements and History

For the serendipitous stimulus that led to this work we are grateful to Frank's graduate student Bogdan Roman, who was investigating efficient MAC-layer techniques for implementing leader election protocols in ad-hoc wireless networks. Frank suggested that he consider the case in which participants cheated instead of cooperating, but this alternative viewpoint seemed less interesting for the student, whose focus was on performance. Frank attempted to caricature the scenario as a game, to make the issues clearer, and subsequently — by then on his own — worked on a financial framework and protocol to implement and play the game. In July 2007 he gave two work-in-progress talks on Cyberdice to the Security Group at Cambridge, where he received quality feedback from several members including at least Richard Clayton, Matt Johnson, Markus Kuhn, Piotr Zieliński, Ross Anderson, Mike Bond and, by mail, Mark Lomas. Frank then teamed up with Richard, who had offered some of the most insightful comments and attacks, to fix further vulnerabilities and consolidate the work into the version presented at the Protocols workshop in April 2008. George Danezis and Emilia Käsper commented on a draft and gave useful advice on related work. Any remaining vulnerabilities are of course still the responsibility of the authors. The sequence of numbered versions listed in the paper is a fictionalised simplification of the much longer litany of attack-defense-counterattack revisions that Cyberdice actually went through.

References

1. Broder, A.Z., Dolev, D.: Flipping Coins In Many Pockets (Byzantine Agreement On Uniformly Random Values). In: 25th Annual Symposium on Foundations of Computer Science, pp. 157–170 (1984)
2. Ben-Or, M., Linial, N.: Collective coin flipping. In: Micali, S. (ed.) Randomness and Computation, pp. 91–115. Academic Press, New York (1989)
3. Dolev, D., Dwork, C., Naor, M.: Naor: Non-malleable cryptography. In: Annual ACM Symposium on Theory of Computing (STOC 1991), pp. 542–552 (1991)
4. Douceur, J.R.: The Sybil Attack. In: Druschel, P., Kaashoek, M.F., Rowstron, A. (eds.) IPTPS 2002. LNCS, vol. 2429, pp. 251–260. Springer, Heidelberg (2002)
5. Faust, S., Käsper, E., Lucks, S.: Efficient Simultaneous Broadcast. In: Cramer, R. (ed.) PKC 2008. LNCS, vol. 4939, pp. 180–196. Springer, Heidelberg (2008)
6. Gennaro, R.: A protocol to achieve independence in constant rounds. IEEE Transactions on Parallel Distribution Systems 11(7), 636–647 (2000)
7. Lamport, L., Shostak, R., Pease, M.: The Byzantine Generals Problem. ACM Transactions on Programming Languages and Systems 4(3), 382–401 (1982)
8. Markowitz, H.: The Utility of Wealth. Journal of Political Economy LX(2), 151–158 (1952)
9. Rabin, T.: A simplified approach to threshold and proactive RSA. In: Krawczyk, H. (ed.) CRYPTO 1998. LNCS, vol. 1462, p. 89. Springer, Heidelberg (1998)
10. Yao, A.C.: Protocols for Secure Computation. In: Proceedings of the 23rd IEEE Symposium on Foundations of Computer Science, pp. 160–164 (1982)

Appendix A — Timeline of Messages in Cyberdice 1.0

Dealer **sends** M_0 (invitation) **to** Dealer's issuer
Dealer **pays** prize MONEY and fees **to** Dealer's issuer $\Big)$ atomic
Dealer's issuer **blogs** M_1 (certified invitation)

Gambler **sends** M_2 (stake) **to** Gambler's issuer
Gambler **pays** stake MONEY and fees **to** Gambler's issuer $\Big)$ atomic
Gambler's issuer **blogs** M_3 (certified stake)

Gambler's issuer **sends** M_3 (certified stake) **to** Dealer's issuer
Dealer's issuer **blogs** M_4 (doubly certified stake)

} repeated for each would-be gambler

Deadline t_2: Gamblers must submit M_2 by this time.
Issuers guarantee to blog and forward the corresponding M_3 shortly afterwards.

Dealer **sends** M_5 (game seal) **to** Dealer's issuer
Dealer's issuer **blogs** M_6 (certified game seal)

Deadline t_5: Dealer must submit M_5 by this time.
Issuer guarantees to blog M_6 (full or empty) shortly afterwards.

All issuers accumulate signatures on M_6 in order, yielding M_7 (multi-signed game seal)
Dealer's issuer **blogs** M_8 (winner announcement)

Winner **sends** M_{10} (prize claim) **to** Dealer's issuer
Dealer's issuer **sends** M_{11} (prize challenge) **to** Winner
Winner **sends** M_{12} (prize response) **to** Dealer's issuer $\Big)$ atomic
Dealer's issuer **pays** prize MONEY **to** Winner
Dealer's issuer **blogs** M_{13} (prize receipt)

Deadline t_{10}: Winner must submit M_{10} by this time.
Issuer guarantees to blog M_{13} (full or empty) shortly afterwards.

Dealer **sends** M_{20} (stake claim) **to** Gambler's issuer
Gambler's issuer **sends** M_{21} (stake challenge) **to** Dealer
Dealer **sends** M_{22} (stake response) **to** Gambler's issuer $\Big)$ atomic
Gambler's issuer **pays** stake MONEY **to** Dealer
Gambler's issuer **blogs** M_{23} (stake receipt)

} repeated for each gambler listed in M_5

Dealer **sends** M_{30} (leftover claim) **to** Dealer's issuer
Dealer's issuer **sends** M_{31} (leftover challenge) **to** Dealer
Dealer **sends** M_{32} (leftover response) **to** Dealer's issuer $\Big)$ atomic
Dealer's issuer **pays** leftover MONEY **to** Dealer
Dealer's issuer **blogs** M_{33} (leftover receipt)

Deadline t_{20}: Dealer must submit *all* the M_{20} and M_{30} by this time.
Issuers guarantee to blog M_{23} or M_{33} (full or empty) shortly afterwards.

Cyberdice
(Transcript of Discussion)

Frank Stajano

University of Cambridge

The game itself is basically a very simple gambling game where you have people round the table with dice, and everyone has put some money on the table to play, the same amount for everybody. They've rolled the dice, and the one who gets the highest dice roll takes all the money that was on the table. Imagine for the moment that nobody rolls the same value on the dice: you have dice with a very high number of sides so it's very unlikely that two people get the same number. So the game is simplicity itself, each player rolls dice, winner takes all.

But we are doing that in cyberspace and the 'cyber' part means that there is no table to put the money on, or roll the dice on: all you see is that you have some network card out of which bits come, and into which you put bits, and all you hear about the other people is that bits come out of your network card. You don't know who they are, you don't know even if they are there, they could all be 'sock-puppets' of someone else. And you have to deal with the issue of rolling dice fairly, and exchanging money, where all you know is these bits that come out of your network card.

We've been talking a lot about modelling the adversary, and here, basically the adversary can do anything that you can do on bit strings. The network is not secure, this is essentially Dolev-Yao at full power. And then, on top of that, everyone else who is playing with you may be a crook, for all you know, because you don't know who they are. And also they may disobey the rules in the most inconvenient way, not just by doing something other than what the protocol says, but also by stopping responding when they're supposed to respond.

Tuomas Aura: So they could be colluding?

Reply: They could be colluding, yes, in fact everybody could be colluding against *you*. And the point is that you don't know if other players are in fact the same player, with different aliases for the same player.

These are the peers of the peer-to-peer situation and any one of them can become the dealer if they like. It's something you decide, you wake up one morning and you decide "I want to make some money, why don't I offer a game of Cyberdice. I'm offering a game with these parameters. If you want to play with me then these are the rules."

The dealer chooses the maximum number of players and if you want to play you must put up perhaps £5 as a player, and he says I will take up to 20 people which means the maximum win that you can make in this game is £100. Up front he is going to put up the £100 in escrow with some issuer that he then announces. In so far as you believe the reputation of this issuer that he has chosen, then you know that if you win that game you can get back the money that you have won, up to

B. Christianson et al. (Eds.): Security Protocols 2008, LNCS 6615, pp. 71–83, 2011.

£100 if 20 people play. Of course if only 7 people play then you can only collect £35. But you know that he has deposited £100 with the issuer, and he can't renege on the fact that he will pay at the end of the game.

Bruce Christianson: Deposit is the same as placing into escrow?

Reply: Deposit is the same as paying into escrow, yes. He chooses acceptable issuers for the players to use in the sense that not everybody trusts all issuers (and so the dealer himself may not trust some issuers that the players may like) to then pay up when it's time for him to collect the fee.

Matt Blaze: Does the game end for everyone at the same time?

Reply: I'll get back to that, the game ends when the winner is designated, and then at that point you can claim your money if you were the winner, or you have lost your money if you were another player, but there are some subtleties there too.

Tuomas Aura: So we have sessions?

Reply: We have sessions, yes. The dealer competes against other dealers on the fee that he charges to play his game. The issuer also charges a fee: there's a fee charged by the issuer, and there's a fee charged by the dealer. Because the dealer collects the fee from every player, and pays out whatever money was on the table, the dealer always makes a profit. His profit is the total of the fees paid by every player, and is independent of the outcome of the game. The dealer doesn't care who wins, he always makes the same amount from the fees that players pay him. The gamblers are players who bite to the lure offered by a dealer: they accept the invitation to gamble and they bid by going to an issuer of their choosing (chosen among the set of those approved by the dealer of that game) and they say: let me put into escrow this £5; of course I'll pay you the fee, in fact I put into escrow £5 plus ϵ, where ϵ is this extra fee that is charged by the dealer, and I get back a bit string that proves that I have put this money in escrow. I can put it on the table, and show how this can then be redeemed by conceptually the winner of the game, but practically the dealer because the winner of the game is in fact collecting money from the dealer's issuer, if you are still with me.

So now we get back to something that Matt mentioned: when does the game finish? Does it finish at the same time for everybody? Since there is a maximum number of players that the dealer accepts, there can be many more players wanting to play than this number: but the dealer at some point will select who gets to play (I'll get into greater detail in a moment). People who did put money in escrow but were not selected to play (i.e. get to the next stage) then get their money back from their own issuer, and they have to prove to the issuer that they were not admitted into that game. Or of course if they can prove that the game was fraudulent then they can also get their money back. And unlike these other two types of principals (dealers and issuers) who will always make a small profit, the gamblers may win more than they put in, or they may lose everything they put in. And of course, as expected value, on average they will always lose, and so you would be excused for thinking: "why would anybody play this game if they always lose?". First of all, this is true of all gambling games, more or less. And secondly there is a non-obvious, subtle and interesting answer to that, which was given by some guy who won a Nobel prize for figuring this out.[1] You are given a choice: "would you rather get 1p or a 1 in 10 chance of getting 10p?" And, "would you rather get 10p or a 1 in 10 chance of getting £1?" and so on. All these things are to be considered independently of each other. You will typically see that people say: "I can do nothing with 1p, just give me the chance of getting 10p and at least it will be worth my while". But by the time you get to, "would you rather have £10,000 or a 1 in 10 chance of getting £100,000", it's: "give me the £10,000 right now". So, depending on how rich you are, there's a switch-over point somewhere in the middle, and your wealth tells something about where you put the breakout point. Anyway, this explains that if the bet is small enough it may be worth your while, psychologically, to go for the gamble instead of just holding onto the 1p. I just put up this slide so you don't worry for the rest of the talk, wondering why would anybody play this game.

James Malcolm: Maybe this is a 0.1 version of the protocol, but it seems to me that at the moment the issuer is implicated in this illegal gambling business, because he's having to look at the log that says who should be paid, which is gambling specific, isn't it?

Reply: No. Well, what I am trying carefully to avoid is having the issuers implicated in that, and the way I claim they are not implicated is that they just make a contract with the player saying, in exchange for the fee that you give me I'll hold onto this money and I will pay it back to whoever gives me a bit string with these properties, and these properties are that some signatures match, and this and that, and it points at some guy that they can prove has a certain public key, and so on, but they're not involved in any of the gambling, they're just honouring a contract about properties of a bit string: whoever presents a bit string with those properties, they will give them back the money that you are depositing now.

James Malcolm: And the properties are not gambling specific?

Reply: The properties are not gambling specific.

Matt Blaze: So it's plausible that that protocol is useful for just general money transfer between people?

Reply: Well, that is the intention, in fact I would love to make this function of the issuer as detached as possible from the Cyberdice game, although as you will see in what I'm presenting now, it is fairly entangled in it in that the contracts have to know a lot about how the Cyberdice game works. But ideally I would like to have the issuers in a position where all they do is just have a very formally defined and detached contract with customers about properties of bit strings where, as a service, they say: you pay me money and give me a bit string with certain properties, and I promise I will pay that back to anybody who presents another bit string with some other properties, and I don't want to know about gambling, because gambling is wicked.

Bruce Christianson: So this could be used for drug dealing and arms running as well as gambling.

---

[1] Harry M. Markowitz, Nobel Prize in Economics, 1990.

Mark Lomas: You appear to be suggesting that gambling is worse than breaching the know-your-customer part of the Anti-Money-Laundering regulations.

Reply: I do; which you think is worse depends on jurisdiction, I guess.

What happens is that each player rolls the dice and gives the (allegedly) random number so that you have a contributory strategy where everyone supplies part of the random number that is selected. You don't want to have someone else choosing your random number for you! This randomness is stirred up, or hashed, and used to decide who will win. The key technical point is that you must commit to your own randomness before you get to see other people's randomness.

So here are the slides with the protocol...

Right, so I guess the bit that isn't solved in those protocols that I've presented there is how to ensure that players actually reveal the values they commit to. The issue here is that gamblers give you the hash of their dice roll and then they don't tell you what it is. When everybody has given their own commit, then you say, OK, reveal what it was, then we hash them all together, and then the number that's closest to that from below will be the winner. But, what if some people don't actually answer? What if some people give you the commitment and then they don't give you the number when they're asked to reveal? In that case you can't compute the final value.

Virgil Gligor: Once they commit to a value, how do they not give you the numbers?

Tuomas Aura: You choose a random number, let's say 73, you give me the hash of 73; I can't work out 73 from that and I say: "so, Virgil, what was your number that gave you this hash?" and you just go quiet. And I don't know who you are, I can't go and beat you up because I just have a public key, so of course you lose your money, but you denied service for everybody else.

Mark Lomas: It's easier to understand why if you think the last person to give a commitment is the only one who actually has something to gain. If you're going around the loop, if you don't know what's going to happen afterwards, you might as well give your commitment, but the last person has an incentive to muck up the whole thing.

Matthew Johnson: Because the last person can change the outcome by deciding whether or not to send theirs in, and if you have a sufficient number of people who do this, then they can essentially make sure one of them wins eventually by withholding their value.

Reply: Exactly this. You have a problem because everybody needs to reveal the value they committed to in order for us to determine a winner, but then you are at the mercy of people not continuing, and then you can't designate a winner. If you say "we will only continue with those who did reveal" then the winner changes depending on whether people participate or don't participate; and, as Mark pointed out, the last person to reveal would know whether, by revealing, they win. I mean, they will know who wins whether they reveal or whether they don't reveal, and they have pointers to two people, one of them could be them, but it could be just two other people, and they can say, OK, I can influence the outcome and make you win, or I can make *you* win, and how about we split if I make you win? Something like that. Or they could arrange to have even more people playing last together and then having all the possible combinations. Actually it's not even necessary to have all possible combinations, just interesting to be able to influence the outcome and point at the people you like.

So we have a problem if we want to use this system because we would like everybody who does commit to be forced to also reveal. But we cannot enforce the atomicity of this, which means that there is an advantage for the last gambler. This is something that is difficult to fix.

One solution that was suggested by Mark by email, if I remember correctly, was to say "if someone doesn't reveal then they have to pay a fine", but on second thought this won't work because if by cheating in this way you could win the whole game, then the fine would have to be a sufficient deterrent for you not to do that, even in case you win the whole game, which would mean you would have to escrow enough money to be fined for the whole value of the game, which you might not be willing to do. You might like to gamble £5 on the game, but you might not want to put up £100 just to play the £5. More so if there are a hundred players or a thousand players allowed by the dealer, instead of just 20.

Tuomas Aura: Even that solution, although it sounds like it would work in theory, has problems if you think of when is the deadline for you to reveal something, because if someone can push you over that deadline, or just pretend not to receive, everyone else says, we haven't heard from you, you keep resending, and they say, we haven't heard from you, and the deadline passes, and now you owe them money.

Reply: That's absolutely correct. In this particular set of arrangements that we have taken, this is taken care of by the fact that the issuers are resistant to denial of service. And so, if you send a message to your issuer, then the assumptions under which we play guarantee that this will be blogged by the issuer, so you have a proof that you did submit by that time. But otherwise in general that would be a valid point: if you could be stopped from sending your message then you would lose all, you would be fined for the whole fee of the game. So we don't like this one.

What about removing the commitment phase, just making it atomic, by making everyone announce the dice roll so there aren't two phases here. Well obviously that can't work because then the last guy sees everyone's dice roll and then he could decide what to roll on his own. So another suggestion that came up, I think this was Richard's idea, was to use a kind of time delay mechanism where you obscure your own roll with some encryption that could be broken if you spent enough time on it, but can't during the normal run of the game. But of course that also isn't very desirable because the capabilities of people for breaking encryption vary by many orders of magnitude so you would never be sure that nobody during that game duration can do that, especially if it needs to be sufficiently breakable that if someone drops out you can then reveal it later.

So what we did instead was to change the way in which the randomness is stirred up to select a winner from the dice rolls. If all these issuers have to sign the messages that they receive anyway, then by signing they introduce some randomness with their own signatures; so why don't we introduce that in the mix as well? The message where all the dice rolls have been revealed is passed around by the dealer to all the issuers involved, which may be many fewer than the players, because several players may have chosen the same issuer, and then each of them signs it, and the result of this is then hashed to produce a target value to designate a winner.

Matt Blaze: It seems to me that you're living in a bit of a state of sin here, beyond the gambling, in that you are depending on a property of signatures that I'm not sure I understand that they have. It seems intuitive that signatures have some sort of unpredictable randomness property to them, but I've never understood that to be a necessary property of signatures.

Reply: Yes, well, as we have written in the position paper, we don't really understand it either, but we believe it's plausible enough, and if you throw some hashes at it, then we think it would work. But I take your point, and I think we just wrote it explicitly in the paper. I'll just quote myself...

Matt Blaze: My excuse is that I haven't read the paper.

Reply: You're not supposed to, but I'll just prove that we thought of that:
"The game can be seen to be fair, in that it is well-known (albeit possibly hard to prove) that signatures made with high quality cryptographic primitives are random. If this isn't believed to be true of signatures in general, then placing their values into a canonical order and then calculating a cryptographic hash of this concatenation will provide an 'even more random' value."

Michael Roe: Are you assuming the signature is deterministic like RSA or non-deterministic like DSS? The issuers might try and cheat if they could do so undetectably.

Reply: We want the signatures to be deterministic for exactly that reason. We want to make sure that once you are given something to sign, there's only one thing that could come out of it.

George Danezis: But how does that go hand in hand with the fact that you want some randomness in the signatures? I was following this debate saying ah, you know, it's all right because secure signature schemes have to be non-deterministic. And now you say, no, we want them to be deterministic?

Reply: Well, random in the sense that you couldn't predict ahead where it's going to point at, but yes.

George Danezis: Unpredictability if you don't know the secret key, effectively?

Reply: Yes.

Bruce Christianson: The signatures don't have to be random, they just have to be unpredictable.

Virgil Gligor: But you can add the randomness to them, you can make signatures sufficiently random artificially, like MACs.

Reply: But we want to be really careful that we are not allowing the signers to make things point the way they want, they shouldn't have any option to make something come out.

Richard Clayton: I think that we're going down a rabbit hole here with randomness, because as part of the point of this paper, we tried to dismiss all of the trivial flaws that people normally find in protocols, so as Frank says, we chuck absolutely everything into every message because we don't want you to start looking at this protocol from the point of view of "where does the randomness come from", or the point of view of "can we pretend using this message in this phase of the protocol instead, and that might break it" *etc*; this isn't what this paper is about. This is about the fact that, because we don't know any theory (we are terribly practical people) if we knew any theory we wouldn't try to do this, because it's impossible. The theory people proved long ago that what we're trying to do is impossible: you can't do a multi-party computation with n people with only one of them being honest, this is a nice theoretical result from the 80s. OK, so we tried to do that. And the other thing is, the theory people know about the property that some of the people go home in the middle (they even gave it a really silly name which I can't even remember now[2]) and they worry about this, and they've written papers about it, full of lots of Greek letters, and you can't understand a word of it, so we're trying to write something simple here. All the theory people suddenly get really excited from this slide, because suddenly we've got n people participating again, at which point it's all possible.

So that's the real point of the paper, it's to draw the attention of this community to the fact that people can go home in the middle of the protocols. Propping up the whole of your paper on Yao's millionaire protocol doesn't work if one of people goes home right at the end of the protocol. And we put some money in here, so people could see that it was important that it didn't work!

Reply: Yes, that's a subtle point. Please don't miss the last bit that Richard said because it really is crucial: in Yao's multi-party computation, at the end one of them knows the result and has to tell the other. What if he doesn't? We try and fix that.

Michael Roe: If the adversary could predict what the secret message was going to be then they could forge signatures, so I think the unpredictability property you want is a natural consequence of the signature algorithm being a good signature algorithm.

Bruce Christianson: But there's still a danger that the person who signs last might have an advantage, using a signature algorithm?

Reply: Yes, and I am shifting who's last from the players to the issuers, who have some reputation. So the people who are slightly more trustworthy do that, and I'm trying to arrange things so that a single crooked issuer can't rig the game undetectably.

Tuomas Aura: So basically what you have here is a kind of trusted third party that can compute a one-way function, but it's deterministic, and everyone

---

[2] *Independence.*

can verify that it was computed correctly. It's important that it's deterministic because otherwise the issuer can cheat.

Reply: Yes, insofar as you want the thing to be auditable. I trust this guy, because he's done it a hundred times, and he was always fine, but if he could hide his tracks, and do it a hundred times and it looks like it's fine but it isn't, then there would be no point in this reputation game.

Tuomas Aura: But it feels there's a need for different cryptographic properties if you want this function, and let's not talk about signatures, because you're not actually signing them.

Reply: Why not? I am signing something aren't I?

Tuomas Aura: But the property that you need is not the signature.

Reply: Well it needs to be something only that guy can generate and everybody else can verify, that looks like a signature to me.

Matt Blaze: But DSS doesn't have these properties, because it's randomized.

Tuomas Aura: Yes, so you're saying it has to be deterministic?

Matt Blaze: Right, so which non-randomised signature algorithm is still considered secure?

Tuomas Aura: Maybe for these purposes you do not need a proper signature, you might just use something like plain RSA.

Matt Blaze: Plain RSA with no pattern, or with deterministic pattern?

Bruce Christianson: But even with vanilla RSA, I'm still worried that a corrupt issuer might force you into a smaller subgroup by having a modulus of the form pq^2 or something.

Matt Blaze: I'm more worried than ever that you're depending on cryptographic primitives that may not exist.

Matthew Johnson: You're moving the "who does something last", to the issuers, and we have previously discussed what the problem would be with crooked issuers. Can the issuer here not do exactly the same as the wicked user just by refusing to sign things?

Can I ask another point about this? You might not need a complete digital signature, but you can't just use a one-way function *per se*, because you need to be able to verify that the issuer has done the correct one-way function.

Reply: The issuers are, to some extent, part of the trusted computing base, and always will be: if nothing else because you give them money that they could always not return, so you have to put some trust in the issuers, whatever happens. But I would like to limit this trust to things that will show if they misbehave in the audit log. Some of these things I still can't, for example, the atomicity of some of the transactions, the fact that if I send them some money I want to get the bit string back. If I don't get the bit string back I have no way to prove that I sent them the money, so I am dependent on that.

Matthew Johnson: But that's you trusting your issuer rather than you trusting anybody else's issuer.

Reply: Yes, but insofar as I take part in a game for which the issuers have been announced at the beginning, I can make a decision on not to participate in one because it contains some issuers that I don't trust.

Richard Clayton: First of all, you are told which issuers will be accepted and they do have a long term reputation, so if you don't like them because they're dodgy then you don't have to play. The second thing is that because they make money from the game they will be interested in looking at the long term.

Reply: I see that I am restoring the original intention of the protocols workshop as a place where you get interrupted all the time.

Tuomas Aura: I may be missing something but don't you get a much simpler protocol by letting the issuer commit to a nonce and the issuer reveals the nonce last.

Reply: I guess we are sliding more and more into grounds where the issuer does the gambling.

Richard Clayton: If people are trying to simplify this then I think that it makes the game run in a different way without all the fluffing around that you need in order to make the thing look like the original throw of the dice, which we've kind of forgotten in all of this. We haven't mentioned throwing the dice and choosing the highest number for some time.

Reply: Roger Needham once said, optimisation is the process of taking something that works and turning it into something that almost works but costs less, and so I apologise, I'm going to do one of these now.

The thing that I am going to optimise away is people throwing dice, so we say, if we are using the issuers' signatures to stir the randomness, why bother even with the dice? We can even save all this "doing the commitment" stuff, since ultimately we need to have it signed by all the issuers anyway. Now why does it become something that only *almost* works? It is because I am no longer fully contributory. At the beginning, I wanted everybody to chip in with their bit of randomness to make sure, but here you just have to make sure that you trust the issuers that are involved, and this is why it is slightly dodgy.

What happens then is simply that the dealer announces the game, the properties of the game, the lines of the game, and so on; the gamblers send their stake, which is their proof of having escrowed the money to play; the dealer selects a subset of the gamblers by the deadline; then this selected subset is signed by all the issuers in a pre-determined order; and then this gives a number which points at one of the people in that selected subset, who becomes the winner.

George Danezis: But can the dealer select the subset so as to influence the outcome?

Reply: Well he can't because he doesn't know the outcome of all these signatures that have yet to happen. The dealer selects a subset of the gamblers, so it includes all these commitment strings of the money, takes it all together, signs it, and then hands it over to all the issuers in turn, sign that, now sign that, now sign that, it comes back to him, he says, OK, now let's hash it and reduce modulo k, and we get a number which points at one of them.

That's why we don't need a commitment any more, because the dealer doesn't know yet what will happen after all these issuer signatures. At that point the winner can go with that lump of stuff to the dealer's issuer and say, look, this proves I am the winner. Actually it only proves that the guy who controls the secret key corresponding to the public key in that slot is the winner, and now I can prove I have that secret key, and then you give me the money. The sub-protocol for that, where again there is a jeopardy for the player with respect to the issuer where he could be doing the proof and signing a receipt, and not having got the money yet, and that is unavoidable because of the position the issuer is in. And then there's the usual thing as before, the dealer goes back and collects the money that wasn't actually played, and all that kind of stuff.

Tuomas Aura: Was there any randomness in there?

Reply: Well there is some randomness insofar as each player selects a new ephemeral key pair every time they play, so the fact that dealer is choosing a new key pair for playing makes this a kind of identifier for that game. In fact the public key itself is also a nonce, and if you are arguing that he could choose the same public key as the previous time, well he could also choose the same nonce.

Tuomas Aura: So do they commit to the public key?

Reply: The first time you hear about that public key for the dealer is when he announces the game: he says, and here is my public key.

Tuomas Aura: OK, so is the dealer the only one who has a new public key?

Reply: No, every player, everybody except the issuers always has a new public key every time they play.

Matthew Johnson: And you need that so that the dealer can't be . . .

Reply: Recycling games, exactly.

Tuomas Aura: So commit to the public keys, and you again have the problem of does everyone play till the end.

Matthew Johnson: No, because you're actually just using the keys them-selves to generate randomness. You don't need them to reveal their private keys, they can start playing whenever they like, and it's fine.

Reply: What's the remaining problem, you have a puzzled face?

Tuomas Aura: It's not showing here the details of the protocols, but at some point there is some order in which people commit to random values, someone will be the last, or maybe someone can just delay till they are the last, so to avoid this you need some kind of commitment phase, and then you then have a problem, who will reveal last?

Reply: Well the point is that if all the randomness you contribute as a player is your public key, then it's going to be very hard for you to rig it up.

Tuomas Aura: But someone is going to sign that.

Richard Clayton: Yes, let's be very clear about this. The threat is that the issuers will cheat. In order to fix the theoretical problem, which is that we can't do this, we give the issuer the property which at the beginning we said we weren't going to give them, and we say, because they have a long-term reputation, we can get away with it. The issuer is trusted to actually do it because of the security economics of the game: the issuers have big incentives not to cheat in order to win one game.

Bruce Christianson: Because the issuer won't go home.

Reply: So the issuers are the only ones with permanent key pairs, everybody else has ephemeral key pairs, so the reputation hangs on the public keys that are permanent.

Virgil Gligor: So the issuer acts as a certification authority for those keys, and that's a commitment to the keys.

Reply: Yes. When you escrow your money you get back something that's signed with the long-term key of the issuer, which in a sense is a certificate that you have this public key insofar as the game is concerned.

Matt Blaze: Just to clarify the security model, the trust model here is that the issuers will not cheat in ways that they can be caught, not that they will not cheat period.

Reply: If they could cheat in a way that nobody sees from the log, then I'm sure they would.

Bruce Christianson: Yes, but going home is very visible.

Reply: Yes, absolutely. And the point is also that if you believe someone is misbehaving then you can choose not to participate because you will know in advance which issuers are involved, because in the announcements of the game the dealer will say, I'm using this issuer, and you can only use one of these issuers. So if you see that, you think I'll be dealing with these issuers, well, I'll just pass on this one.

Tuomas Aura: I'm still worried about, what determines which players get within that subset, maybe some players will be flooding in at the end.

Reply: We are taking away any chances for the players to mess things up by only giving them one thing to do, to say, I want to play, and I have deposited my money. Do I get selected, I don't know, this depends on the dealer, if I get selected I can't decide not to play any more because I've already said I'd play, and that's it, which removes most of the screw-ups they could introduce in previous versions.

Virgil Gligor: I want to understand more about the commitment to the keys by the issuer. Two players chose one issuer, and two players chose a different issuer, what does that commitment to the key mean? Do the issuers talk to each other? I get my key signed by you as an issuer, so you are my certification authority, somebody else has a different certification authority whom I don't trust. Does the fact that it's a different issuer make a difference?

Reply: Well it's slightly different from what you say, insofar as you are taking part in a game where various issuers are involved, and you have to, to some extent, trust all these issuers, otherwise you wouldn't take part.

Matthew Johnson: You see the list of issuers before you join because it's published.

Reply: Yes, it's in the game announcement, the dealer says, this is the list of issuers that I will accept for the players.

Virgil Gligor: So that's one of the fundamental assumptions?

Reply: Yes.

Richard Clayton: The trust is not just in their public key, the trust is that they are saying, the dealer has given me £100, and you can collect it. So the trust is very real, and if you don't feel that the St Petersburg Trust Issuing Authority is the right one to use, then you don't want to play this game.

Virgil Gligor: If everyone trusts this group of people this is no longer a decentralized problem.

Reply: Well the trust placed in the issuers is slightly different for the issuer of the dealer, and the issuer of the player. The issuer of the dealer, you have to trust him to actually hand out the prize money, because that's the whole point for you to play. The issuers of the other players you have to trust them to do the signature without rigging it up, they're not going to give you back any money, so it's slightly different, but you still have to trust them.

Virgil Gligor: But there is central trust in this dealer's issuers and this core of issuers.

Reply: Yes, that's the cheating bit.

Virgil Gligor: That's the cheating bit, that's because you haven't been able to solve the original, impossible problem.

Tuomas Aura: You could do the same with nonces again, by letting the issuers commit to nonces, and then once the dealer decides on his nonce, and now you just have the original game, but with a difference since the issuers have to continue to the end of the game by the rules that they're guaranteed to finish it.

Reply: So what advantage did we gain?

Bruce Christianson: I don't think that works because the issuers can dishonestly share their nonces.

Tuomas Aura: No, the issuers can also share their private signature key, or they can act as oracles for whoever wants the key, so it's just as if you wanted to share the nonce.

Bruce Christianson: But if I share my private key with someone ...

Tuomas Aura: No, but you might give someone access to your private key for the purposes of this protocol by acting as an oracle.

Bruce Christianson: But in this protocol they sign in order, so I don't know what I'm going to sign till I get it, so I can't reveal the signature until I'm going to have to anyway.

George Danezis: It depends on how many potential players there are. If there are exactly as many candidate players as there are going to be players playing the game, then the attack that Tuomas describes would work, because you could have a crook issuer that will give you access to their key as an oracle, and then they will be able to choose whether to participate or not depending on what kind of values they would sign.

Bruce Christianson: Maybe I haven't understood the protocol, there's a block that goes round all the issuers, each one signs on top of the other one.

Richard Clayton: There were various schemes with only one signing, and they don't work.

George Danezis: Aha!

Matt Blaze: Perhaps I'm uneasy about this protocol because it seems very complicated and specific to solving two things at once. One is establishing the outcome of the game in a distributed fashion with the appropriate deniability among parties, and the second is settling the payments after the outcome of the game, where the game is a simple guessing game. Well it seems that gamblers have historically solved the establishing the outcome of the game, that is having a secure random number generator, long before computers and distributed computation, by simply relying on a published source of randomness that everyone agrees is unpredictable. For example, the classic numbers game in the United States, and maybe elsewhere, uses to establish the outcome things like horse races, or the lower bits of the closing stock price on the Stock Market, or some other widely published readily agreed on, and hard to influence or predict, number. If you have a source of such numbers does your protocol become simple, does it simply reduce to the settlement part of the problem and is that simple?

Reply: Well I like this comment, I guess it might. I can't answer on my two feet like that, but if we could separate it out and have a way of dealing with the money in cyberspace, and then just use the random number you mentioned as a pointer, reduce modulo k among the people who have played, we would still have most of the issues here: selecting who plays, in which order, so that we are arranging them and so on.

Matt Blaze: Right, maybe it doesn't make it simple well, maybe it does.

Reply: Well yes, because there isn't that much else in this game other than, putting the people in order, and then selecting one. I'd be happy if we found a way of simplifying that, and especially separating the payments out of that.

Matt Blaze: I think the published sources of randomness have a long history in gambling, and there's something poetic if you can employ them here.

Reply: It's nice to separate concerns, and the thing that would be even nicer for me would be to separate as much as possible the action of the issuers from the working of the Cyberdice game protocol itself, so that the issuers offer a service that could be used for many other things as well. It's basically always the same service, you give me some money, I'll give you a bit string, and there are certain conditions.

James Malcolm: I think maybe the problem with Matt's suggestion is, in the Internet everybody has access to the same random number, which is not big enough, and they can collude. In the real world, a bunch of gamblers in Texas cannot collude with a bunch of gamblers in New York, so that the two games can use the same random number, can't they?

Matt Blaze: Yes, they can. For example, if I'm using something that depends on the global economy, or that depends on some likely observed natural phenomena . . .

James Malcolm: Choosing enough different such numbers might be difficult.

Matt Blaze: That's right, these numbers may be in limited supply.

Problems with Same Origin Policy

Know Thyself

Dieter Gollmann

Hamburg University of Technology, Hamburg, Germany
diego@tu-harburg.de

In the tradition of distributed systems security, access control equals authentication and authorisation, where *obtaining the source of the request is called 'authentication'* [4]. In web applications, the source of a web page is a host known by a DNS name. Web browsers attempt to enforce *same origin policies* on scripts executing within a web page or on the dissemination of HTTP cookies. To enforce same origin policies, the browser must be able to authenticate origin.

Current browsers only keep track of the host they have received a page from, but there is no fine grained authentication of the individual parts of a web page. *Cross-site scripting* (XSS) attacks exploit this deficiency by using a 'trusted' server, *i.e.* a server with more access rights than those granted to the attacker, as a stepping stone [2]. A malicious script is either placed directly in a page on the trusted server or in a form in a page on the attacker's server that launches a request to the trusted server with the script hidden, *e.g.*, in a query parameter. When a user visits either page and when no additional precautions are in place, the browser will execute the script with elevated access rights. Authentication of origin has failed as it did not correctly capture the true origin of the attacker's contribution to the page received from the server.

Cross-site request forgery (XSRF) attacks follow a similar principle but target a server [1]. The server is 'trusting' a client, *i.e.* there is an authenticated session where the client has more access rights than those granted to the attacker. The attacker uses the client as a stepping stone to send actions to the server in HTML request within this session. These actions are then executed with the access rights of the client. The server had authenticated the origin of the entire HTML request but not of its individual parts.

To fix this access control problem authentication could be improved. For example, client and server could establish a secret at the start of a session; the client stores the secret in a place out of reach for attackers and uses it to compute message authentication codes for HTML requests (a.k.a. XSRFPreventionTokens).

Alternatively, access control policies could be based on attributes that can be checked. We may take a cue from the inscription $\Gamma N\Omega\Theta I \ \Sigma A\Upsilon TON$ ("know thyself") written in the Temple of Apollon at the Delphic oracle.

An entity unable to authenticate the origin of data provided by others may still be able to authenticate its own contributions. This gives us a new elementary security primitive "recognizing oneself" around which a new theory of access control can be built. An example for this approach is the RequestRodeo proxy that provides a client side defence against XSRF attacks [3]. It marks all URLs

B. Christianson et al. (Eds.): Security Protocols 2008, LNCS 6615, pp. 84–85, 2011.
© Springer-Verlag Berlin Heidelberg 2011

in incoming web pages with an unpredictable token and keeps a database associating tokens with domains. Outgoing requests are checked for the presence of a token:

- If no token is found, the request is locally generated ("know thyself") and can be sent in authenticated sessions.
- If a token is found and the origin of the request matches the domain it is being sent to, the request is permitted by the same origin policy and can be sent in authenticated sessions.
- Otherwise, all authenticators (SIDs, cookies) added by the browser are stripped from the URL before sending the request.

The research challenge put forward in this position paper is the exploration of access control models for mash-ups of web applications that are based on authentication primitives such as "know thyself".

References

1. Burns, J.: Cross site reference forgery. Technical report, Information Security Partners, LLC (2005) (Version 1.1)
2. CERT Coordination Center. Malicious HTML tags embedded in client web requests (2000), http://www.cert.org/advisories/CA-2000-02.html
3. Johns, M., Winter, J.: RequestRodeo: Client side protection against session riding. In: Piessens, F. (ed.) Proceedings of the OWASP Europe 2006 Conference, Departement Computerwetenschappen, Katholieke Universiteit Leuven, Report CW448, pp. 5–17 (May 2006)
4. Lampson, B., Abadi, M., Burrows, M., Wobber, E.: Authentication in distributed systems: Theory and practice. ACM Transactions on Computer Systems 10(4), 265–310 (1992)

Problems with Same Origin Policy
(Transcript of Discussion)

Dieter Gollmann

Hamburg University of Technology

Basic point, if you want to enforce the same origin policy, you have to be able to authenticate origin. In many cases, as you will see, one might be unable to do so for whatever reasons. But you might still be able to authenticate yourself, and that could be a useful security primitive, and that is one of the purposes of this talk, to discuss this security primitive of knowing yourself. I will use examples from web application security (which some of you might be much more familiar with than myself) to illustrate this point, and I could quite often refer to mobile network security, I see great similarities.

My first example of a problem is cross site scripting. Simple background: we have an attacker, we have a client, and we have a server trusted by the client. Attacker places malicious code somewhere on a webpage. If the webpage is directly at the server, this is known in the trade as stored cross site scripting; if the attacker somehow persuades the victim to submit this data himself to the server, this is known as reflected cross site scripting. When the server constructs a webpage, sends it back to the client, the malicious code the attacker had placed at the server comes back to the client, and is executed at the client side as coming from the trusted server, so it's running with the permissions of the trusted server. The attacker somehow manages to create an interesting webpage at the attacker site, the victim clicks on something, something is transported from the attacker to the victim containing the malicious code, the victim might add more information, then sends it to the trusted server, the trusted server sends back a response and the malicious code will now be executed on the client as coming from there, and not from here, and that's why it's called cross site scripting.

Ultimate cause, fundamental problem: failure of origin based policy. Those who know me, know authentication is a topic I've been beating up on for a very long time. We've only authenticated the entire page, we have not been looking at the bits and pieces in the page, and in this case some of those pieces came from the attacker.

The first defence I would classify as saying, OK, origin based policy doesn't work here, the problem really is we're executing code when we don't like to execute code, therefore let's try to differentiate between code and data. Very good. The server might sanitise the output it sends out. We might use escaping so the dangerous characters that initialise the script, or start the script, are somehow blocked. I am tempted to call this a band-aid because it works in many cases sort of reasonably well, but not always. And I have an example, which I hope some of you might find interesting and educating, and might raise

B. Christianson et al. (Eds.): Security Protocols 2008, LNCS 6615, pp. 86–92, 2011.

general discussions about abstraction security. It's admittedly slightly tangential to my topic, it's about SQL injection attacks.

There is a defence against SQL injection called the `addslashes` function, which adds a slash in front of every dangerous character to escape that dangerous character. And the other part of the story is the GBK character set for simplified Chinese. The story I found on this website from Chris Shiflett[1], as part of a discussion. What he observed is that hexadecimal character BF27 is not a character in GBK. If we look at it byte by byte, it's BF and 27 and 27 is a single quote, and single quote starts a string, so it's a dangerous character, and we have to escape it. So we add a slash which is 5C in hexadecimal representation. However, what we get then is BF5C which happens to be in the GBK character set, so we have this character, followed by a single quote, despite the fact that we've just tried to put a slash in front of the single quote. So something very interesting is happening here with abstractions. You have the abstractions in the character set, you have the byte level representation, and somehow inserting slashes at the byte level doesn't insert slashes at the level of the abstraction. So that is something to think about.

Second defence, which Martin Johns called session-safe. The idea is a simple one. At the time the server starts a session with the client, the server sends unpredictable one time URLs. The server is now able to recognise its own URLs because it has created those URLs in some unpredictable way, and if it has kept track of who has received those URLs, it knows who has been sending these requests. So in the cross site scripting example an attacker would have to include a URL in the request to the server. If it's an unpredictable URL that had not been compromised at the client, the attacker would not be able to do this, and in this way we would get authentication of origin, courtesy of this know thyself primitive.

Next example in my list: cross site reference. In essence you see the same players involved, the same flow of information. The main difference: in this case the user has an authenticated session with the server, the server is the target system, so the request coming from the attacker will be treated by the target as a request coming from the user, and again you have a violation of an origin based policy. Exploit the trust, trust the target website has with the user. The user is authenticated, be it through cookies, be it through an authenticated SSL session, or something else. And again, the user has to go to the attacker's website to start the attack. When the user goes to the attacker's website the client browser will submit the attacker's data to the server, and the server will treat this as coming from my authenticated user. Violation of the target's origin based security policy, and the same story as before. Ultimate cause: the server only authenticates the entire page, or the entire request, I should have said, and not the individual parts in this request.

In the literature I see two types of defences, one is a server initiated defence. Here the interesting thing is that, to authenticate the request as coming from a particular user, or a particular client, you go up above the level of the browser to

---

[1] `shiflett.org`

the application running on top of the browser, and you do it through standard cryptographic mechanisms, hash functions, random tokens. In each case at the time the session between client and target is being established, the server sends the secret to the client, and in the attack model here, to come back to the topic of the workshop, we are not worried in the least about how the secret is protected on the way from the server to the client, you can even send it in clear text. We are worried about an attacker compromising the client machine and finding the secret there. Interception of traffic over the Internet is not an issue.

Second defence I have seen, again, by Martin Johns, on the client side, and it is to me again an example of the same principle. Put the proxy between the browser and the network. Any incoming URL you mark with an unpredictable token and you keep a database associating the token with the domain this particular URL came from. For every article you request, you look at the URL, has it got a token, then it wasn't mine, anything I receive from anybody else I have tagged, so I'm already able to recognise myself those requests that come from somebody else. I can further check whether this is a request matching the same origin policy, meaning, is this request going back to the domain it came from? That's what we want in the same origin policy. If yes, and the proxy can check this using the database, then this is OK. If not, strip away any session identifiers that would authenticate this request as coming from the client. And this works only if you use cookies or session identifiers, but it doesn't work if you go down to SSL, because if you use SSL you do authentication at the lower layer, and all these defences at the level of the web application, HTTP, are not able to touch the authentication information. So one might argue that in this respect that using SSL might be less good than other ways of authenticating at the application layer.

Final example, DNS rebinding. I came across this in a paper from Dan Boneh and others, "Protecting Browsers from DNS Rebinding Attacks" submitted to ACM CCS last year[2]. Same origin policy, applet can only connect back to the server it came from. We have two abstractions: domain names and IP addresses. For the client browser to connect back it needs an IP address. Where does it get the IP address for a domain from? It asks the authoritative DNS server for that domain. To use the T word, the client's browser *trusts* the authoritative DNS server to give it a correct IP address. And you know my view on this subject, trust is bad for security, and you will see in a moment why. Because trust can be abused, it's the authoritative domain server of the attacker, and in the first example of this going back a very long time in our history, Drew Dean, Ed Felten and Dan Wallach at Princeton found the following way of attacking an early version of a Netscape browser in 1996. In the first instance the attacker's domain name server binds the attacker's domain name to two IP addresses: to the correct IP address, and to a victim IP address. When the client gets the applet from the attacker, the applet will ask to connect to the IP address of the victim, the browser checks with the authoritative DNS server, is this a good IP

---

[2] 14th ACM Conference on Computer and Communications Security (CCS), pp 421-431, 2007.

address for the attacker to make the attack, it says, oh yes, go ahead, and the connection to the victim is made in violation of the same origin policy, and the defence suggested at that time was, well we should do this at the level of IP addresses, same origin policy at IP level. And one can discuss whether that is really a meaningful way of doing things the way we're using the web today.

Next round, I have this from Dan Boneh's paper, and he's referring to a talk at the RSA Conference 2001. We are changing coordinates, we're moving from space to time, and the attacker's DNS server now gives the correct IP address initially, but with a very short time to live. Then the attacker rebinds the domain name to the victim address. By the time the malicious code connects to attack.com the binding has expired, the DNS server is asked again, and is redirected to the victim. What is the fundamental problem? The client trusts the attacker on time-to-live of associations, and the solution is not to trust the server, but do it yourself. And in technical terms, pin the host name for an IP address. Then you can discuss or can look at current browsers, for which period do they do this pinning? And again, Martin Johns, who've I mentioned already two times, made the following interesting observation: I am the attacker, I take my machine which my applet tries to connect to, off the net. When the client browser deals with my applet's request to connect to my machine, the browser will be told, the machine cannot be found. Some browsers will then say, why should we keep a pin for a machine that's no longer there, drop the pin, and then ask the DNS server again for a new binding, this machine might have moved, and then the attack works again.

Mark Lomas: There's a problem if anyone's using round robin in DNS in order to have multiple servers with the same name for availability.

Reply: Absolutely.

Pekka Nikander: I'm wondering why we are binding the applet to the domain name, why not directly to the IP address?

Reply: Well the applet originally connects to the IP address, but there is no machine at this address anymore, and then the browser reverts, so it will say, well, I'm trying to be helpful, I'm trying to rectify the situation, I'm going back to the DNS server and asking the DNS server, what has happened to this machine, have you moved it, has it gone offline, is there an alternative machine I should go to.

Matthew Johnson: It's precisely this round robin event that means you have to do it like that otherwise it doesn't work, and having round robin DNS availability stuff is vital but dangerous.

Reply: Yes, I think that's interesting.

Third iteration of this, the browser plugin is doing the wrong pin, and then (I would say, repeating the same mistake that had been made ten years ago) the client browser asks the domain name of the attacker for acceptable sites for this domain, and of course the attacker says, yes, all of these machines, they are mine, that's OK if you connect back to this. And you now have a very interesting constellation, you have with the browser a communication path between the plugins, individual plugins do the wrong pinning, so they link or associate the same domain name with different IP addresses. So you go from one IP address, the one in the browser, to a different plugin, and then go to a different IP address. That was the attack discussed in this Stanford paper.

One defence would be the classical security strategy of centralised control. Problem would be the pinning has been separated too much, go back to one pinning database, let plugins, for example, use the browser's pin. For me the more interesting suggestion, or observation was, why do we ask the DNS server about good IP addresses for this domain? Shouldn't we ask the IP addresses whether they want to be in this domain? And that reminded me of Tuomas Aura's comment in the past on defences against binding attacks: you shouldn't ask the sender for permission to change location, you should ask the target address whether it really wants me to reside on that address. And so the same suggestion is being made here, reverse the direction of authentication, which brings me to the end of the talk.

If you want to enforce a security policy you have to authenticate the attributes you're using in your policy. If you're not able to do that, it gets you the problems you have seen being sketched in my talk. With respect to same origin policies, I think the fun is only starting now. There are many more clever ideas around about doing very sophisticated interactions in the browser between different web pages, and to clear up this mess, and understand what one is doing actually, will be an interesting topic for the next two years. Challenge: how to authenticate location, where something comes from? Data items have potentially travelled quite a way. And going back to my cross site request issue, what is the end point we are authenticating? I am by now deeply confused, and deeply troubled by any paper saying, the server, the client. What do you mean? At which level do you work, is it the IP address of this machine, is it the browser, is it the application making use of the browser, is it a particular user running through the application on this browser, on this machine? Different authentication techniques have different endpoints, and if one isn't very precise in language, one will keep suffering from these problems. So thank you very much.

Mark Lomas: I like your observation that you should ask the server with a particular IP address if it really is the one with the name, because it reminds me of an observation that Bruno Crispo and I made about certification authorities. Too many certification authorities will issue a certificate with a key, when they ought to insist upon a signature under the corresponding private key that says, I allow my key to be bound to this name, and then that should be included in a certificate. But very few people ever do that.

Reply: Yes.

Pekka Nikander: If I understand correctly, quite a lot of this stuff comes from the confusion that we have when we are trying within a single application to handle data which is coming from multiple sources, from multiple origins, and it's been relatively well known for a long time that browsers are really bad at that. If you have multiple webpages open at the same time, you are looking for trouble because the implementation can't really keep them separate. And now what seems to get more complicated, if I understand correctly, is that in a way we are composing a new message from these bits and pieces that have been gathered from multiple origins, and we are sending this new message to another machine, and if we want to go to the root causes, I guess we may even need to change the programming languages that we are using for these kinds of network applications, where we are dealing with data coming from multiple origins. If we could have the origin of the data at the programming language level, internally to the language, and then enforce that these taggings are added to the messages going out, quite a lot of this might go away, but of course there will be even further tricks of getting around. But that reminds me of the situation where, originally we had C and now we have Java, and C#, and whatever, which in a way prevents us from doing some of those bad things, so by developing a new language we could probably alleviate the situation a little bit.

Matthew Johnson: There are other attacks which have come out recently where you use Javascript to rewrite the page content, to contain links to websites which the browser will follow itself, rather than being done by the client side code, so you can cause it to create an image tag, which the browser then requests, and then in Javascript you check whether or not that succeeded, so you can use that to scan your intranet to find things. And you can do similar tricks to get requests to places which don't have passwords, it's like a lot of stuff you can do with the client side code only altering the tag of the website, and not actually making any connections, so you even if you're restricting completely what the code can do in terms of sending out connections, typically in the web browser because images and so on are used all the time, that make links to other domains, you can't really restrict that to a same origin policy so easily.

Reply: Interesting.

Richard Clayton: You haven't said anything about cookies. Cookies have an interesting same origin policy because they not only belong to exactly where they came from, they belong to one level up or down as well.

Reply: The fun is starting.

Richard Clayton: Well cookies have been around for well over ten years, so the fun has been going around for that long, because it occured to the people who wrote the initial specification that it would be a good idea not to let people try and set cookies into ".net", because then it would apply to all ".net" things, and they made a rule for that. Unfortunately over here we have things like ".net.uk", and in order to deal with this Firefox ends up with a blacklist of some three thousand exceptions to the rule which says, that it's obvious that people can work out exactly where the authority is. Furthermore, some people worked out that if you produced a URL which was ".net" then a number of browsers decided whether or not you had enough components in the thing by counting the dots, and therefore validating it and saying, setting that cookie in ".net" was alright, but right at the last minute the resolver inside of your machine takes an address, and says, ah, this is somebody who's read a dud, and throws it away, and then resolves it properly. Somebody in 2004 reported that you could set a cookie on ".net", and then discovered that it had been originally reported six years earlier and was still not fixed.

Reply: I would be interested in references for that because that fits into my story of abstraction, and things we're not very good at yet. Coming back to your point about languages, I think you're right, and I also see this parallel to buffer overruns. In my view of security, it's about broken abstractions, with buffer overruns if the abstraction was broken. And now the abstraction "location" is very badly defined, and some of the attacks build on the fact that either you don't trace the true location of all the parts in a document, or that you are translating between different addresses, and allowed the attacker to help you in doing so.

Pekka Nikander: I guess most of the programmers don't even understand the threats that come from having data coming from various origins.

Sandy Clark: You often don't get to find out exactly where you're getting your information from.

Hardened Stateless Session Cookies

Steven J. Murdoch

University of Cambridge, Computer Laboratory
http://www.cl.cam.ac.uk/users/sjm217/

Abstract. Stateless session cookies allow web applications to alter their behaviour based on user preferences and access rights, without maintaining server-side state for each session. This is desirable because it reduces the impact of denial of service attacks and eases database replication issues in load-balanced environments. The security of existing session cookie proposals depends on the server protecting the secrecy of a symmetric MAC key, which for engineering reasons is usually stored in a database, and thus at risk of accidental leakage or disclosure via application vulnerabilities. In this paper we show that by including a salted iterated hash of the user password in the database, and its pre-image in a session cookie, an attacker with read access to the server is unable to spoof an authenticated session. Even with knowledge of the server's MAC key the attacker needs a user's password, which is not stored on the server, to create a valid cookie. By extending an existing session cookie scheme, we maintain all the previous security guarantees, but also preserve security under partial compromise.

1 Introduction

Many websites require users to authenticate themselves before permitting access. Reasons include customising the appearance to meet user preferences, restricting access to confidential information, limiting who can change site configuration, and tracking who contributes to the site. The protocol used for web page access, HTTP [1], does not provide a session layer. If needed, websites must implement a mechanism for securely linking a series of requests together and back to a user account. This paper discusses the construction of a session management system which is robust against disclosure of the authentication database.

1.1 Web Authentication

Users almost universally authenticate to websites by providing a username and password. Both are sent as a HTTP form submission, optionally encrypted with TLS [2,3]. The website will then retrieve the specified user's account details, typically from a SQL [4] database, and check if the password is correct.

It is prudent engineering practice not to record the cleartext password in the database; instead the result of a one-way function should be stored. This allows the site to verify whether a presented password is correct, but an attacker who can read the authentication database cannot directly retrieve the password. It

B. Christianson et al. (Eds.): Security Protocols 2008, LNCS 6615, pp. 93–101, 2011.

would still be possible for such an attacker to test all common passwords, and time-space trade-offs such as rainbow tables [5] can perform this attack almost instantaneously. To resist these attacks, a per-account random value, the *salt*, should be additionally fed into the one-way function, and stored. Adding a salt makes pre-computing a dictionary infeasible (hence each account must be brute-forced individually), and hides whether two users share a password [6].

1.2   Session Management

Following successful authentication, the website must be able to link HTTP requests to the relevant user account. This is achieved by the website returning a byte string to the client on login, a *session cookie* [7]. The client will include this cookie in the headers of subsequent HTTP requests to the same domain, until the cookie is deleted by the user or it expires. Cookies may be set as persistent, and otherwise will be be deleted when the web browser exits. The structure of the cookie is opaque to the client.

There are a number of standard approaches for constructing session cookies. One common technique, supported by web frameworks such as PHP, stores session state on the webserver, in a file or database. Here, the cookie contains a randomly generated session identifier which allows the website to retrieve or save the relevant session state. The cookie contents should be a cryptographically secure pseudo-random number and be sufficiently long to make guessing a valid session identifier infeasible.

Many users will have multiple sessions associated with their account, for example one for work and one from their home PC. Also, unless users explicitly log out, the server state associated with a session must be retained until the session times out. This means that the space required on the server for maintaining state can grow much faster than the number of users. This also introduces a denial of service vulnerability, in that attackers could create many sessions and fill up the filesystem. CAPTCHAs [8] can restrict automated account creation, but it would significantly harm usability to require them for login.

It is thus desirable to implement stateless session cookies. Here, the server does not need to store any session state — all necessary information is stored in the cookie held by the client. With this approach, load balancing is easier, as session state does not need to be replicated over multiple front-end servers. This paper will discuss how to implement such cookies securely, so that attackers cannot spoof authenticated users or alter critical session data. While previous work has assumed that an attacker has no control of the server state, here we show how a limited version of the security guarantees can be retained even when the attacker is able to read the account database.

There are a number of ways in which unauthorised read access to a database can be gained. For example, a simple Google search can find several database backups for blogs unintentionally left on the web[1]. Also, one of the most common

---

[1] I have contacted the site operators in question, recommending they remove the backups and change their passwords.

security vulnerabilities in web applications is the SQL injection attack, which we will show can often grant read, but not write, access.

1.3 SQL Injection

Storing website data in a relational databases is a very common design choice made by developers. This approach permits convenient and efficient querying of data, and allows the now stateless front-end webserver to be replicated for scalability and redundancy. However, the use of a database introduces the risk of SQL injection attacks, one of the most problematic classes of web application vulnerabilities. Here, improperly sanitised user provided information is used in constructing a SQL query, allowing the attacker to inject malicious SQL code.

For example, suppose the following SQL query is executed by a web application, in order to retrieve the account details for a user[2].

```
SELECT * FROM wp_users WHERE user_login = '$user_login'
```

The value of $user_login may be chosen by the attacker, and if it contains a ' character, the string literal will be terminated and the remainder of the value interpreted as SQL. To exploit this vulnerability the following value for $user_login may be chosen:

```
' UNION ALL SELECT 1,2,user_pass,4,5,6,7,8,9,10 FROM wp_users
WHERE ID=1/*
```

Now, the SQL executed will be:

```
SELECT * FROM wp_users WHERE user_login = '' UNION ALL SELECT
1,2,user_pass,4,5,6,7,8,9,10 FROM wp_users WHERE ID=1/*'
```

The result of this query will be the concatenation (union) of rows returned from the two subqueries. As no rows fulfil the `user_login = ''` expression, the only row retrieved will be where the user's ID is 1, which is by convention the site administrator. The /* starts a comment, preventing the trailing ' from causing a syntax error.

As will be shown in Section 2, with Wordpress, knowing the contents of the user_pass column is sufficient to impersonate the respective user. If the result of the above query can be retrieved, the attacker can then exploit further security weaknesses to eventually escalate privileges to user-level, and potentially root access, on the web server.

At this point, it is useful to note the structure of the queries above — the attacker can only append SQL into the existing string. In particular, the attacker cannot convert a SELECT query (for reading data) into UPDATE or INSERT (which modify data). The SQL syntax does support executing multiple queries

---

[2] This example is a simplified version of the exploit code for CVE-2007-2821, a SQL injection vulnerability in Wordpress 2.1.3, written by Janek Vind: http://www.milw0rm.com/exploits/3960

in a single call, by separating them with a ; character, however the standard database API rejects such queries[3]. Effectively, the attacker has read-only access to the database.

In many cases, the ability to read the database is sufficient to totally compromise the security of a web application. Web servers are, for security reasons, commonly prevented from writing any data to the filesystem, other than via the database engine. Thus all secrets, whether randomly generated or entered into the management web interface, are at risk from SQL injection vulnerabilities.

As with buffer overflows, the theory of preventing SQL vulnerabilities is well understood but poorly applied in practice, especially in legacy applications. Identifying potentially dangerous code is difficult, especially when user input is processed by several layers of escaping and unescaping, by partially undocumented libraries, before the string is passed to the database engine. Prepared statements [9] improve matters, but these cannot be used when the user input defines the structure of the query itself.

It appears that SQL injection vulnerabilities are inevitable in large web applications — even if they do not exist when the system is written they could easily be introduced later by less-experienced programmers or carelessly written libraries. Therefore, following the principle of defence in depth, in addition to efforts to eliminate vulnerabilities, the application should be structured to limit the harm caused by exploits.

Previous proposals for stateless session cookies fail completely if the database can be read, for example through SQL injection. This is understandable, given the common attitude that a website vulnerable to SQL injection is a hopeless case and so there is no need to consider further layers of defences. Nevertheless, we have shown some cases where an attacker has read access, but may find gaining write access more difficult, or even impossible. This paper will show how to leverage this read-only property into limiting the potential damage.

2   Weakness of Existing Proposals

Due to the lack of stateless session cookies in standard web frameworks, a wide variety of ad-hoc solutions have been developed. Fu et al. [10] showed that several of these were seriously flawed, due to weak or non-existent cryptography, using a counter when a cryptographically secure pseudo-random number is needed, and inappropriate padding. Their paper demonstrates how the schemes were reverse-engineered, without any access to the server code, simply by observing the cookies returned and sometimes through generating specially constructed usernames. It then describes how the schemes can be exploited, including spoofing cookies for chosen accounts and even extracting the system-wide key from one website.

Another ad-hoc solution is implemented by Wordpress, where the authentication cookie is of the form MD5(MD5(*password*)). The account database stores MD5(*password*) in the user_pass column, so on subsequent accesses, this value

---

[3] http://www.php.net/mysql_query

can be hashed a further time and compared with the cookie. This approach suffers from three main weaknesses, which are the subject of CVE-2007-6013 by the present author [11]. Firstly, no salt is applied before storing the hashed password in the database, easing brute force attacks. Secondly, if the attacker can read the hashed password in the database, it is trivial to generate a valid cookie. Thirdly, a cookie will never cease to be valid — if the database is compromised or a cookie is leaked, the affected users must change their password to a different one.

In their paper, Fu *et al.* [10] make a number of suggestions for improving web authentication, including proposing an improved structure for stateless authentication cookies:

$$\texttt{exp=}t\texttt{\&data=}s\texttt{\&digest=}\mathrm{MAC}_k(\texttt{exp=}t\texttt{\&data=}s)$$

Here, t is the expiry time for the cookie and s is the state the web application needs to be maintained, such as the username or the user capabilities. The digest is a message authentication code, such as HMAC-SHA-256, under a key known only to the web server. This scheme prevents a valid cookie being generated by an attacker and also prevents existing cookies being modified. Liu *et al.* [12] extended this proposal to also encrypt s and optionally bind the cookie to a particular TLS session. However, in either scheme, if the MAC key is compromised, for example through an SQL injection attack or insecure backup, an attacker may spoof cookies for any account, until the compromise is detected and the key revoked.

3   Stateless Session Cookies

The motivation for the scheme proposed in this paper is to maintain the security properties of the previous work, while also remaining secure even if the attacker has read access to the database. In essence, we suggest including an iterated hash of the user's password in the database and its pre-image in the session cookie. Thus, someone with the correct password can calculate a valid cookie, and this can be verified using the database entry, but it is infeasible to generate a cookie given access to the database alone.

In the following section, we use the following recursive definitions, based on the fall-back password hashing algorithm of the phpass library [13]:

$$a_0(salt, password) = \mathrm{H}(salt \| password)$$
$$a_x(salt, password) = \mathrm{H}(a_{x-1}(salt, password) \| password)$$

Where *salt* is per-account, cryptographically secure pseudo-random number, long enough to resist brute force attack (*e.g.* 128 bits), and *password* is the user password. $\mathrm{H}(\cdot)$ is a cryptographically secure hash function (*e.g.* SHA-256).

(1) Account creation: On requesting an account be created, the user specifies the desired username and password. The web site then generates the random salt, and calculates the authenticator $v = \mathrm{H}(a_n(salt, password))$ both of which it stores in the database. The public value n is the hash iteration count (*e.g.* 256).

(2) Login: To log in, a user presents their username and password. The web site retrieves the user account details, including the salt and authenticator. Using the supplied password and retrieved salt it calculates $c = a_n(salt, password)$ and compares it to the stored authenticator v. If $H(c) \neq v$ the user is denied access and c is discarded. If $H(c) = v$ the web site concludes that the supplied password was correct and returns a cookie, constructed as per the Fu *et al.* scheme, but with an extra field `auth`:

$$\texttt{exp=}t\texttt{\&data=}s\texttt{\&auth=}c\texttt{\&digest=}\text{MAC}_k(\texttt{exp=}t\texttt{\&data=}s\texttt{\&auth=}c)$$

(3) Subsequent accesses: Following login, as the client requests further pages, the server reads the submitted cookie, checks the MAC, extracts c, and compares $H(c)$ with the authenticator v from the database. If they match, access is granted.

3.1   Security

In the conventional threat model, an attacker does not have access to the authentication database, so does not know the salt, password or MAC key and here our proposal performs just as well as the Fu *et al.* scheme. Even though it is likely that many users will select poor passwords, the inclusion of a large salt prevents operation (3) being of help in brute-forceing the password. This property is desirable because rate-limiting, to resist online brute-force attacks, need only be applied to the login procedure (2), not every page that requires authentication. This could be particularly valuable in load-balanced situations with one login server and multiple application servers — only the login server need retain state on the number of failed login attempts.

   If a cookie is retrieved, for example from a compromised or stolen computer, or through XSS [14], the attacker may use it to log in, until the cookie expires. The MAC prevents the expiry time from being modified. However, as the attacker does not know the salt, the cookie cannot be used to confirm whether a particular brute-force guess at the password is correct. It is for this reason that the salt in the scheme must be fairly large. In conventional password hashing schemes the salt is only to make a precomputed dictionary infeasible to store, and so a few tens of bits are adequate. In this scheme the salt is additionally used to prevent the attacker learning any information about the password from a cookie, so must be as large as a cryptographic key, *e.g.* 128 bits.

   If the attacker is able to read the database, *e.g.* through unsecured backups or SQL injection, it can discover a user's authenticator, salt and global MAC key. This is still insufficient to generate a valid cookie, as doing so would be equivalent to discovering the pre-image of a hash output. Of course, the attacker can still brute force the password, and if it is weak the attacker can gain access. This task is made more difficult by the salt (preventing a rainbow-table attack) and is further slowed down by iterating the hash function n times (*e.g.* 256).

   With knowledge of the MAC key, an attacker can alter cookies, so user capabilities cannot be safely stored there and instead must reside in the account database. If an attacker compromises the MAC key and can intercept a cookie for a privileged user, its expiry date can be extended until the compromise is detected and key revoked. Regularly rotating the MAC key would require the attacker to gain access to a recent copy, limiting the vulnerable period.

An attacker with write-access to the database is outside the threat model of this scheme. With such access, the attacker could simply create a new account with chosen password or escalate an existing account to high privilege. We see no way to defend against such an adversary in the general case.

3.2   Efficiency

The scheme proposed in this paper is not significantly more computationally expensive than one based around the Fu *et al.* [10] proposal. At account creation and login, the only additional step is one invocation of $H(\cdot)$, as the iterated computation is present in any salted password authentication scheme. If the salt needs to be extended, there will be a increase in size of data hashed, but as the salt is only added once, this increase is negligible. On each subsequent access, where authentication is required, an extra invocation of $H(\cdot)$ is needed, in addition to the two already required for HMAC verification.

We also require a database read to retrieve the authenticator and user access rights. In contrast, the Fu *et al.* scheme can operate independently from the database after the login stage, because the site-wide MAC key can be cached in memory. Our scheme introduces more complexity in load-balanced environments because front-end servers need access to the database, however, unlike standard session cookies, only read access is required so maintaining consistency is easier and on-disk indices need not be updated.

4   Variations

A large variety of possibilities for variations on this scheme are possible, and may be desirable in certain deployment environments. Any sufficiently secure password hashing mechanism may replace $a_n(salt, password)$, provided the salt size is adequate to also prevent offline brute-force password-recovery attacks on cookies. For example bcrypt [15], with its 128-bit salt, would be a good candidate. If possible, the password hashing function should be written in an efficient compiled language, allowing a higher value of n, so as to reduce the advantage of attacker with a custom implementation.

If the available password hashing functions do not permit a sufficiently long salt to be added, an alternative is to encrypt the cookie under a server key before sending it to the client [12]. This means that the cookie alone is still not helpful for attempting a brute-force password recovery attack. Both the extended-salt and encrypted authenticator schemes are vulnerable to brute force, if the user's salt or encryption key respectively are available to the attacker.

We have not selected the encrypted authenticator option because standard web libraries do not come with symmetric encryption libraries, possibly due to export regulations. Also, if the salt is sufficiently short for there to be collisions, a user who has the same password on multiple sites might have the same authenticator on some of them. In this case, if an attacker compromises one site, obtaining a user's cookie along with the cookie encryption key, he can replay the cookie to a different site for which he has compromised the MAC key if the user has both the same password and salt. This weakness can be defended against by selecting a long enough salt such that collisions are unlikely, or by incorporating the site URL in the calculation of the authenticator (for example, by appending it to the salt when calculating v).

Fu *et al.* suggest a number of other hints for maintaining secure web sites, which complement the authentication proposal in this paper. Their recommendations include prohibiting weak passwords, requiring re-authentication before changing passwords, using HTTPS to encrypt login, and binding cookies to IP addresses. We add a further recommendation, of storing two MAC sub-keys if possible — one in a file and one in the database, which are combined at runtime. To compromise the key an attacker would need to obtain both sub-keys which mitigates certain vulnerabilities.

In addition to security, usability is another important consideration for an authentication scheme. Enforcing an expiry time on cookies reduces the risk of cookie compromise, but requires users to re-authenticate periodically. This could be especially annoying to users if they compose a long blog post, only to find out that their cookie has expired when they submit the form, potentially losing their changes. A simple way to reduce this risk is to require users re-authenticate a few hours before the expiry time if a GET request is made, but to permit POST requests up to the hard deadline.

5   Conclusion

In this paper, we have described how an attack resulting in read-only access to a website authentication database is a plausible scenario, motivated by the examples of a badly-protected database backup and SQL injection vulnerabilities. We have shown how to harden existing stateless session cookie schemes, which were previously vulnerable to such attackers, thereby greatly limiting the potential damage. The new scheme we have presented has negligible overhead, when compared to existing proposals, and can leverage existing password authentication libraries, yet provides good security guarantees even when the attacker has read access to the full website state.

Acknowledgements

Thanks are due to Richard Clayton, Markus Kuhn, the attendees at the Security Protocols Workshop (especially Mark Lomas), and the contributors to Light Blue Touchpaper, for their valuable discussions on the topics discussed here.

References

1. Fielding, R., Gettys, J., Mogul, J., Frystyk, H., Masinter, L., Leach, P., Berners-Lee, T.: Hypertext Transfer Protocol – HTTP/1.1. RFC 2616, IETF (1999)
2. Rescorla, E.: HTTP over TLS. RFC 2818, IETF (2000)

3. Dierks, T., Rescorla, E.: The Transport Layer Security (TLS) protocol version 1.1. RFC 4346, IETF (2006)
4. JTC 1/SC 32: Information technology – database languages – SQL. ISO/IEC 9075:2006 (2003)
5. Oechslin, P.: Making a faster cryptanalytic time-memory trade-off. In: Boneh, D. (ed.) CRYPTO 2003. LNCS, vol. 2729, pp. 617–630. Springer, Heidelberg (2003)
6. Morris, R., Thompson, K.: Password security: a case history. Communications of the ACM 22, 594–597 (1979)
7. Kristol, D., Montulli, L.: HTTP state management mechanism. RFC 2109, IETF (1997)
8. von Ahn, L., Blum, M., Hopper, N.J., Langford, J.: CAPTCHA: Using hard AI problems for security. In: Biham, E. (ed.) EUROCRYPT 2003. LNCS, vol. 2656, pp. 294–311. Springer, Heidelberg (2003)
9. Fisk, H.: Prepared statements. MySQL Developer Zone (2004),
   http://dev.mysql.com/tech-resources/articles/4.1/prepared-statements.html
10. Fu, K., Sit, E., Smith, K., Feamster, N.: Dos and don'ts of client authentication on the web. In: Proceedings of the 10th USENIX Security Symposium, Washington D.C., US (2001)
11. Murdoch, S.J.: Wordpress cookie authentication vulnerability CVE-2007-6013 (candidate) (2007),
   http://www.cl.cam.ac.uk/~sjm217/advisories/wordpress-cookie-auth.txt
12. Liu, A.X., Kovacs, J.M., Huang, C.T., Gouda, M.G.: A secure cookie protocol. In: Proceedings of the 14th IEEE International Conference on Computer Communications and Networks, pp. 333–338 (2005)
13. Solar Designer: Portable PHP password hashing framework (2006),
   http://www.openwall.com/phpass/
14. CERT Coordination Center: Malicious HTML tags embedded in client web requests. Advisory CA-2000-02, CERT/CC (2000),
   http://www.cert.org/advisories/CA-2000-02.html
15. Provos, N., Mazières, D.: A future-adaptable password scheme. In: USENIX Annual Technical Conference, Monterey, California, US, pp. 81–92 (1999)

Hardened Stateless Session Cookies
(Transcript of Discussion)

Steven J. Murdoch

University of Cambridge

Pekka Nikander: Maybe I'm missing something, but what's the advantage of a double hashing here, or first supplying a and then $H(\cdot)$, instead of having, for example, two different hash functions?

Reply: If the cookie was another hash of something then the server wouldn't be able to verify whether that cookie is correct.

Pekka Nikander: Oh, OK.

Reply: So I'm considering, let's start with the medical principle of do no harm, what is this compared to previous schemes? The thing that makes me suspicious about this is I'm sending the password in a cookie, which is probably not a good idea, but the function includes the salt which is kept secret from the database host, so I claim that it should not be possible to go from the cookie back to the password. This is important because users share passwords over multiple websites, and if the client is a victim of a cross scripting vulnerability, it shouldn't be possible for the attacker to go back to the password and then use that to attack another site.

Pekka Nikander: So you're saying your attacker has read access to the data?

Reply: Yes.

Bruce Christianson: So previously it was assumed that the attacker cannot see v or s, is that right?

Reply: Yes, and that was the scenario that all of the previous schemes were meant to be secure under, the attacker has no access to the database. But then let's suppose that the attacker does have access to the database, so he has v and he has s, so with these he can brute-force the passwords, but that was always the case because this is how the password hashing algorithm works. But he shouldn't be able to get from v to c unless he brute-forces the password, so if your password is strong then this scheme should be secure even if the attacker has read access to the database.

Bruce Christianson: And the s is there now simply in order to prevent cookies from being transported from one server to another?

Reply: The s is there for the same purpose as normal password salting, which is stop a brute-force table from being built up. The thing I've missed out from this (which is in the paper) is actually all this is MAC'd under a static secret, which I am assuming that the attacker will get access to as well: but if the attacker doesn't have access to that key he can multiply the cookies. Another aspect of that is, there's an expiry thing in the cookie, and if the attacker gets access to the database and a valid cookie, they can extend that until it compromises the data, but if they don't have a cookie to start off with, they shouldn't be able to

B. Christianson et al. (Eds.): Security Protocols 2008, LNCS 6615, pp. 102–106, 2011.
© Springer-Verlag Berlin Heidelberg 2011

generate a new one. I can't think of a way to be able to get any better security properties than that, if you can, I'd be very interested to hear.

Feng Hao: I'm not very sure of these a functions, so it's just a hash?

Reply: Yes, you will get all the same properties if you use a various small hash options. I suggest that it be implemented is based on the `phpass` algorithm, which is, you take the hash of the salt and the password, and then take the hash of that and the password, and a hash of that and the password, and then do that 256 times. This is because you want the attacker to work as hard as possible, if they have access to the database and the salt, and want to get back to the password.

Feng Hao: Oh I see, but if the attacker is able to read a cookie and read the database then basically . . .

Reply: If they can read the database, they can brute-force the password, so you do have to use good passwords. But they can't build an offline database because of the salt.

Matthew Johnson: And there are two scenarios given. If the attacker has access to a cookie which is valid, then they can extend them a little because it's a stateless system so all of the state has to be in the cookie, but you can't really defend against that if they have access to those. But they still can't get the password without brute-forcing it.

Reply: Yes. Maybe we can look at it in three examples. One is the attacker has access to the cookie only, and then I think this is cryptographically secure, one is that the attacker has access to the database, and I think that's secure. The third option is the attacker can brute-force the password because the password is poor, and then if the attacker has access to the database it's not secure.

Michael Roe: What do you do if your server receives a very large number of cookies which don't match, as in somebody trying to do an online search for the password?

Reply: There needs to be rate-control at the login stage, I don't know if I need to do a rate control at the cookie verification stage unless the attacker has the salt.

Michael Roe: That is exactly the case I was thinking of.

Reply: Well if the attacker has a salt then they probably have access to the database anyway, so they can do an offline attack. In the database, with the salt and v you can then do an offline brute-force attack, so I don't think online brute-force buys you anything extra.

Matthew Johnson: It buys you part of the hash algorithm, which is a lot.

Reply: Yes.

Bruce Christianson: How stateless are you? Does the server even know which clients are logged in?

Reply: Yes, I don't think the server needs to know what clients are logged in. The slight different in state to the Fu *et al.* scheme is I do require that the client on every request is able to read the user login interface, whereas the Fu scheme doesn't require that, it just requires that you read a login database on login, but everything else doesn't need to touch the database at all.

Bruce Christianson: Why do you need to do that?

Reply: Because v is stored in the database, and the server needs to access v.

Bruce Christianson: So it's the server that needs to do that?

Reply: Yes. Reading a database is not so bad, it's only a read, which is much simpler because you don't need built-in indexes, and there's less problems of . . .

Bruce Christianson: And there's no concurrency problems, yes.

Tuomas Aura: There are two hashes in use, but I don't think that's necessary really if you want a more abstract version of the protocol. You have two kinds of secrets. You have the long-term secret, which is a password, and then you have the short-term session secret, which is the hash, and you can keep these completely separate.

Reply: The problem with that proposal is that servers would have to store state per session.

Tuomas Aura: So then you would rather just store the random cookie?

Bruce Christianson: If you allow per session state to be stored then you can solve the cookie extension problem as well, that was why I asked my question.

Tuomas Aura: But isn't there a problem now with this key that the sessions don't expire?

Reply: There is also an expiry time which I haven't mentioned in this slide, it is in the paper. There is a MAC of the expiry time and the cookie, and MAC over everything, so when that hits the server, if the hacker does not have access to the server they can't extend the cookie, if they do have access to the server and a valid cookie, they can extend it indefinitely until the problem is detected in the key exchange.

Bruce Christianson: If you want your session to be encrypted though, the server has to be able to work out which key to decrypt that session with. So there has to be a control block somewhere, mapping session to key. Well, if you're storing keys, and keys are state, then you can store a bit more state in the same control block.

Matthew Johnson: Oh, you're thinking about SSL session state aren't you?

Bruce Christianson: Yes.

Matthew Johnson: The SSL session is not done by the code that does this. Although that might be done.

Tuomas Aura: I suggest still doing stateless key, and generating the two keys as hash of the server's secret key, and the username or IP address, or whatever it is, that I have mentioned. That way you don't need to store session secrets, but the advantage you get if you do is that you can't use the cookie to do a brute-force password search.

Reply: So in that case if the attacker gets access to the server's secret, they can generate new cookies. Or are you thinking of per session servers?

Tuomas Aura: So the idea is that there's no secret on the server?

Reply: There is a secret on the server.

Tuomas Aura: So if that secret is compromised that would be that.

Matthew Johnson: But the bad person can't create new cookies if they don't know the password.

Reply: I agree that it is a bad idea to use the password, but a nice property that the password has is that the server only knows it at the correct time, provided it throws it away. If they use anything other than the password, then where can the server get it, other than it being stored in the database? The password comes from the user, and then once it's been used the server can throw it away, I can't think of anything else that has this property.

Pekka Nikander: So making an analogy, is the password a kind of a weak private key which you're using for computing c, which is a kind of a weak public key which you then include plus signature into the cookie.

Reply: Yes, but I'm strengthening it with SSL.

Tuomas Aura: I think you have to, because one of your attackers gets the cookie, and in that case you'd have a weakness that it is possible to brute-force, even though you have a salt which means it more difficult.

Bruce Christianson: Salt is not usually intended to be a protection against online brute-force.

Reply: The cookie's only the function of the salt, so given the cookie you have the brute-force case and the password, and s is 128 bits.

Virgil Gligor: It seems that some man-in-the-middle of the client end of the server could replay the request of the cookie without having to log in, is that a concern?

Reply: Yes, that is a problem, so if the attacker does cross side scripting, for example, and steals a cookie, they can use it again, so you would really want to be running this using POS as well. But certificates are so expensive and users get scared off by self-signed certificates, so most websites don't do this, even the best ones.

Pekka Nikander: I don't know if this could be done, but I'm wondering if when the attacker gets the password you could perhaps derive the hash chain, and use the anchor of the hash chain in the cookie, and then when you get the re-trust you can reset the cookie using the next element from the hash chain. But of course then you would have a vulnerability that you need to store something on the database, so it wouldn't work directly in that way.

Reply: I like the idea of the hash chains, maybe there is something in that.

Pekka Nikander: I think there might be something in that direction, but it's not straightforward.

Tuomas Aura: A server will need to store the hash.

Bruce Christianson: It all comes down to first of all, exactly how stateless you insist on being, and secondly whether you want to do things at the same or different levels of abstraction because you've got particular properties.

Pekka Nikander: But the converse is that if your database is really read-only then you can't change anything on the server, so in a way you can then do your sequence with the hash chain. The legitimate user could probably do a sequence of enquiries or whatever, and the attacker could recreate some of those enquiries but it wouldn't matter.

Bruce Christianson: Well if the server was really stateless he wouldn't have been able to upload his database onto the server.

Reply: This is one point on the continuum, so yes, it's more stateless than the session IDs but it's less stateless than the two keys. But I think it's a useful point, so assuming that I can't come up with any more breaks on this we'll try to push people into deploying this, because it's better than what we've got at the moment, and it doesn't break any of their software.

Bruce Christianson: The nice thing is that it then fits exactly into the niche that's already provided.

Reply: Yes.

TPM-Performance Sensible Key Management Protocols for Service Provisioning in Cloud Computing

Haibo Chen[1], Jun Li[2], and Wenbo Mao[2]

[1] Fudan University
[2] EMC Research China

A Trusted Platform Module (TPM) is a small and hence low-performance hardware chip whose main function — at least for the service provisioning topic of this paper — is to play a trusted third party's role inside a service provisioning computing platform so that the platform will have what we call a behaviour conformity property. The property of behaviour conformity is most needed in service oriented applications, such as utility computing, grid computing and the new notion of cloud computing, where a resource-scarce user (guest) submits jobs to be computed at computational resource providers (hosts). It is inevitable that prior to a session of service provisioning, security protocols will run between the guest, the host, and the TPM. For service provisioning to have scalability albeit TPM's low performance, such a protocol needs to be carefully designed not to place the TPM in a bottleneck position. We propose a protocol mechanism by remodelling the original TPM being the trusted computing base (TCB) into two sub-components: a high performance software TCB which is a measured virtual machine monitor to delegate most of the functions of the TPM, and the original low performance TPM TCB which retains the software measurement function inside itself for low frequent uses. Our result has an independent value for wide deployment of TCG technologies.

1 Problem Statement and Threat Analysis

Fig. 1 illustrates an abstract protocol view of a service-oriented computing problem. Here, Alice is a resource-scarce user who wants to compute her jobs on a resourceful service provider Bob. In the rest of the paper we shall consider Alice as a guest, and Bob as a host. In this service provisioning problem, a guest's process/application running on the host needs protection, both in terms of data/code confidentiality and integrity.

This service provisioning problem has a somewhat unusual threat model. Usually a guest is viewed as a potential adversary which may cause damage to the host and to other guests on the host. However, the unusual direction of the threat we want to emphasize in this paper is the following: the host is a partner of the guest, as well as a potential opponent. There are different ways to view the latter direction of the threat. First, with the host providing services to many guests, it is possible that a guest makes use of the host to launch attacks on other guests. This is particularly possible if the host makes use of commercial-off-the-shelf systems to

B. Christianson et al. (Eds.): Security Protocols 2008, LNCS 6615, pp. 107–114, 2011.

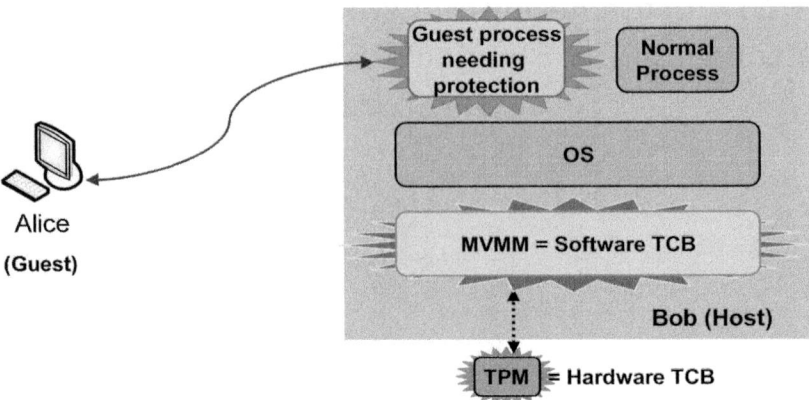

Fig. 1. An abstract protocol structure for service provisioning and host protection (only part of the host components need protection and are marked as "wrapped")

build its service provisioning environment, such as commodity operating systems and third party software which the host has little control about their trustworthiness. Second, the system administrator at the host may also be an adversary, and indeed, with a root-level privilege, the owner adversary is a formidable one! A potential threat from the host to a guest can be unauthorized disclosure of guest's proprietary code/data. This sort of threat is less of a concern in traditional ways of service provisioning which are only affordable from reputable hosts. However, it is nowadays becoming problematic in more and more popular ways of service provisioning like Grid [1] or Cloud [2] computing that service providers are ad-hoc recruited, and the relationship between a guest and a host is in a "one off pay as you go" manner. Serious guest users such as small and medium enterprises and hosts such as seasonally resource abundant financial institutes may not wish to "join the cloud" if strong protection is not in place.

2   Our Contribution: Separation of Trusted Computing Base

We will use Trusted Computing Group Technology to provide the needed protection. In our emphasis on the host provisioning not only computational services, but also strong security services, we use the TPM [3] to provide an integrity measurement on an important and privileged software component: the virtual machine monitor (VMM) [4]. A measured VMM [5] is denoted MVMM which is considered an extension of the TPM as a trusted computing base (TCB). The measurement takes place when the computing platform is booted. The reason we measure a VMM is because this software will be providing most security services, such as process isolation [6,7,8], to materialize the needed property of behaviour conformity at the host.

MVMM is considered the software TCB delegated from the TPM which is the hardware TCB. The separation of software and hardware TCBs is a very

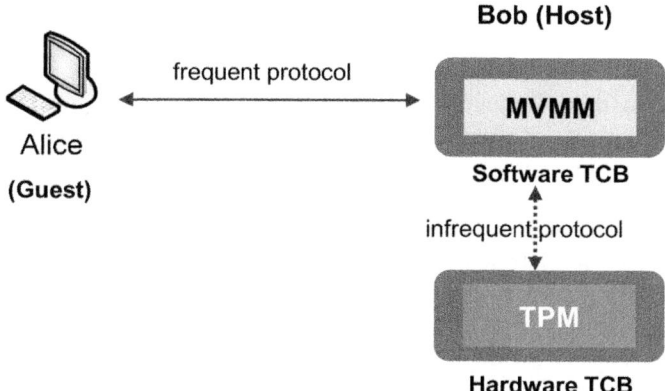

Fig. 2. Protocol separation to minimize the use of the TPM

important and the key point of this paper. The software TCB is in high performance to delegate much of the functions of the hardware TCB which is in low performance. However, as the key point of this paper, there is one important function of the TPM that will not be delegated on to the MVMM: that is the measurement of the very software TCB: one cannot measure itself. Fig. 2 depicts the protocol view abstracted from Fig. 1.

The protocol suite consists of several protocols of which we emphasize two. Most of the time, such as when the host accepts a guest application (most of the time because there can be a large number of guests to be served by one host), a usual protocol (we shall term "frequent protocol") is to run between the guest and the MVMM in the host without involving the TPM. That protocol involves a delegated attestation of the MVMM to the guest. The delegation is possible because MVMM is the software TCB certified by the TPM, and the chain of trust works just in the TCG defined manner.

However, occasionally, a guest application which is already running at the host will enter a state of indecision whether or not the software TCB has been properly measured. These occasions typically include the following situations: to roll-out a guest application to the persistent external storage for processing at a later time (maybe because the host needs to schedule processes on it to achieve a better performance), or to checkpoint a VM image to prevent power loss, among others. We will argue in a moment that in these much rarer occasions, a guest application rolled out to the persistent storage will enter a state of indecision, and we will let the TPM kick in to make the needed judgement. Since the guest application needs "wrapping" (see Fig. 1) outside the memory (inside memory protection is achieved by the memory arbitration function of the MVMM which we will not discuss in this paper), the rolling out of a paused application will involve cryptographic algorithms to be applied to the guest application, such as code/data encryption plus integrity protection. In our design, this rarer case of cryptographic protection is served by applying an "infrequent protocol" which should use key material of the TPM rather than that which has been delegated to the software TCB.

One may ask why the use of the TPM key material is necessary for "wrapping" the rolled out guest applications. Why not just use the delegated key material of the MVMM, which will later permit the MVMM to directly re-admit the rolled out application in an efficient manner? As an important point of notice, we observe the necessary stateless design of the software TCB: the MVMM which has rolled out a guest application and the application to be resumed needs not to be the same session run of the software (may even not be the same version of the software in case software upgrading). Consider the checkpoint case followed by a power loss for instance. The software TCB is rebooted after power back on must already be a new session run. With the stateless design of the software TCB, the new session run (version) of the MVMM already uses a new set of delegated key material, and hence can no longer decrypt the previously rolled out guest application.

3   TPM-Performance Sensible Key Management Protocols

3.1   Notation and Terminology Agreement

To describe the protocol clearly, let's first provide a notational and terminological agreement.

Integrity Measurement: The integrity measurement [9] is a term of TCG technology. In the measurement of a VMM, it is by the TPM computing a cryptographic hash value of VMM code. The measurement can only be done by TPM and will not be delegated to any party external to the TPM. In the TCG specification, an integrity measurement value is stored in a PCR register in the TPM. However in our TPM-performance sensible design, the TPM shall hand a certified copy of the measurement of the software TCB to the software TCB. The certification uses the AIK of the TPM.

Delegation of the software TPM: The delegation takes place in the boot time when the VMM is measured and loaded. The result is that the measured PCR value of the VMM will be digitally signed by the TPM and handed over to the MVMM. Later the MVMM can be attested by a remote guest to verify the delegation using the attestation identity key (AIK) of the TPM. Notice that this step of attestation verification needn't involve the TPM. The MVMM contains a new pair of AIK' with the public part being certified by the AIK of the TPM.

AIK: Attestation Identity Key (AIK) is a TCG term for special purpose public-private key pair inside the TPM for attestation use. In our remodelling, after each measurement of the VMM, a new pair of the session AIK' will be made available to the MVMM which is certified and verifiable by the AIK of the TPM. This AIK' is for the MVMM to run delegated attestation between the MVMM and the guest.

Binding: This is a TCG term for traditional public-key encryption using the public key of a TPM. Decryption using the matching private key inside the TPM is called unbinding. In our intentional design for sensible use of the TPM, this pair of operations will be delegated to the MVMM.

Sealing: This is another TCG term for conditional public-key encryption using a public key of the TPM (usually related to the storage root key SRK). The condition is that encrypted messages are bound to a set of platform metrics PCR values which are specified by the message sender. Decryption using the matching private key inside the TPM requires the TPM to check whether the PCR values inside the TPM and those in the sealing match. Sealing/unsealing operation can only be conducted by the TPM itself and will not be delegated to any party outside the TPM.

3.2 Protocols Description

The protocols description has four parts: (in 3.2.1) the establishment of the software TCB in the boot time (an "infrequent protocol"), (in 3.2.2) the deployment of the guest application which is the frequent case of using delegated functions in the software TPM (a "frequent protocol"), (in 3.2.3) the rolling-out and -in of the guest application which is the infrequent case of using the TPM, and finally (an "infrequent protocol"), and (in 3.2.4) the migration of the guest application (a "frequent protocol"). Of these four cases, only protocols in 3.2.1 and 3.2.3 involve infrequent uses of the TPM (the latter case has only the rolling-in half needs to use the TPM) while the other cases of the cryptographic services should only use the delegated services provided by the software TPM. Throughout the paper in all the figures we shall use dash lines to indicate "infrequent protocol" communications with the TPM, and solid lines, those frequent ones with the software TPM.

In the following protocol descriptions, phase numbers are the line numbers shown in Fig. 3.

3.2.1 The Establishment of the Software TCB
Phase 0: Measurement and delegation

This phase has been described in "integrity measurement", "delegation of the software TPM" and "AIK" paragraphs in 3.1. As we have remarked, this is an "infrequent protocol".

3.2.2 Deployment of the Guest Application
The protection of online guest application involves the first three dash lines in Fig. 3.

Phase 1: Alice attests Bob's platform

In this phase, Alice checks the trustworthiness of Bob's platform by attestation. The attestation is done by MVMM of Bob as follows:

Bob runs a challenge-response protocol with Alice to prove that his AIK' is certified by the TPM, and he also produces to Alice the signed PCR value of the MVMM. In the run of challenge-response protocol, Alice will verify the AIK'

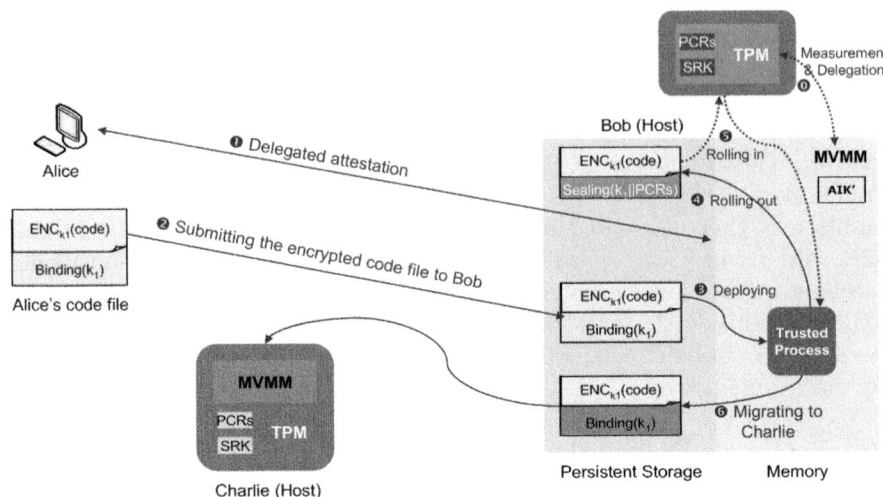

Fig. 3. Key Management Protocols

certificate and check the correctness of the PCR value with respect to the desired VMM code.

If succeeds, Alice should believe that Bob's platform is loaded and running the expected MVMM.

Phase 2: Alice submits encrypted code/data file to Bob

Alice encrypts her code file by using a randomly generated symmetric key k_1, and appends the encrypted file with a meta-data of encrypted k_1 by using the public key of Bob's platform. This encryption is the binding which we described in 3.1.

We know that the encrypted code/data file can only be decrypted by the same MVMM which has been attested and running in the host. We notice that if Bob's platform reboots after receiving encrypted code file, then the new session run of the MVMM will not be able to decrypt the file because each boot will render the new session run of the MVMM to use new key material. This follows the principle of the stateless design of the software TCB.

Phase 3: To load a guest application at the host

When invoking `execve()`, the OS will load the guest program code into the memory. Before transferring the control to the user process, the MVMM will unbind the code.

This protocol is a "frequent protocol".

3.2.3   Rolling Out and in of the Guest Application

As we have discussed, the guest application may need to be rolled out or check-pointed to the persistent storage. We use phase 4 and phase 5 to describe these steps.

Phase 4: To roll out a guest application

If the running guest application needs to be rolled out, the code/data will be saved to the persistent storage. We shall use the sealing function in stead of the binding. To make sense, we formulate the new meta-data as the ciphertext of data "$k_1 \| PCRs$" which is encrypted by the public key public key of the TPM.

Phase 5: To roll in a guest application

When the rolled out program code/data need to be rolled back in, the TPM will have to perform the decryption (unsealing). The TPM firstly decrypts the meta-data by using its storage related private key, and then checks if the decrypted PCRs values match the PCR values inside it. If the checking succeeds, the TPM will output k_1 to the MVMM. Otherwise the TPM will output nothing. In this case, we can say that the TPM acts as a protector of empty-headed program code/data.

We remark that only Phase 4 involves "frequent protocol" while Phase 5 is "infrequent".

3.2.4   Application Migration

The application migration is shown in phase 6. If the program is about to be migrated to Charlie, Bob will be in the position of a guest and do the attestation regarding the host Charlie's platform and then prepare for the encrypted code/data file to be deployed to Charlie. This is a regular operation and it uses the same method as the deployment of Alice's code/data to Bob as described in the protocol in 3.2.2.

4   Conclusion and Follow-Up Work

With the very privileged position of the VMM in the bottom of the software stack, it is very reasonable that the TPM delegates most of its performance critical functions on to the measured VMM to make it the software TCB of a high performance. The TPM only retains few critical functions which are directly related to the measurement of the software TCB. Then thoughtful protocol design mechanisms permit the use of the TCG technologies with most performance critical functions delegated to, and served by, the high performance software TCB to minimize the performance penalty related to the typical low performance of the TPM. The particular showcase of the service provisioning use case for Grid and Cloud Computing in this paper actually manifests our work's independent value beyond our particular embodiment: the TCG technology's performance potential needn't be limited by the low performance of the TPM.

A follow-up work for the two protocols designed in this paper can be a formal proof of correctness with respect to a set of carefully deliberated specifications.

References

1. Foster, I., Kesselman, C.: The Grid: Blueprint for a New Computing Infrastructure (1999)
2. Weiss, A.: Computing in the clouds. NetWorker 11(4), 16–25 (2007)

3. Trusted Computing Group. Trusted platform module: TPM Main Specification (2010),
http://www.trustedcomputinggroup.org/resources/tpm_main_specification
4. Goldberg, R.P.: Survey of virtual machine research. IEEE Computer 7(6), 34–45 (1974)
5. Garfinkel, T., Pfaff, B., Chow, J., Rosenblum, M., Boneh, D.: Terra: A virtual machine-based platform for trusted computing. ACM SIGOPS Operating Systems Review 37(5), 206 (2003)
6. Chen, H., Zhang, F., Chen, C., Yang, Z., Chen, R., Zang, B., Yew, P., Mao, W.: Tamper-resistant execution in an untrusted operating system using a virtual machine monitor. In: Parallel Processing Institute Technical Report, Number: FDUPPITR-2007-0801, Fudan University (2007)
7. Chen, H., Chen, J., Mao, W., Yan, F.: Daonity-grid security from two levels of virtualization. Information Security Technical Report 12(3), 123–138 (2007)
8. Chen, X., Garfinkel, T., Lewis, E.C., Subrahmanyam, P., Waldspurger, C.A., Boneh, D., Dwoskin, J., Ports, D.R.K.: Overshadow: a virtualization-based approach to retrofitting protection in commodity operating systems. In: Proceedings of the 13th International Conference on Architectural Support for Programming Languages and Operating Systems, pp. 2–13. ACM, New York (2008)
9. Sailer, R., Zhang, X., Jaeger, T., van Doorn, L.: Design and implementation of a TCG-based integrity measurement architecture. In: Proceedings of the 13th USENIX Security Symposium (2004)

TPM-Performance Sensible Key Management Protocols for Service Provisioning in Cloud Computing
(Transcript of Discussion)

Wenbo Mao

EMC Research China

Matt Blaze: You're considering just currently available commodity OS, it's not an intrinsic property of commodity OS?

Reply: Current or past. We don't want to touch the OS, OS is a monster. It's a good monster, it provides many good services, but for security we don't trust it.

Matt Blaze: Right, but this isn't an intrinsic property of the fact that it's commodity OS, it's just what the market has produced?

Reply: True, well that's why you can do nothing, the market is a superpower.

Matt Blaze: And apparently malicious.

Bruce Christianson: So the market is the attacker.

Reply: So now let's consider the market. If it is commodity OS, then the TCG chain of trust won't work because going back, you consider virtual machine that comes with this stuff, Linux, whatever you think about it. TCG will measure upwards, even at the applications, that so far nobody believes, so the chain of trust is not working. Of course the next question would be to consider developing a secure OS, somebody did it, several people in Stanford, including Rosenblum, Boneh, and their students. Well it's called closed box OS, and I think it's concluded it's a model, it's not real. It's a model saying, virtual machine monitor, and a closed box OS, that would do good, I believe, if you do have closed box OS. But still I don't think, in terms of developing a commodity OS like a Vista like thing, that they have got far. So if you consider, I suspect even big players won't be able to do so. Of course Vista was protected by TPM, and supposed to be a trustworthy operating system, if that were true, trusted by whom? Of course, could be trusted by the Vista maker, even without using the TPM. So this road won't work.

Pekka Nikander: I'm still trying to understand what's going on here. In a way, is the trusted trap running on a different virtual machine, in some sense, so whenever it does a trap, to make a system call, that would be caught by the virtual machine monitor which will re-route it to a different virtual machine?

Reply: Correct, yes, so it is running on VMs, even inside VMs. The VMM down there, the hypervisor, can insert different system calls. It will open wide all the system calls which are related to the files: opening, reading, writing. Once it sees this it will do the bookkeeping. Other things it will not touch, it will forward to the OS. So once it sees that these IO, input/output related file open read/write, it will keep it, it will do the encryption: saving encryption, reading

B. Christianson et al. (Eds.): Security Protocols 2008, LNCS 6615, pp. 115–117, 2011.
© Springer-Verlag Berlin Heidelberg 2011

encryption, that's all the VMM will do. So this is called isolation inside memory control. Inside memory, don't worry, this guy can control the memory.

Pekka Nikander: Is there a reason why the TCS is part of a virtual machine monitoring stuff, couldn't it be a separate virtual machine which is doing all this?

Reply: No, it is a component inside the VMM we're adding.

Pekka Nikander: What's the reason for that? If I intercept all the system calls coming from the trusted process, and then I forward them to the operating system on a different virtual machine by default, couldn't it be simpler to have multiple virtual machines that can serve the system calls, so that I would have just a policy within the virtual machine monitor saying that these systems calls go directly to the Linux kernel, while these other system calls will go first to this other virtual machine which is running the cryptographic functions.

Reply: That's what they do, but this one, I am criticising, virtual machines need OS, it's on top of OS, but which OS?

Pekka Nikander: But the virtual machine can run without OS, you can just in a way create a very simple ...

Reply: Yes, you want this guy to provide protection, you want this guy to be trustworthy, but the chain of trust is not right.

Pekka Nikander: The reason why I'm asking this is that now you are blocking the virtual machine monitor. So when you're adding functionality to the virtual machine monitor, you are making it harder to verify the virtual machine monitor itself, and you might want to have different policies for different protected processes. But now basically you are just enforcing a single policy for all protected processes because it's built into the virtual machine monitor.

Reply: I'm with you. Single policy, indeed, the only policy about a file opening, file reading, file writing, that's all. Any other complex policy indeed can use your way, but for this, what we really are concerned with is the processes data privacy integrity, that's all we're concerned with.

Pekka Nikander: But I can't see there are any big differences. What people tried to do with MAC back at the end of 80s and so on, was to try to build a very small kernel, a virtual kernel, and that would put all the services into processes. Now in a way the virtual machine monitor is more or less like the micro kernel of the 80s and 90s, and instead of putting new functionality to the virtual machine monitor itself, if there are some trusted service processes, in addition to the trusted client process, which you already have, then in that way you could gain some of the flexibility that people try to do with the micro kernels, but now you should probably do it in a secure way, given that we have some more hardware there, and the virtualisation.

Reply: I agree with you. This talk is about building the full trust chain, so this is a big assumption we dare not touch. Yes, one day somebody will do it that way you say, I think the VM way is doing it with this protection, as a VM it will do, you see this, if you look at the animation, just do a lot of services, much more than what we do, but we don't know how to do this with a commodity OS, we don't know how to do it.

Pekka Nikander: You don't have to have an OS, it could be a very simple thing without any OS at all.

Reply: So indeed we do hypervisor thing, the VMM is like a hypervisor, we work on that level, and we do not touch anything above.

Virgil Gligor: So does VM here support virtual memory? Then it's probably not a hypervisor. Hypervisor typically is extremely small, they go under the virtual memory management mechanism. In a hypervisor you do not want to do resource management if at all possible: management policies, memory, IO, processes, and all that, should be outside, so you can avoid that complexity.

Reply: In our case, whether you call it hypervisor or the virtual machine monitor, it does the memory management. OK, let me concentrate a bit more on this. This is the bottom line here for keeping down complexity. If the trust process wants to be protected, it will not mess up with the hypervisor, oh no, let me change name, VMM. It will try to say, give me good service, if I do not mess it up, then the bookkeeping here is possible, but by the VMM. So it's a layered design, I've seen many things since computer science started.

Stepwise refinement is the principle, this is applied to TCG using a measured VMM as a software refinement for the hardware TPM. And now the TPM becomes a fake TPM: consider a complex TPM has a mistake, has an error, needs to be patched, how can you patch a TPM? Maybe there is a way to patch, but then the trustworthiness of TPM becomes questionable. TPM is hardware plugged into the platform, the patching would be a nightmare. So a fake TPM which only does the measurement would be a good solution. And then VMM as software patching is a much less a problem issue. And we should also consider layering the design of VMM as well: a TPM facing layer, which does the delegation thing. And an OS which does the more semantic management of IO memory management. So far our experiment says the VMM works well (though maybe too many files opening at a time by application may be troublesome). But I think of this as a pre-echo to you guys scepticism: in future indeed we need to work on it.

Handling New Adversaries in Wireless Ad-Hoc Networks

S. Farshad Bahari[1] and Virgil D. Gligor[2]

[1] Electrical and Computer Engineering Department,
University of Maryland,
College Park, Maryland 20742
fbahari@umd.edu

[2] Electrical and Computer Engineering Department and CyLab,
Carnegie Mellon University,
Pittsburgh, Pennsylvania 15123
gligor@cmu.edu

A common threat in many networks is the capture of network devices by an adversary. Stajano's "big stick principle" which states that whoever has physical control of a device is allowed to take it over, suggests that such an adversary is more powerful that the Dolev-Yao and traditional Byzantine adversaries, and hence difficult to counter. Protecting device secrets (*e.g.*, cryptographic keys) via physical security mechanisms, which currently range from those employed by smartcards (very little tamper resistance), to IBM 4758/64 crypto co-processors (highest FIPS 140 evaluation), and to Physically Unclonable Functions (very good but not perfect physical security) will continue to require network security measures. We argue that "good-enough" measures in the face of node capture by adversaries can be obtained by using "emergent properties." Intuitively, these are properties that cannot be provided by individual network nodes — no matter how well-endowed nodes might be — but instead result from interaction and collaboration among multiple nodes. Such properties can be used to detect, often probabilistically the presence of an adversary within a network and to pinpoint with reasonable accuracy the affected network area (*e.g.*, identify a specific captured node, a particular property of captured nodes). However, all such measures require periodic network monitoring in normal mode to detect a somewhat rare event (*i.e.*, node capture, replica insertion) and hence their cost can be high.

Wireless sensor networks, mesh networks, and embedded networks pose unique security challenges due to the fact that their nodes operate in an unattended manner in potentially hostile environments. A particularly difficult problem not addressed to date is the handling of node capture by an adversary. A key goal for solving this problem is that of limiting the damage caused by captured nodes. This is important since node capture cannot be prevented: by definition, there is no practical physical mechanism that could keep an adversary from physically accessing the internal state of a sensor node discovered in an unattended area. Hence, the presence of the adversary within such a network must be detected, and of course, the earlier the better. Adversary detection is predicated on the fact that access to a captured node's internal state, which includes secrets such as cryptographic keys, requires a nodes removal from the network in an

B. Christianson et al. (Eds.): Security Protocols 2008, LNCS 6615, pp. 118–119, 2011.

operational (*e.g.*, physical) sense and a non-zero time delay for internal-state access. This suggests that adversary detection can be achieved, in principle, if the node absence from the network exceeds the node monitoring period during which the node has to respond to neighbours' queries regarding its status.

In this paper, we propose two probabilistic schemes called the "pair-wise pinging protocol" and "consensus-based pinging protocol," whereby the network continuously monitors itself in a distributed and self-organizing manner. We investigate the trade-offs between the network cost-performance and security of these protocols via a Markov chain model, and present analytical solutions that allow us to choose appropriate performance parameters, such a the expected residual time-to-false-alarm, and security, such as the probability of a missed detection. The consensus-based protocol, whose outcome is an "emerging property," outperforms the pair-wise protocol for an interesting range of security parameters, including cost of messages (and implicitly energy consumption). Furthermore, we show that both protocols are scalable with network size and their complexity is linearly proportional to the average node degree, as opposed to the maximum size of the network.

Handling New Adversaries in Wireless Ad-Hoc Networks
(Transcript of Discussion)

Virgil D. Gligor

Carnegie Mellon University

I was extremely happy to see this year's theme. In 2005 I had a talk here about redefining the adversary, and I still believe that that's a good topic to think about. Let me first say a few words about the adversary, and whoever gets whom I am paraphrasing will win a beer. A system without a definition cannot possibly be insecure, it can only be astonishing, and of course astonishment is a much under-rated security vice.

Mark Lomas: Could it be Bob Morris?

Reply: You have a beer, so it's obviously Bob Morris Sr., who came several times to this workshop. What he really said was that a system without a specification can only be surprising.

In 2005 the claim was that limited physical node protection in networks, such as in cellphone networks, mesh networks, embedded networks, really introduced various new and unique vulnerabilities, and at that time I argued that this requires that we use new methods and tools for handling the adversary. Today I'd like to go to a consequence of what Frank Stajano calls the big stick principle, which says essentially that whoever has physical access to a device is allowed to own it. Frank wrote this in his PhD[1], and what I think he meant (he can always tell us what *he* thinks he meant) is that an adversary's physical access to a device can always get to the internal state of the device. And the moral is that a long-term secret held on devices captured by an adversary are not secret for the long-term. And the second moral is that we should never bind secrets to devices, particularly devices which are unattended, or devices that could have malware on them, or are plagued by malicious insiders.

I'm saying that because I listened carefully to Wenbo's talk about TPMs[2]. In my opinion TPMs have a fundamental flaw in them: it's not the fact that they use a secret key, the fundamental flaw is that there is no easy way to change that key, the procedure to change the key in a TPM is extremely cumbersome. If we go back to the beginning of distributed system security (which was in the 70s as far as I can tell), one of the things that we realised in those days was that we actually need to use secret keys and crypto only for distributed components of a system. In other words, you only need cryptography because of that mythical man-in-the-middle, who basically is somewhere in-between your

---

[1] Security for Ubiquitous Computing, University of Cambridge Ph.D. Dissertation, also available from John Wiley and Sons, 2002, 0-470-84493-0.

[2] Mao, these proceedings.

B. Christianson et al. (Eds.): Security Protocols 2008, LNCS 6615, pp. 120–125, 2011.

client and server. You shouldn't use secrets for things that you don't need to use secrets for, such as protecting internal resources of a system, if you can help it. So what I'd like to do today is to point out what you should do when in fact your secrets are being captured by an adversary, and if there is anything that we can really do in practice.

Matt Blaze: At the risk of revealing my hardware ignorance, can you elaborate on this 10% error property. I'm certainly willing to be surprised, but I would imagine a scenario in which on average you see up to 10% of an error, but under extreme environmental conditions, what you get is completely different behaviour from each of the outputs.

Reply: That's absolutely true. As a matter of fact that's exactly why they do this extra check using the stored hash of the correct key, because you may get more than 30 errors under the conditions that you are talking about, and what should you do then. So in order to detect that you generated the wrong key, and to stop using it at that point, you take the output, which may be corrupted, hash it, and compare it against the stored hash of the correct key.

Matt Blaze: OK, so the device just fails.

Reply: The device fails, right. The way the author suggested we retry this a number of times to generate.

Matt Blaze: Right, but if the environmental conditions stay then the device fails?

Reply: Yes.

Frank Stajano: If you are storing in unprotected memory why are you doing it in the first place?

Reply: Originally the device was not used for generating secrets, it was used for generating challenge response pairs. So suppose I am the owner of the device, I get a large number of paired challenge response, which are unique to the device, I store them somewhere, I installed the device remotely, and then if I want to authenticate it I send a challenge, I get a response, if it's the right response I accept that the response comes from my device. So it was basically a physical authentication method, OK. So the authors of the scheme, or at least one of them, decided to publish this paper about how to generate this secret using this key. So I'm referring to the use of this scheme to generate stored secrets on devices, which I actually think is an extremely bad idea as I mentioned already. Essentially you should actually store in the memory of an unprotected system, only quantities which are presumably not useful to an adversary.

Frank Stajano: But I thought you said the key was in the store?

Reply: Ah, no, you store the hash of a key, not the key. So you have two hashes, one is here to mask the timing pattern, and one is the hash of the response. Actually that's not in the drawing, thank you for pointing that out.

Matt Blaze: I just want to make sure I understand, this is intended to be a small tamper resistant chip, but all the memory is outside?

Reply: Right. Essentially the idea is that you take this circuit and if you want enclose the area that you really want to be protected, so that to get to that area you have to physically tamper with the circuit. I thought originally that this was a brilliant idea, and it really is very good for device authentication, but when they went past that and starting using it, at least in published papers, to generate secret keys, I didn't think it was good any more. In particular, if anything goes wrong, if this key gets compromised, and it looks like it might be compromisable, there's absolutely nothing you can do here, you just have to discard the device, you bound the secret to the hardware.

Frank Stajano: Could it switch to using a different key?

Reply: Well but then you launch the same attack, and you get the same property. If you compromise this key, you compromise the secrets on the device, so you have to start everything from scratch, in other words, the device is essentially gone.

Michael Roe: You have to do an authentication, because there can be a lot of those challenges, and if they capture a device they can see what those challenges are.

Reply: That's right, the challenges and responses are held remotely and you can randomly pick a pair, and the adversary wouldn't know what you'd done.

Frank Stajano: With secret generation, do you store the challenges within the black box?

Reply: The challenges cannot be stored in the black box because otherwise you don't have access to it to generate it, so the challenge comes from the outside along with the syndrome.

Frank Stajano: So who supplies the key?

Reply: Whoever wants to generate the key, it's stored in the memory of the node, and that's OK, those are public values, there's nothing wrong with having them public. The point is that, the fact that the challenge and the syndrome are public doesn't really give you much advantage.

Frank Stajano: But the secret responses come up there, outside the black box?

Reply: It goes up to the encryption device that's connected to it.

Frank Stajano: It's outside the tamper resistant boundary. What about an attack at that time?

Reply: Indeed. It is most likely to be outside the tamper resistant boundary unless you can somehow protect it physically. So you can actually tap it here, that's a second problem that you have with it. If you have to verify the response, the key, then somehow you have to use not just the encryption box, but the hash function. The outside hash function is out here, and even if you don't want to tamper with this area, maybe you can pick the first round in the iterated hash function, and then you work your way backwards, and you find what the response is.

Frank Stajano: For this to make sense, you have to extend to the part that uses it.

Reply: Exactly, the black box would have to extend to the part that has the hash function, and the encryption function, completely to be safe. In other words, this has to be protected physically, so that if you physically touch that interconnection, then you don't get the right key.

Tuomas Aura: The syndrome isn't an error correcting code, so why does that have to be sent into the black box? Why can't the correction be done outside? Why not hash a response, and then have the error correction code, which supposedly doesn't give away information?

Reply: Yes, it can be, but then you still have to protect that part of the circuit, with a circuit itself, because if you can tap in there, you've obviously used the output from here if you can tap in there, so then you get the secret out. So it doesn't matter where you do it provided that it's physically protected, and it would have to be physically protected as roughly the same circuit.

Matt Blaze: This seems equivalent, except for perhaps fostering complexity, to simply having a statically stored randomly generated key and a little crypto processor in the tamper resistant boundary. So the central advantage here is that what we have to put inside the tamper resistant boundary is very small. But now we keep extending the tamper resistant boundary to include the output of the secret response. So does this in fact make things simpler?

Reply: I don't know that it makes things simpler, it's just an alternate way of doing it.

Matt Blaze: OK, so I should stop asking you hostile questions about this, because you're about to start agreeing with me.

Reply: I'm in violent agreement, I said at the beginning I thought that this was a brilliant idea, but it turns out not to be. Your questions are making my point.

All right, so now the question is, since we established that we really don't have anything useful to protect this secret, and the secret should not be bound tightly to these boxes, what do you do about an adversary that actually captures these nodes, and captures all your secrets, that's really the subject of the talk.

So, for example, if you take a sensor which is not physically protected, you take it out, you can actually download all its secrets in about a minute and a half. On the other hand, if you have reasonable protection, it doesn't have to be perfect, good enough obfuscation (and we know how to do that from published literature), then we can delay the adversary for say two hours. OK, so if we do that we might have a chance to detect the adversary's capturing action by observing that the node is taken offline. Of course this doesn't work with cellular phones, for example, because cellular phones, you can take out the battery and put it back in for good reasons, so it doesn't mean that your cellular phone was captured. If you really want to have a private conversation of course you must take the battery out of your cellular phone, otherwise your conversation will not be private even if your cellular phone is turned off. So essentially the scheme doesn't work for the kinds of networks where the node can be legitimately offline without being captured, but for all the other cases I think this approach in principle would work.

So the idea is that we try to detect that the node is offline in this capture period. So now the question is, how do you actually do that detection? We take a network that monitors itself. Say a sensor network, for example, it could be a mesh network. Each node is monitored by its neighbours in some way, we can use a very simple pinging protocol where each neighbour pings the target and measures the response that it gets from the target in terms in time. And after you do that for a single node pinging, we want to have a quorum of nodes to figure out if say M out of N neighbours run this protocol, and if M of them signal that this node has been captured or is not responding, then essentially they broadcast this to all the neighbours, and they all revoke the keys. So essentially the node becomes automatically revoked from the network so the adversary has no ability to exploit the keys that it finds.

Matt Blaze: I'm imagining the sensor network used for alarms in a building, to detect burglars. If a burglar arrives he can simply jam with enough RF to cause the nodes in that region to become suspects, and then after they've been taken offline he can burglarise the area.

Reply: Well yes, you could do that, but the point that I am trying to make is that once a neighbour has detected that this node is not responding, for whatever reasons, the action that they take in this protocol is that they revoke the keys. But they could take other actions. There is a very good question what happens when you have multiple adversaries, but the burglar by itself would not be able to do this undetectably in one single area, he would have to be in multiple places of the building roughly at the same time. You want to figure out the absence of the device in that particular interval, so if the device is protected well then the adversary would have to put foil around it, and do his physical attacks.

Tuomas Aura: But if the adversary wants to, the adversary can make the node look unreliable.

Reply: Well that's always possible.

Tuomas Aura: But normally you have to do something physically that would cause permanent failure of the nodes, but here you can cause the permanent failure without touching the nodes physically.

Reply: Yes, but our problem is to detect that the adversary has done that, and revoke the node so the adversary cannot actually reinstall clones, for example, that the adversary controls. That's the problem that we want to solve.

Tuomas Aura: There may be another, less sophisticated adversary that only can break things. I think there is a difference between going to a node in the centre and destroying it, and everyone who comes back can see that it's destroyed, and just physically trying to replace it.

Reply: Right. The point is, if you take a network of unattended nodes, they are always subject to a variety of adversarial attacks. The attacks that I'm worried about here are not attacks where as a result the node is permanently disabled, because that's a highly observable event.

My protocol doesn't have to have observable physical damage at all, it will disabled the node if the is taken offline in any way. The point is, if an adversary really wants to disable a network of 10,000 nodes by launching the attack that you mentioned, the adversary would have to go and attack it physically in a way that doesn't scale. He would have to put his aluminium foil, or Faraday cage, around each node, one at a time. That's perfectly fine with me, but what I don't want to happen, I don't want the adversary to be able to take the node out, get its secrets, install code in it, place it back in the network, and have unobservable unreliability for a long period of time, maybe even for the lifetime of the network. That's really the threat that this protocol deals with, which is a different attack from the one that you postulate.

Richard Clayton: I was going to say that potentially your scheme is fail-safe, a lot of the objectives are, hey look, it's fail-safe, is this inefficient. The observation I was going to make was that in real life where people have used systems like this, like for example when we were parachuting agents into Holland during the war, in practice the Germans could turn them round faster than we realised they could turn them round, and despite all the evidence that they were then corrupt, everybody in London kept on believing that they weren't, on the basis we couldn't possibly have that rate of failure.

Reply: Right. By the way, I thank you for putting me on to the book by Leo Marks[3] many years ago[4], I did read it, and I found it extremely interesting. Yes, that's exactly what happened, so the idea here is that to turn a node will take a certain period of time, and if you can figure out that the node was turned in the time then you can isolate that node, roughly it's the same philosophy.

---

[3] Between Silk and Cyanide.
[4] See LNCS 4631, pp 266–275.

Problems of Provenance for Digital Libraries

Michael Roe

Microsoft Research

Introduction

In 2007/2008, both Google and Microsoft were involved in separate projects to digitally photograph a large number of library books and make them available over the Internet. At about the same time, several hardware manufacturers brought out devices that were specifically intended for reading books. These included the iRex iLiad, Amazon's Kindle, and the Sony eBook reader.

There are also a number of companies and organizations that add value to an eBook by converting it into a different format:

Feedbooks provides eBooks in PDF format, typeset for comfortable reading on the screens of dedicated hardware readers such as the iRex iLiad. Feedbooks stores the book internally in a private database format, and can automatically retypeset a book for the screen size of each manufacturer's device. Authors can upload their own book to Feedbooks, and users can contribute out of copyright works. Many of the books on Feedbooks are based on text provided by Project Gutenberg.

Project Gutenberg provides eBooks in plain text and HTML format. (A few books are available in other formats, such as Latex). Project Gutenberg eBooks have been corrected by proof-readers, and so the text is much more accurate than the raw output you would get from an optical character recognition (OCR) program. Project Gutenberg is one of the oldest sources of eBook on the Internet, having been in existence since 1971. Project Gutenberg's eBooks have been prepared by many different volunteers, but a large proportion of them were provided by Distributed Proofreaders.

Distributed Proofreaders is a web site that allows the work of proof-reading a book to be shared among several volunteers. Each volunteer takes one page at a time from the sever, proof-reads it, and submits the result back. The site takes as input photographic scans of books, and produces as finished output proof-read text in plain text and HTML format. The photographic scans come from a variety of sources, but a large proportion come from Google and Microsoft's scanning projects.

The Internet Archive provides on-line access to books from a variety of sources, in various formats. Many of their books are photographic scans from Google and Microsoft's scanning projects.

From this short description, it can be seen that the contents of a paper book passes through several format conversions, several stages of manual (human-controlled) correction and several organizations before the user gets to read it. A book might be owned by a library such as the New York Public Library;

B. Christianson et al. (Eds.): Security Protocols 2008, LNCS 6615, pp. 126–133, 2011.
© Springer-Verlag Berlin Heidelberg 2011

scanned by Google; archived and distributed by The Internet Archive; OCR'ed and proof-read by Distributed Proofreaders; archived and distributed by Project Gutenberg; then reformatted into PDF by Feedbooks. At each stage, metadata such as the book's title, author and date of publication is also reformatted (or simply discarded).

Advantages of eBooks

Digital copies of books offer several advantages over the original paper edition:

- Search engines (such as Google or Microsoft Live Search) can search the content of these digitized books. For example, it becomes easy to produce a list of nearly all books containing a particular word or phrase. As search engines are Google's main business, the motivation for their involvement should be clear.
- The electronic copies can be downloaded much more quickly than a librarian can fetch a book from the stacks, and are available from distant locations, and at times when the library is shut.
- If readers use the electronic copy, it protects the original book from wear and tear (being lost, stolen, written on, heavily thumbed and so on). The process of scanning involves some risk of damage to the book, but this can be reduced by the use of scanners that are suitable for rare books. (In cases where the book is easily replaceable – for example, new books – destructive scanning can be used: cut off the binding of the book and run the cut sheets through a sheet-fed scanner).
- The electronic copies provide a back-up in case the original books are destroyed by fire or flood. (For example, the Herzogin Anna Amalia library had a fire in September 2004).
- Paper books physically decay, especially if the paper contains sulphuric acid.
- It is very expensive to provide storage space for books in major cities (for example, the British Library is in central London). It might be cheaper to store the books somewhere where rent is lower, and provide readers with remote access.

Advantages of Proof-Read OCR

The Google and Microsoft projects provide access to a digital photograph of the book. Project Gutenberg takes a different approach, and provides access to an accurate, proof-read, transcribed text of the book. The Project Gutenberg approach has several advantages:

- Searching will be more accurate. Google's Book Search is based on an automatic optical character recognition (OCR) scan of the book, which is often inaccurate, especially for unusual languages (e.g. Latin), unusual scripts (e.g. Ancient Greek) or unusual typefaces (e.g. German Blackletter). In consequence, it may miss some books containing the searched-for text.

- Transcribed text can be much easier to read. The low resolution of Google or Microsoft's scans can make them difficult to read. In addition, the fonts in which some old books are typeset can be difficult for many modern readers to understand. This is most obvious in German, where old books are often typeset in Blackletter (Fraktur) fonts, but there have also been changes in English typography: for example, long s is no longer used.
- Transcribed text can be reflowed to a different page size, making it easily readable on eBook readers that are of a different size from the original book.

The disadvantage of Project Gutenberg's approach is that it is much more labour intensive. In effect, it is more costly, although it can be hard to see just how much more costly it is because Project Gutenberg's books are produced by volunteers giving their time for free. Project Gutenberg could be regarded as targeting a different market from the other two: high-quality versions of a relatively small number (20,000 or so!) of popular titles, versus lower-quality versions of a much larger number of titles.

Relative Popularity

The Internet Archive (www.archive.org) provides access to both Google and Microsoft's scans, and to Project Gutenberg texts. By 22 May 2009, the 50 books which had been downloaded the most times from The Internet Archive were: 14 Project Gutenberg texts; 4 in-copyright works made available by permission of the author; 1 collection of sheet music; and 31 photographically-scanned books. Of the photographically scanned books: 23 were in Arabic; 1 in Persian; 6 were heavily-illustrated; and 1 was an edition of Saint Augustine's *De Civitate Dei* published by Nicholas Jensen in 1475.

Many readers will obtain Project Gutenberg texts directly from Project Gutenberg, or Google scans directly from Google, rather than going through The Internet Archive, so these numbers may not be representative of their relative popularity. However, it gives an indication that Project Gutenberg texts are the preferred format when available, while photographic scans (usually from Google or Microsoft) are being used for picture books, musical scores, books in scripts other than the Latin alphabet, and books where the typography is important (such as the Jensen edition of De Civitate Dei).

Photographic scans should also be useful for works that were not sufficiently popular to have been transcribed by Project Gutenberg.

Problems

However, there are several potential pitfalls with electronic books, including the problem of provenance. If you download from the Internet something claiming to be the Encyclopedia Britannica, how do you know that it really is the Encyclopedia Britannica? It is worth mentioning at this point that trademarks can outlive copyright, so that the publishers of a book can still have the rights to the trademark, even after the copyright has expired. It might be regarded as a quirk of the law that the two kinds of "intellectual property right" can persist for different periods of time, but it also strikes to the heart of the problem: even after copyright has expired, the reader of the book has an interest in knowing that what they are looking at is, in some sense, authentic.

Integrity

The process of scanning books and putting them online is vulnerable to errors at several stages.

Popular books have often been published in several editions, and some editions can be of higher quality than others. The book might not have been proofread very well in the first place, and some U.S. editions of British books have had the dialect translated into American English. The editions that are scanned are often selected on practical grounds (e.g. they are out of copyright, the library has a surviving copy), and may not be the "best" ones.

The copy that is scanned may have previously suffered damage, such as comments written in it by library users, or torn pages.

"Missing pages" are a serious issue with many of the book scanning projects, especially Google Book Search. Typically, books are scanned by a human being turning the pages in front of a digital camera. Common errors include turning over two pages at once, or accidentally putting your hand in front of the camera when it takes a picture.

In the next stage, a grey-scale image is quantized to a 1 bit per pixel black and white image. The quality of the algorithm used to do this can affect both the legibility of the image, and the accuracy of the output of the OCR stage.

"Despeckling" algorithms remove from the image marks that are due to dust or defects in the paper. This improves data compression ratios and OCR accuracy, but if it is done too aggressively punctuation marks such as commas and full stops are removed as well.

The optical character recognition (OCR) algorithms can have quite a high error rate. Depending on the level of subsequent proofreading, these errors may or may not have been corrected. Modern OCR software uses a dictionary to know which words are probable, and so can commit errors in which an obscure word is replaced by one which is visually similar and statistically more likely. Such errors aren't caught by spelling checkers, and are hard for human proofreaders to spot, too.

There are some checks that can be done without knowing the provenance of the scans. For example, books usually have page numbers, and if your scans go from page 58 straight to page 61, you might suspect that pages 59 and 60 are missing. Books printed in the eighteenth century often have catchwords, in which the first word of each page is repeated at the bottom of the previous page. These were originally intended to detect mistakes made by the printer in assembling the book, but also serve to detect missing scanned images. However, these checks aren't reliable. Books often contain pages that lie outside the numbering sequence (e.g. full page illustrations), or that form part of the page numbering sequence but don't bear a number (e.g. when the chapter title is on a page by itself). I have seen errors in Google's scans where one unnumbered chapter heading has been replaced with a different unnumbered chapter heading from elsewhere in the book.

In general, you cannot tell that you have a complete copy of the book just by looking at a set of scanned images. You have to know something about their provenance: were they scanned using a highly reliable process? what quality-control procedures were followed? etc.

This problem is worse if you only have access to the OCR output and not the scans themselves. Without knowing something about the quality of the OCR used, you don't know how accurate the text is.

If you don't even know which edition of the book was scanned, you don't know likely it is to contain printer's errors. Previously, Project Gutenberg did not identify which edition of the book was used for their etexts, although this information is provided for books they have added more recently.

Rights

The copyright on the original book has often expired. But there can be additional copyright claims. The scanner of a page might claim a photographic copyright on the digital scan. The person doing the OCR might claim a copyright on the OCR'd text. The person adding HTML markup might claim a copyright on the markup. There appears to be some disagreement as to whether U.S. law grants a new copyright to someone who scans a page of an out-of-copyright book. I'm not a copyright lawyer, so I won't comment on whether or not this is the case. But if such copyrights exist, they are potentially a problem for digital libraries.

Someone who wants to make use of a scanned book (e.g. using the scans to print a new paper book) needs to know what legal rights they have to make use of the scans, and to do this they need to know when and by whom the scans were made, and which contracts (if any) restrict their use.

Reader Privacy

On 26 November 2007, an FBI special agent served a National Security Letter on The Internet Archive, demanding the name and address of one of The Internet Archive's users. The letter also prohibited The Internet Archive from publicly discussing its existence; the only reason we know that this happened is because The Internet Archive were able to successfully challenge the request in court (*Internet Archive et al v Mukasey et al*, No. 07-6346-CW (N.D. Cal)).

This clearly raises some serious privacy issues. An online library can record more information about its readers' activities that the paper equivalent. (A paper library may record who has borrowed a particular book, or requested it to be fetched from the closed shelves, but will typically not have a record of which readers have looked at books on the open shelves. With some technologies, an electronic library may even be able to record which *pages* of the book have been viewed).

Censorship

When each library held a separate physical copy of a book, this provided some measure of protection against censorship: if the book isn't available at one library, it might still be available elsewhere, perhaps in another country. The number of large-scale book scanning projects is quite small, so a capricious decision to suppress a book by one of these projects could easily result in it becoming completely unavailable.

As an example of the potential risks, in April 2009 over 57,000 books on amazon.com had their "sales rank" removed, effectively hiding them from user's searches. A spokesperson from Amazon blamed an "embarrassing and ham-fisted cataloguing error". Most of the affected books were on lesbian or gay subjects.

Interactions

These problems can interact with each other:

1. Missing pages can be fixed by rescanning the missing page.

When this is done, the resulting set of images contains some that were taken by a different person, at a different time, and possibly using a different copy of the book. (Or worse yet, a different *edition* of the book. Project Gutenberg e-texts come with a standard disclaimer that this may have been done, although in practise it is strenuously avoided).

This is a potential problem for integrity. To start with, there is the possibility that the different copies of what was allegedly the same book might actually be different, for example if the printer made changes between printings without updating the title page. But also, there may have been different levels of quality control applied on the two occasions. It is not safe to assume that the same level of quality control applies to all images in the scan set.

This also causes problems for copyright. Suppose that most of the book was scanned by Google, except for page 37, was was scanned by the Bibliothèque Nationale. When redistributing the scan set, you may need to know that different pages came from different places. It is a further problem for integrity if you subsequently find that you actually have all of the book, but that copyright law prevents you distributing page 37 of it.

2. Missing pages as a copy-protection measure.

There is a rumour that some image sources deliberately omit pages as a copy protection measure: this prevents a publisher from reprinting the book. If this is not adequately recorded in metadata, it potentially a serious problem for integrity. Imagine that the library forgets that some pages have been deliberately omitted, and then disposes of the only remaining paper copy of the book, believing that it has a good electronic copy. Similarly, a publisher who is not aware of this may reprint the book with pages missing.

3. Page images versus OCR.

It is easier to check a digital photograph of a page than it is to check the OCR of a page. This is because OCR is much more likely to introduce errors. However, the copyright on the two may be different. You may find yourself in the unfortunate position of being able to redistribute the OCR, but not the page scans, because the holder of the photographic copyright on the scans does not permit it. This is a problem for integrity, because the user of the ebook is then unable to verify that it was scanned correctly.

Versioning

Electronic books often exist in several versions, even though each version is based on the same physical book. For example, if it is discovered that the photographic scans of a book have a page missing, and the missing page rescanned, then this creates a new version of the online copy. OCR'd text can also exist in multiple versions, if residual OCR errors are detected and corrected, or if the text is line-wrapped using a different algorithm.

This means that a electronic book is not uniquely identified by the paper book it is based on. To give an accurate reference to the electronic book you actually used, you need to specify which version.

Maxims from Distributed Proofreaders

Volunteers at Distributed Proofreaders often quote the following two maxims:

"The book, the whole book, and nothing but the book."

This is the principle that the online OCR'd eText should contain all of the text from the original paper book (including, for example, advertisements), and should not have any new introductions, commentary or illustrations added to it.

"Match the scan."

This is the principle that, by default, the words in the OCR'd eText should be the same as those in the photographic scans of the paper book. Distributed Proofreaders sometimes departs from this principle in minor ways. For example, obvious typos are sometimes corrected, usually with a "transcriber's note" at the end of the eText to explain what corrections has been made; the spacing around punctuation is often changed to conform to the modern convention for English-language books, even for books in languages such as French that have traditionally followed different spacing rules. However, it mostly followed.

One of the advantages of this principle is that it is possible to check that it has been done correctly. The author may have meant to say something else, or even written something else in the manuscript they supplied to their publisher, but this can be hard or impossible to check (e.g. if the author is dead, you can't ask them what they really meant). The printed book is the artefact that we have.

Conclusions

1. The requirements for electronic *archival preservation* of books are very different from the requirements for *search engines*. Libraries who have scan sets that are only suitable for search need to be aware that they cannot get rid of the paper copies.

2. A quality control check for missing pages in scan sets is essential for archival preservation. (Search engines can work quite effectively with books that have missing pages.)
3. For reasons of both integrity and copyright, digital scans of books need to be accompanied by metadata describing their provenance: exactly which copy was scanned, who scanned it, when it was scanned, and what quality control checks were performed.
4. This metadata needs to apply to individual pages, not just the book as a whole. Clearly, the encoding of the metadata can be optimized for the case when most of the pages have the same history.
5. The online scans or OCR of a book can go through several different versions, even though the paper book they are based on is unchanged. References to online texts ought to include which version was used. (e.g. if an eBook is created by converting a Project Gutenberg eText to a different format, should record which version of the PG eText was used).
6. OCR'd text should have metadata that enables the corresponding page images to be retrieved. Importantly, this means that those page images need to remain accessible.
7. For archival preservation, steps need to be taken to ensure that the digital copy will continue to be available. It is not sufficient, for example, for the book to be put on some random guy's personal web site. Care also needs to be taken that the data format will remain readable: will web browsers still render the HTML the same way in 50 years time? (For that matter, will web browsers still render HTML the same way next month, never mind 50 years?)
8. Online libraries can record more information about their user's activities than paper libraries (who looked at which book, and when), giving rise to new privacy concerns. (e.g. Can law enforcement ask the library who has read which books?)
9. In the move to digital media, a small number of organizations (e.g. Google, Amazon) have become dominant. This raises concerns about the possibility of censorship: what happens if Google or Amazon don't want to stock the book?

Problems of Provenance for Digital Libraries
(Transcript of Discussion)

Michael Roe

Microsoft Research

I'm Michael Roe from Microsoft Research. I'm going to talk about the problems of putting library books online. This isn't a crypto protocols talk in the usual sense. There's going to be absolutely no cryptography in this talk, so I hope you'll forgive me for that.

Over the last year or two both Google and Microsoft have been making deals with various libraries where they'll digitally scan all their books and put them online. You can see Google's scans at books.google.com and www.archive.org has Microsoft's scans. This talk is about some of the issues that become apparent when you do something like that.

The first point is that it's absolutely great, having library books online. You have full text search of all the books, so you can do a search and find a book that answers your question, even if the relevance wasn't apparent from the book's title. Of course this is why Google is interested — they're in the search engine business, and they want to search these books.

It also gives you really quick access to the book. Even when the book's in your own local library it takes maybe half an hour for a book to be fetched from the stacks. When it's online you can pull it up on your screen within seconds, even if the library is far away. I might be able to easily walk across town to the Cambridge University Library, but if I wanted a book from Harvard, that would be a big deal, whereas online within just a few seconds it's on my screen.

It also preserves books. Scanning the book in the first place puts a certain amount of wear and tear on the book, but once you've done that you can keep the book out of the hands of library users who might not treat it as carefully as they should. Books just wear out anyway from use, but also there are people who do barbaric things like write in library books, and we want to discourage this very strongly. And finally, paper decays, particularly if the paper contains sulphuric acid, which will start eating the paper away. For preservation purposes, you would like to take copies of these books in a long-lasting form before the paper falls to dust.

And finally, finding space to store books is extremely expensive, particularly in a location like central London where your readers are. What many libraries would like to do is move these bulky, expensive to store, paper books to somewhere where it's a lot cheaper to store them. This somewhere cheaper might actually be a landfill site when they finally get rid of the paper copies. Wherein lies much of the risk.

So I've said why it's good, but there are problems. When you see a representation of the book on the screen, how do you know that what you're seeing

B. Christianson et al. (Eds.): Security Protocols 2008, LNCS 6615, pp. 134–143, 2011.

is a faithful representation of the original book? What is this that I'm looking at? And secondly, if you want to do something with the electronic data — you might want to republish it and print it as a new paper book, or reformat it as an eBook for some new device and sell it — how do you know who's got the rights to it?

Some examples of what can go wrong, from one of the oldest projects doing digital books, Project Gutenberg. (It dates back to 1971). The route they've taken is to put online the text of the book rather than digital photographs of its pages. They started with it being typed in, and more recently use OCR software. Since the start of the project, they've upgraded from the ASCII character set to using Unicode so they can represent non Latin characters, and they now have HTML encoding so they can do exciting things like bold and italic text, but basically it's just text. They've done around 20,000 titles, which in some ways is a large number, but is nowhere near as many as the number of books in the holdings of a big library like the British Library.

So what can go wrong? It's contributed to by volunteers, which isn't bad in itself, but there's a potential variation in quality. Many of their books have been done by one person, and you as a consumer, looking at the online text, don't know whether the person who did it was good at proofreading or not. It may be that the text you're looking at is well proofread and a faithful representation, or maybe it was done by somebody who was a less competent proofreader, and it's full of errors — you don't know. The other thing you don't know is which edition they scanned. Recent practice is to be upfront and tell you this, but if you look at many of the earlier Project Gutenberg eTexts, no indication is given at all of which edition of the book was used to form the eText. You've just got the text minus the original title page and verso from the original book that said where it was and where it came from. And finally there is this absolutely terrifying disclaimer you get from Project Gutenberg, that the eText you look at might have been created from several different editions; so what you're reading might be some Frankenstein's monster that has been patched together from several different editions of the book, with no indication to you of which bits of the thing you're reading came from which edition. Again, this is currently discouraged, but nevertheless they reserve the right to do this to you without warning.

Google has taken a somewhat different approach. They actually photograph the book, and so what you'll get from them is a PDF with a photograph of the book. Essentially these are done by hand. There are rumours out there that they have some clever robot that will automatically and rapidly turn the pages and photograph them, but you can see from the errors that this is not what happens, because a frequent failure is that you'll get a photograph of the hand of the guy who turns the pages, rather than the page itself. This is rather convincing evidence that the process is not totally automated, and there is a person in there. The other thing that can go wrong with this is that the guy doing the scanning turns two pages over at once. This is very easily done, but then you've missed two pages from the book. They also get the pages out of order, I'm not quite sure why this happens, but empirically it happens quite a lot. What you'll see in the scan set is all the pages, but not in the right order.

Mark Lomas: It's because they actually spotted the earlier error . . .

Reply: . . . and tried to fix it. Quite possibly.

Sometimes images are cropped too closely. For example, books can have tight bindings so the text that is close to the spine is missed. Or the image can be cropped too high so you've missed the bottom couple of lines on the page, or cropped too low and you missed the top two lines.

Other things that can go wrong. Books can have pages in colour and you might scan those as black and white. There's a rather famous set of maritime records in the Public Records Office that were originally on nice colour coded index cards which were microfilmed in black and white, and the colour coded index cards destroyed, so now you only have the black and white.

Robert Watson: This is also true of the 18th century newspapers in the British Library, which were in colour but were scanned in black and white.

Reply: Yes. Colour illustrations.

Bruce Christianson: The trouble with the shipping registers is that the colours were used to encode, for example, what capacity people were sailing in, whether it was an outward voyage, and that information is just gone.

Reply: Yes, that's exactly what I was thinking of.

Scanning one bit deep is just fine for text, but often not adequate for illustrations. You often find that illustrations have only been scanned one bit deep, which is possibly not enough; for example, the Bibliothèque nationale has done this.

You can also have a scan of the page with not enough resolution for anybody to be able to read the text. If you're scanning one bit deep you have to choose a threshold between what's a black pixel and what's a white pixel. And you can see sometimes, comparing the same book as done by the Bibliothèque nationale and by Google, that although Google have fewer pixels, they can make the text more readable because they've managed to have better algorithms for choosing where the threshold between black and white is. And there's de-speckling. Old paper often has texture to it, or little ink spots, or flecks, or whatever, and there are algorithms that look for little dots and remove them from the image. Unfortunately commas and fullstops also look like little dots, and if you do this too aggressively you loose all the punctuation marks.

And finally, even if all the current process was right, there are the problems in the original book. A good example to look at is George Bernard Shaw's *The Miraculous Revenge* — a rather nice short story — as reprinted by the Haldeman-Julius Company. This was a very famous publisher of radical pamphlets; it's worth keeping the Haldeman-Julius edition because it's interesting in its own right, but nevertheless you can see that their attempt to render George Bernard Shaw into American English from British English has introduced a substantial number of errors into the text. And as someone wanting to read this, you actually do care that the text on your screen is Haldeman-Julius' translation of George Bernard Shaw into American English rather than what George Bernard

Shaw originally wrote. The way the statuette of the Virgin Mary becomes a statute of the Virgin Mary is particularly amusing.[1]

Copyright. Now I'm a not a copyright lawyer, and this isn't a talk on the legal situation, just how the legal environment may potentially affect what you have to do technically. There's the copyright on the book itself. Maybe the photograph of the page has a copyright independent to the copyright on the work itself, possibly dependent on your legal regime. There's some considerable argument about this, so I don't want to give a definitive opinion, but you might have to take into account technically that photographs of books have their own copyright separate from the books themselves. Then there's OCR that you produce from a photograph, and then there's the HTML markup of it. There may be considerable creative input in deciding how to format a book for HTML display, which has it's own copyright, which is completely separate from the original book.

Why does this cause you integrity problems? Firstly you'll see that most of the books that have been scanned are from the US and Canada rather than from Europe, although there have been some books done from the Bodleian Library. Part of the reason for this is different copyright laws in the UK and US. In the US, although the rules are many and complex, one of the main things you want to know is whether the book was published before 1923. This is really easy because books usually have a publication date on the title page, so you can just look at it, see whether it's before 1923, and you know. In Europe, copyright expires 70 years after the death of the author, which means you have to know when the author died, which is not conveniently printed in the front of the book because the author typically wasn't dead at the time it was printed. This leaves you with a big problem if you have a million books and you want to cheaply and efficiently work out whether it's over 70 years after the death of the author for each of them. Google has taken a very conservative approach on what it shows to readers who are accessing their site from an IP address that their database thinks is in Europe. They will only show you books that are sufficiently old that it is highly improbable that the author lived until 70 years ago, even if the author lived a very long time after publishing the book. They're taking a very conservative approach, which means a lot of books that are actually out of copyright in Europe you can't see.

Robert Watson: There's also a difference with scanning for preservation. In the US, some libraries say that fair use allows them to take preservation efforts, including scanning, and so you will scan books up until the current day, but will not present them to anybody — even people in the library — on the grounds that this might not be fair use. Fair use doesn't of course exist in the UK.

Reply: As previously discussed, US reprints can be terrible, so one consequence of this is that the only electronic copy of the book may be a scan of an American translation of a British book, rather than the original British publication. This isn't really an integrity problem, but with some European languages, you just don't get to see the book at all, because Americans weren't all that

---

[1] For the Project Gutenberg eText, *statute* was then erroneously amended to *statue*.

interested in reading books in Swedish (say) and so there are no copies in US libraries to scan.

The second interaction, at least if you're in a legal regime where the images have a separate copyright, is that you can be in a bad position where you can distribute the OCR text, but not the images, because somebody else has rights to those images and isn't going to let you distribute them. This means that your poor unfortunate reader has no way to check that your OCR was right.

Matthew Johnson: Why would the OCR text be a derivative work if the image isn't covered by the same copyright?

Stephen Murdoch: The person who scanned it can give permission to people to distribute the OCR'd version. So being a derivative work means that you have to say what the owner wants to happen. It doesn't mean you can't do anything with it.

Reply: Yes, so the person who scanned it might have given you a licence to distribute the OCR but not the image.

Robert Watson: But copyright of photos is a little weird though, because it has to do with things like composition and stuff like that. OCR's aren't really photos, so they're not derivative photographs. Which doesn't mean that your point doesn't hold. The thing that was copyrighted in the photograph was not the contents of the text.

Reply: There's an interesting discussion the lawyers can have, over whether you can end you up in a situation where you have permission to copy the words but not the photograph of the words. It also possibly contributes to some nervousness about admitting which edition was OCR'd. If you have a book for which it is obvious that some editions are out of copyright, but possibly not the one that was OCR'd, then the source of the eBook may be slightly coy about telling you exactly which edition it's from.

And lastly you will discover that some libraries have missed out pages as a copy protection mechanism. It's a very effective way of stopping other publishers reprinting the book, to randomly miss out pages in the middle. The problem with this is that if you don't announce you're doing this then people will reprint the book anyway, or possibly you'll forget yourself and despatch the original to the landfill site mentioned at the beginning of this talk, and only then remember that you randomly left out one percent of the pages.

Trademark also causes problems with metadata. For example, the Project Gutenberg Encyclopaedia. The book that was OCR'd to create it came from a very well-known publisher of encyclopaedias. The text is out of copyright in the US, so Project Gutenberg can republish it, but the name of the well-known publisher of encyclopaedias is still a valid trademark, so they are reluctant to mention it in case they are accused of passing off. So the metadata is very coy about where exactly this encyclopaedia came from.

Mark Lomas: That's only if you're claiming it is it. You'll say, this is a suitable alternative to the Encyclopaedia Britannica.

Reply: For example, yes. But you have to be careful. You have to be very careful about what your metadata says and implies. You certainly don't want to use somebody else's trademark in a way that implies that what you're selling is their product, you have to be careful about the claims you make.

Matt Blaze: I'm not any more of a lawyer than anyone else in the room, but my understanding is, at least under US law, anybody is entitled to utter or use a trademark even in a commercial context. The issue of infringement only comes up if the trademark is being used in a way that is misleading, that is, it's perfectly good to say, this is an alternative to the Encyclopaedia Britannica, which is a registered trademark of Britannica. What I can't do is claim that I am selling an Encyclopaedia Britannica, that would certainly be a trademark infringement.

Reply: As Mark has mentioned, attempts to fix up the problems can make things worse. There's a nice button on Google's website where you can report problems with the book to them, and indeed they do fix it. This means that the scan sets aren't constant over time, that you can look at an eBook from Google at one point in time, and somebody else might look at it later, and they might see a different set of pages, or possibly the same pages in a different order. So in terms of giving a reference to things you've got a problem. Different pages might be scanned with different technology, so by the time that they've got round to rescanning the missing page 73 they're using a different scanner with a different number of pixels, and a different software process. If you care about photographic copyrights, they're then different for this rescanned page from the rest of the book, and in particular you could imagine a situation where many years hence the photographic copyright has expired on all of the scan set except page 73 which was done five years later. Another thing you might do is you could get from another library what you really hope is the same edition of the same book, scan the missing page, and patch it in, and then you really hope the publisher didn't make subtle changes to the book, like renumbering the pages or something, without changing the information on the title page. Or if you're really, really desperate, you can get a different edition of the same book and just copy it in and hopefully the editors didn't change very much in-between. Hence the Project Gutenberg disclaimer that they might possibly have done that.

OK, conclusions. The first is that scanning books for preservation is a completely different problem from scanning for a search engine. If all you want to do is drive a search engine then you want as many pages as possible, so you've got as much chance as possible for a successful match, and you don't mind very much if the pages are in the wrong order, or there are gaps. But if you want to preserve the book so somebody can read it, you do care about the pages being all there and in the right order. So if you're a library wanting to collaborate with a search company, you had better understand the difference, and be clear about what it is that you're hoping to do with the digital copies.

The second thing is that you absolutely need some kind of quality control process. I'm not blaming the guys doing the scanning who put their hand over the page — I've scanned books myself and it's an easy mistake to make. The thing is, the whole organisation doing the scanning need to have some quality control process that is checking for this, and rescanning the missing pages.

And lastly you need decent metadata, that goes right down to the level of the individual page. That says, which book was scanned, when was it scanned, who did it, and so on, so that later on you can answer questions such as, who has the right to reproduce it, and can I trust it given what I know about the history of how it got to me.

Mark Lomas: To give you another example, which supports what you've just been saying, Bell Labs published a book which was supposed to be the collected papers of Claude Shannon. It's a very good book, but one of Shannon's papers was classified, so he published two different versions of it. There was the one that was classified, and one with the same title that was public. It was subsequently declassified and put back into Bell Labs library, so if you ask the librarian for that paper you get a different paper to the one that appears in their collected set of papers. And it's well worth asking for the declassified one because it has all of the declassification notices in it as well, so you know the entire distribution list.

Robert Watson: I know a group of social historians who are looking at the effects of digitisation on the study of history, and they have a rather interesting set of problems. When they went to speak to Google about the Google Books project there was a clash of cultures. For example, historians are very interested in which specific instance of a book it is, not just which specific version of a book it is: Which publisher, which publication date. They were interested in marginalia, and Google did not have a way to track the fact that there were different instances of the same book. They simply went to the libraries, and said to the libraries, please give us one of each book, and the libraries took them all off the shelves, and shipped them off in big crates, and then they scanned them all. The marginalia may not be something that the OCR will recognize, it may only exist in the particular original object, and if you don't keep track of what is actually scanned, you'll never know if you've missed the marginalia.

Richard Clayton: We all know margins are never big enough to contain the proofs which we'd like to see. But there's a related thing which is that in the 60s when there was a great push for microfilming and so forth, not only did they throw away the cover, in some cases when they scanned all of the newspapers from the 19th century they scanned all of the news stories, and they didn't scan the ads on the basis that nobody is interested in that. Whereas now when we look back at it we are not interested in the Times' account of the Battle of Waterloo, and which day it appeared, because there are lots and lots of books that can tell us that, and what that particular account says. We're interested in what the price of hats was in the adverts next to it. Which unfortunately weren't scanned, and the newspapers went off to the landfill, and the social historians are far more interested in adverts than the news stories. When we're scanning books there's a built-in assumption that we know what is important.

Reply: There's a running argument at Project Gutenberg as to whether to include the adverts at the back of the book in the OCR'd text or not. Usually — for the reasons you mention — the adverts are included these days.

Bruce Christianson: A cynic might say that this obsession with version control is quite a modern thing. For example, when the King James Bible came out, several different plates were used to print the different signatures and they were all different, and because of the binding process, which involved selecting signatures essentially randomly from the different piles, it's entirely possible that no two copies of the first edition of the King James Bible were identical. The question of what Shakespeare actually wrote, or more to the point, what he actually published, is something that still goes on and on, and keeps lots of people in a job. Is it possible that the new technology is just going to put us back the way we were in the 16th century when the press was first invented?

Reply: One of the things that was different with printed books from manuscripts is the correction process is invisible. With manuscripts you can see the crossings out, so the reader of the manuscript is well aware that there is a process of duplication, errors and correction going on. Whereas with a printing press you can fix up the plate until it looks OK to you, and then bang, you put out lots of identical copies all of which look untouched by human hand.

Mark Lomas: Even that's not strictly true, because they've done some historic analysis on how some of Shakespeare's plays were printed, and they said there were two different forms of the letter A, and the typesetter would use one of them until he ran out, and then he'd use the other, and if he had to edit up a page, make corrections, the prevalence of a particular style of the letter A showed that that page had been edited even though it's entirely printed.

Reply: That reminds me... There is a problem with interpreting semantic markup from a printed book. If you're writing HTML yourself, you know the meaning of what you want to write, and you can put in the appropriate semantic markup. But if you're trying to infer semantic markup from whether the original printed book used a roman face or an italic face, you rapidly hit the problem that in metal type days they had boxes of the letters, and when they ran out of italic type, they would start using the roman type instead. An algorithm that is trying to infer some kind of semantics from this can go badly wrong.

Bruce Christianson: I quite like significance of the black and white passages in the film *If...* If you haven't seen the film there's passages in black and white. The reason was they had gone over budget and they couldn't afford coloured film.

George Danezis: I think to some extent the historians are very focused on the preservation of books, and I can understand that because this is mostly due to them preserving their jobs. What we maybe should be caring slightly more about is the new culture that has been developing that is not actually printing books any more. The visual culture: CD-ROM's, DVD's, web content, but also more functional stuff such as software. These will probably be of some cultural value in the future, and it is not just cultural value, it could be of some practical value, because in order to decode the Excel spreadsheet to find out what was the cost of wheat on the day the Iraq war started, people will need some software to be running in 200 years time, and it's not quite clear how we preserve this kind of stuff.

Robert Watson: There is legislation that can prevent us from doing that kind of thing. Copyright law actually gets in the way of preserving all sorts of media today.

George Danezis: In much more insidious ways, yes.

Reply: Yes, the newer types of media have much bigger problems than just printed books.

Robert Watson: It's too bad. The National Archives in the UK used to preserve all paper products that came out of government, and then within four years they had to decide what to reduce it to, and what to actually keep. Today they consider quickly if this is an archive form. They can no longer wait four years; they have to start pushing the reduction activity onto the officers that produce the paperwork, and the officers that produce the paperwork have a very specific view about what should be saved, and what doesn't, in a way that the National Archives didn't, because the National Archives was interested in the long view. In particular, they didn't mind keeping around some of the more controversial things, but officers that do controversial things may feel much more strongly about discarding them.

Sandy Clark: I find myself brooding on something that's tangential, you allude to it on one of your earlier slides, and that's about the loss of information. What's to prevent someone from maliciously removing something that they don't want people to remember. Suppose, for example, there is a bad press report, and you have the power to remove that, so that people who are looking at it later get an entirely different picture of the way that the world was. You could really control what people knew, you could control actually what people thought about history if you could remove this information, and there doesn't seem to be any digital controls on this.

Robert Watson: There weren't any controls before either.

Sandy Clark: But now it's so much easier to just cut out a piece of digital data than it was to alter every copy of a book.

Robert Watson: It was pretty easy before, too. The archives most of the archivists are interested in exist in only a few places in the world, and they're heavily edited. One of the resources that's not heavily edited is the censors office from the Imperial British Empire, where you can see copies of all documents that were printed in India. Now it's a fascinating source for historians who want to go and see what was being censored at the time, which is exactly the opposite of what you would expect. Not a very flattering view of the Empire.

Reply: We see the after effects of 19th century censorship in that there are now books that are missing from the online collections because we're going back to old books in the library, and back in the 19th century the libraries didn't want to stock those books. So even though now, you might not find those books particularly objectionable, we're missing electronic versions because many of the libraries didn't keep them.

Matt Blaze: So to put this very specifically into a security protocols context, one of the things that Google may inadvertently do is break a very good security protocol. I am reminded of Stuart Haber's company Surety[2], which provided a digital time stamping service by doing a kind of hash tree thing, and they would sell you digital time stamps, and the root of their hash tree would be published weekly in an ad in the New York Times. And the rationale was that this would be a very difficult artefact to change in the future because it would exist in paper form, or in an archival form, in many, many libraries throughout the world. You know, this is an old stodgy medium, and it would be hard to erase it. Well, you know, thanks to Google books all this data is suddenly becoming centralised again. Sandy's talking about rewriting history in a broad political context, but you know, we could also do some interesting damage by changing very, very small facts.

Bruce Christianson: Like who owns your house.

Reply: Yes, now the only record of that hash value is just one bit-map on a Google server.

Matt Blaze: Suddenly you've taken something that's decentralised, and as a side effect, recentralised it.

Bruce Christianson: Yes, on the grounds of access to that central repository is easy from anywhere.

---

[2] www.surety.com

Towards Understanding Pure Publish/Subscribe Cryptographic Protocols

Pekka Nikander[1,2] and Giannis F. Marias[3]

[1] Ericsson Research Nomadic Lab, Hirsalantie 11, 02420 JORVAS, Finland
pekka.nikander@nomadiclab.com
[2] Helsinki Institute for Information Technology,
Metsänneidonkuja 4, 02015 TKK, Finland
[3] Department of Informatics, Athens University of Economics and Business, 10434
Athens, Greece
marias@aueb.gr

Abstract. In this paper, we pursue towards understanding how to design and analyse cryptographic protocols in a (large) network setting where all communication is solely based on the publish/subscribe paradigm. That is, we expect a stack and network architecture where all message passing is based on publish/subscribe rather than send/receive, all the way down to the link layer. Under those assumptions, it looks like that the majority of present work on cryptographic protocol analysis applies to an extent, with only minor modifications mostly on the notation side, while the protocol design aspects will need larger modifications. Furthermore, the paradigm shift opens a number of interesting problems, requiring modifications to many of the traditional intuitions guiding protocol design and analysis.

1 Introduction

With the advent of serious proposals for moving from the present inter-networking of computers to inter-networking of information as the primary communication paradigm [11,20], the publish/subscribe model [7] has been raised again as a potential primary communication method, replacing the present send/receive model.

In this paper, we take the first baby steps towards understanding how to design and analyse cryptographic protocols when the underlying network is solely based on the publish/subscribe paradigm. Interestingly, while many of the intuitions and traditional ways of designing protocols appear to need changes, the actual formalisms underlying the various analysis methods appear to be better equipped to encounter the new reality.

2 Towards a Pure Publish/Subscribe Paradigm

Consider a network built solely up using the publish/subscribe paradigm instead of the commonly used send/receive paradigm. In such a network, there are no

B. Christianson et al. (Eds.): Security Protocols 2008, LNCS 6615, pp. 144–155, 2011.

receiver or sender names. Only messages have names. We expect the message name space to be very large and essentially random, making it virtually impossible to guess a message's name. Whenever receivers or senders need to be named, *e.g.*, in order to be able to argue about authentication of principals, it must be understood that such names are given outside of the networked system. This also means that there is no primitive that would allow a message to be sent to a given principal. The only thing a sender can do is to publish the message and hope that the intended principal has subscribed or will subscribe to it.

As an example, in a pure publish/subscribe system the routing and forwarding tables could be based on the reachability of the subscribers. That is, at each intermediate node there would be a forwarding table that indicates the physical port or radio characteristics of the next hop(s) for each message. A publication tag in the message would be used to find the right entry in the table. In other words, when a message arrives over a physical link to a forwarding network node, the forwarding node looks up the next physical link(s) where the message needs to be delivered and re-sends the message over that (those) link(s).

Each individual message can be considered as a primitive publication, having an unique name (an identifier). For a message to be meaningful, some node must publish it, and there must be one or more nodes that have indicated or will indicate their interest to receive it. Hence, when Alice and Bob agree that Alice will send a message to Bob, they must have an a priori agreement of the name of the message that Alice will send.

In reality, such a simple model does not scale; it is unrealistic to assume that all subscribers will explicitly subscribe for each message they want to receive. On the other hand, as a conceptual model, it has some very appealing properties. First, it requires that each principal explicitly expresses what messages they are interested about, with the assumption that the network will deliver them only messages matching with their interests. Second, it requires one to think more thoroughly some of the underlying assumptions, as one can no longer assume messages to be delivered by simply sending them. Together, these seem to map nicely to a number of existing protocol analyses tools.

2.1   Recursive Composition

A key structure to enable pure publish/subscribe are recursively composed publications; without them the system would not scale. Basically, a composed publication is one that consists of a collection of more primitive publications, such as messages. For example, at the implementation level the forwarding table entries might contain such publication identifiers instead of identifiers of single messages, thereby allowing the routing and forwarding system to scale to more realistic dimensions [19].

Let us now consider some recursive publication structures, starting from file transfer. (We are ignoring a number of very interesting but thorny issues related to reliability for the moment, assuming that message delivery is error free.) Typically, today's networking technology places an upper limit to the size of messages, requiring one to use multiple messages to send a file. Using the publish/subscribe paradigm, we can accomplish that by first publishing a separate "meta" message containing the names of those messages that form the segments of the file. Hence, if a subscriber wants to receive a file, it can first subscribe to the meta message, learn the identifiers of the file segments, subscribe to each of the segments, and reconstruct the file from the segments.

In a similar manner, we can imagine a media stream (*e.g.* a voice call) to consist of a number of tiny messages (segments), each of which the receiver conceptually subscribes to individually. However, opposed to the previous case, the number and content of the messages is not known a priori. Hence, it would make more sense to create the segment identifiers algorithmically instead of listing them in the meta message. Instead, the publisher of the media stream could publish a meta message containing an algorithm that allows the receivers to compute the subscription identifiers for the media segments that will appear in the stream at well defined points in the future.

As a third example, let us consider scalability at the network level a little bit deeper. Given that in our model each message is (conceptually) a separate publication, a global publish/subscribe network would have a huge number of publications. Hence, it would be unrealistic to assume that each intermediate node separately has a distinct forwarding table at the message granularity. To solve this problem, consider wrapping the message level publications into separate coarser granularity publications that each corresponds to a subscriber group. These group-granularity publications can further be clustered into even coarser-level publications, creating a partially redundant multicast forwarding table[1]. Using this structure, each forwarding node has a fairly simple forwarding table that contains only the identifiers and next-hop information for a relatively small number of these coarser-grain publications.

From a security protocols point of view, it is important to understand that such composed publications consist of multiple messages, separated by time. Hence, from a protocol analysis point of view it is an open question when exactly they should be considered as simple composed (concatenated) messages, when as separate steps in the protocol specification. Apparently, both cases will appear, *e.g.*, depending on how the message names are used or how they are bound together.

2.2   Unifying Forwarding and Storage

Returning to the publish/subscribe paradigm, we can further enrich our total system by adding a (persistent) caching function to the publish/subscribe network and providing an API that unifies storage and forwarding.

Let us return to our previous file transfer example. With caching, the network can now cache the file in addition to forwarding it to the present subscribers. Such caching allows the network to forward the file to any future subscribers more efficiently[2] by simply sending the packets from the closest cache instead of

---

[1] In practise, such recursive wrappings could be implemented with MPLS-like labels.

[2] For brevity, we ignore some the very interesting problems related to cache consistency.

re-requesting them from the original publisher. If the cache is persistent (enough), even the original publisher can take advantage of this, as it can now discard the original file and request it on demand by subscribing to it.

2.3 Multicast and Concast

While traditional two-party protocols can be easily implemented even in a publish/subscribe network, publish/subscribe as a paradigm makes multicast and concast (reverse multicast) natural modes of operation. In the multicast case, there is one principal who publishes new messages belonging to a known publication, which in turn may be subscribed by several receivers. Conversely, in the concast case, there is just one subscriber but there may be multiple principals that add messages to the publication. In that case, the network may be expected to merge multiple messages before they reach the subscriber, or at minimum make sure that the flood of messages does not overload the network, as the traffic may require more resources closer to the subscriber [5].

From the cryptographic protocols point of view, in both cases we enter the domain of group communication. Furthermore, in the latter case, where the network acts actively on the messages, it may be necessary to include parts of the network to the analysis, moving even further from the traditional Dolev-Yao intruder model.

2.4 Main Differences from the Present Model

The main differences of our publish/subscribe model from the present send/receive model can be summarised as follows:

- The messages are not directed to any explicitly named receiver; the expected receiver or receivers must be understood from the context.
- The primary mode of communication is one-way rather than two-way. Two-way communication requires at least two explicit channels.
- The senders and receivers have no network-provided names.
- All data is conceptually identifiable; each message has an (unique) identifier.
- The basic message-passing primitive is based on multicast rather than unicast.
- Network nodes are able to and are expected to cache messages.

3 An Initial Formal Model

Based on the ideas above, let us outline an initial formal model to present publish/subscribe communication. Herein we focus on the exchange of single messages, leaving issues related to message names and composition for later.

Adopting notation from [4], we will use upper-case letters $A, B, C, ...$ to denote principals, N and I to denote numbers, and M to denote an arbitrary message. All of these symbols may be annotated with subscripts or superscripts.

Messages are built inductively from atomic messages (identifiers and number symbols) by pairing, encryption, inversion, and hashing. For M, M_1, and M_2

messages, we write the pairing (concatenation) of M_1 and M_2 as $M_1; M_2$, the asymmetric encryption of M_1 by M_2 as $\{|M_1|\}_{M_2}^a$, the symmetric encryption of M_1 by M_2 as $\{|M_1|\}_{M_2}^s$, the asymmetric inversion of M by M^{-1}, and the application of a hash function H to M as $H(M)$. As conventional notation for keys, we will write K_A to denote a public key of the principal A, with the corresponding private key K_A^{-1}, and we will write K_{AB} to denote a symmetric key that is shared by the principals A and B.

Given the above, a protocol specification consists of a finite sequence of message-publication steps, each of the form $(p_q) \rightarrow: (N_1, ..., N_i).M$, where (p_q) is a name of the protocol step, M is the published message, and $N_1, ..., N_i$ are distinct number symbols (nonces). Note that we have dropped the traditional principal symbols indicating the alledged sender and intended recipient, as they would be completely misleading. For example, a publish subscribe protocol should work even when the messages are published by some intermediate third party (*e.g.* a message cache) and received by multiple subscribers.

A step of this format indicates that the original publishing principal generates fresh random numbers (nonces) $N_1, ..., N_i$ and then publishes the message M. This notation does not indicate who the original publishing principal is or who the intended recipient(s) are. This is to reflect the different nature of publish/subscribe as opposed to send/receive.

Moving forward from a specification to the actions of the principals, we can define three basic actions, roughly corresponding to those in [4]:

- $p(I, M)$ – publication of the message M with the distinct message name I,
- $r(I, M)$ – receiving the message M with the name I, and
- $f(N)$ – generating the fresh number N (note that the number can be a name).

These actions reflect the fact that the underlying network is both publish/subscribe in nature and may also be hostile. A publication action does not name the intended recipients; in some cases the set of recipients may not even be known by the publisher. The receiving actions do not name the message's publisher either, it may not be known or the message may originate from some other than the expected principal[3]. For example, one can assume that the network is controlled by a Dolev-Yao intruder [6] who can compose, send, and intercept messages at will, but cannot break cryptography.

Using these notations, we can now express the principals' action sequences using a direct interpretation by simply composing the permissible runs (or traces) for the principals.

Example. Consider the Otway-Rees Authentication/Key-Exchange Protocol (OR) [17], adopting from Example 9 in [4], where A is authenticating herself to B using a trusted server S:

---

[3] Naturally, the contents of specific messages may reveal the participants' identities, as is typically the case in many traditional authentication protocols.

$(or_1) \rightarrow: (N_1).\ I_R; A; B; \{|N_1; I_R; A; B|\}^s_{K_{AS}}$

$(or_2) \rightarrow: (N_2).\ I_R; A; B; \{|N_1, I_R; A; B|\}^s_{K_{AS}}; \{|N_2; I_R; A; B|\}^s_{K_{BS}}$

$(or_3) \rightarrow: (K).\ I_R; \{|N_1; K|\}^s_{K_{AS}}; \{|N_2; K|\}^s_{K_{BS}}$

$(or_4) \rightarrow: \qquad I_R; \{|N_1; K|\}^s_{K_{AS}}$

where I_R is the Otway-Rees run identifier.

With this, realising that B passes some messages verbatim, we can describe the permissible actions by B as follows:

$$r(I_{AB}, I_R; A; B; \gamma_1).$$

$$f(N_2).$$

$$p(I_{BS}, I_R; A; B; \gamma_1; \{|N_2; I_R; A; B|\}^s_{K_{BS}}.$$

$$r(I_{SB}, I_R; \gamma_2; \{|N_2; K|\}^s_{K_{BS}}.$$

$$p(I_{BA}, I_R; \gamma_2)$$

where I_{AB}, I_{BS}, I_{SB}, and I_{BA} are message names[4]. $\gamma_1 = \{|N_1; I; A; B|\}^s_{K_{AS}}$ and $\gamma_2 = \{|N1; K|\}^s_{K_{AS}}$ represent sub-messages that B cannot interpret due to not possessing the key K_{AS}.

Of course, this is essentially the same as in the formalisms based on send/receive, as neither the protocol nor the semantics have changed. The only obvious change is that this version explicitly needs the four "channels", or pre-agreed message names I_{AB}, I_{BS}, I_{SB} and I_{BA}, instead of relying the network to "magically" deliver the messages to the intended receiver. Some of the intuitions may have changed, too, due to the recipients being replaced with (unique) message names. Furthermore, as we will note further down, the way protocols are designed may need more fundamental changes.

In the light of the early formalism and the example above, the basic elements of traditional cryptographic protocol analysis appear to be essentially the same in publish/subscribe and the more conventional send/receive worlds. The only difference is that the sender need not know the network-level topological identity of the intended recipient. However, as most "standard" cryptographic protocols do expect that the sender simply must know some (cryptographic) identifier for the recipient (*cf. e.g.* [21]), such an "insight" does not lead us far.

Hence, we have to look at other intended purposes (beyond simple authentication) that a cryptographic protocol may have. For example, instead of knowing the identity of the communication peer, it may be enough to know that there is only one peer (*e.g.* a group of fully synchronised nodes) that remains the same throughout some session. More generally, it may be necessary to look at the intention more from the application point of view, and try to understand the

---

[4] Note that the generation and distribution of these message names remains an open problem, and probably requires protocol changes, perhaps even fundamental ones. For example, one could imagine that while I_{AB} and I_{BS} may need to be (algorithmically) pre-agreed names, at least I_{BA} and I_{SB} could be carried within the protocol.

economic mechanism, contract, or other purpose which the protocol has been build for. Some of the properties from more traditional protocols may still apply though, such making sure that the holder of a particular key is currently reachable (freshness), *etc.* (*cf.* also *e.g.* [21]).

Another aspect that we haven't yet considered adequately are message names. As we explained above, in a pure publish/subscribe network all messages are supposed to have a distinct name. If these names are cryptographically meaningful, they per se create a set of implicit protocols, needing explicit design and analysis. For example, in a publish/subscribe network it may be meaningful to establish a cryptographically strong relationship between a certain (application-level) principal and a set of message names[5].

4   Towards a Problem Statement

Given the publish/subscribe communication model and its constraints, we tentatively can make the following observations.

- While the traditional Alice & Bob like protocols with the Dolev-Yao intruder model still pertain, they form only a small subset of the interesting problems. Furthermore, the existing models may need to be extended and enriched by the facts that all communication in the publish/subscribe network is naturally multicast and that two-way communication requires explicit establishment of a return channel (message name).
- Moving focus from authenticating principals to various security properties related to the data itself may require completely new methods.
- The group communication aspects of publish/subscribe seem to change the nature of many problems, and lead focus from typical Alice & Bob two-party protocols to protocols traditionally used for group communication.
- Another set of open problems can be found from within the infrastructure. Apparently, a number of new publish/subscribe based protocols are needed. A large open problem in designing such protocols is that of resource control, including issues related to fairness, compensation, and authorisation.

Given this all, it becomes necessary to reconsider what we mean with authentication goals and assumptions. As the network provides no names for the active entities (nodes), the next generation applications are likely to be more interested in the ability to receive correct and properly protected information rather than communicating with predetermined nodes.

The threats and security goals can be divided, in a perhaps more standard fashion, as follows:

- Secrecy of security-related entity identities and identity protection.
- Secrecy of keys and other related information, typically needed for confidentiality and data integrity of the transmitted information.

---

[5] Kudos to Dieter Gollmann for this observation. Additionally, he writes: "It will probably be an interesting question to identify useful identifiers [in this context]".

- Denial of service, including unsolicited bulk traffic (spam).
- Threats to fairness, including mechanisms such as compensation and authorisation.
- Authenticity and accountability of the information, including its integrity and trustworthiness, reputation of the origin, and evidence of past behaviour, if available.
- Privacy and integrity of subscriptions to information.
- Privacy and integrity of the forwarding state (as a result of subscriptions).

At the mechanism level, there must be in place mechanisms to enable communication through potentially malicious networks and nodes, as well as to establish mutual trust between different administrative domains. This may require new kinds of cryptographic protocols that draw insight from micro-economics, *e.g.* algorithmic mechanism design [16], and have explicit structures for handling compensation, authorisation, and reputation instead of relying solely on more traditional identity authentication and key distribution.

4.1   Design and Modelling of Cryptographic Protocols

The majority of work in the area of cryptographic protocol design and modelling has been based on the two-party communication model, with a Dolev-Yao [6] intruder. As discussed above, such a model appears insufficient for pure publish/subscribe networks, where the network provides no identity (other than the implicit identity provided by the location-related forwarding information) for the active parties. Furthermore, the set of interesting security problems goes beyond the standard end-to-end examples, such as authentication, key distribution, and secure file transfer; in addition to those, we need to consider group communication, denial of service, security goals related directly to data or database transactions, and the overall security of the network infrastructure itself.

In this section, we briefly look at existing work, trying to figure out possible ways to enhance them to cover some of the new challenges.

4.2   Adversary Model

The standard attacker model in cryptographic protocol design and analysis is that of Dolev and Yao [6], often enriched with the correspondence assertions by Woo and Lam [23]. The Dolev-Yao model assumes two honest parties that are able to exchange messages through a powerful adversary that is able to intercept, eavesdrop, and inject arbitrary messages. Given that in our model primary communication is expected to be one way data transfer rather than two way transactions, requires two distinct channels for two way communication, and that in a more realistic model the attackers are typically able to compromise only part of the infrastructure (a byzantine model) instead of having complete control over it, a richer attacker model is needed.

Given the primarily multicast nature of the publish/subscribe paradigm, some insights may be attainable from the work on group protocols [13]. It may even turn out that discrete attacker models are not sufficient, but that instead one has to turn attention to probabilistic or micro-economic models, such as Meadows' model for analysing resource-exhausting denial of service [14] or Buttyán and Hubaux micro-economics flavoured models [3].

4.3   Modelling Logic and Beliefs

To our knowledge, the vast majority if not all the work on logic-based modelling and verification of cryptographic protocols is inspired by the Alice & Bob two-party setting (see *e.g.* [4,21]), sometimes enriched with a Server. Considering the publish/subscribe paradigm, this does not appear very useful. In the case of a single publication (channel), the publisher basically knows nothing, or, rather, does not gain any new knowledge when publishing. The subscribers, on the other hand, may learn new knowledge from the message contents. However, some properties, like freshness, appear impossible to implement without either two-way communication or additional, external data (such as roughly-synchronised clocks).

Digging slightly deeper, it becomes evident that also in the publish/subscribe world there will necessarily be two-party or multi-party protocols. Using our basic model, the initial messages will contain information that allows the receivers to subscribe to some messages expected to be published in the future, or publish messages in a way where they can expect there to be a subscriber. Hence, already here we have some basic beliefs:

> Alice believes that there is a party ("Bob") that is subscribed to a message named M and will do some well-specified action X once it receives a valid M.

As this belief expresses expectations about the allowed future states of the system, an open question is whether adding temporal modalities some of the existing modal-logic based approaches would be sufficient.

4.4   Spi Calculus

Process algebras, such as Spi calculus [1], and especially Pattern-matching Spi-calculus [9], seem to be readily capable of modelling our basic model, including multicast communication and explicitly named messages. However, in order to derive useful and interesting results, one may want to consider various richer description for the net. That is, instead of assuming a Dolev-Yao type all-capable intruder, one may want to model an intruder that is capable to subscribe to (eavesdrop) any messages and message sequences (publications) that it knows about, but has limited capabilities of eavesdropping messages whose names they do not know or publishing messages on message sequences that they do not know about.

4.5   Strand Spaces

Like Spi calculus, strand spaces [22] appear capable for basic modelling. For example, multicast is naturally modelled, requiring no extensions. However, as in the case of Spi calculus, an open question is how to model the network and the penetrator in order to derive interesting results. One approach might be to continue using the basic penetrator model, but add new strands that model the publish/subscribe nature of the network in between.

4.6 Information-Theoretic Models

At the time of this writing, it is an completely open problem how the more information theoretic models, such as the one underlying Huima's tools [10] or developments thereof (*e.g.* [15]), could be applied to publish/subscribe.

5 Discussion

The publish/subscribe paradigm being completely different from the prevailing send/receive paradigm, with the starting point of naming information instead of principals of actors, we expect that much of our intuition on how to efficiently build security protocols will fail. As a reference point, consider the intuitions behind circuit-oriented and packet-oriented communication and the affect of those intuitions to the definition of authentication, as discussed by Dieter Gollmann [8]. Basically, there are subtleties in how, exactly, to define "authentication" depending on the intuitive model of the network between Alice and Bob, *i.e.*, whether the network is expected to be a circuit with Mallory sitting there in between or the network delivers packets that may (sometimes) be intercepted by Mallory.

That exemplifies the problem we have with our intuitions; we expect the difficulties to be much larger when moving from send/receive to publish/subscribe. That is, the problem appears to go deeper when the entities (principals) are no longer the primary objects of communication. Most intuitions based on thinking about the principals in terms of humans fail. In addition to the necessity of focusing more on other security goals but authentication, even the very concept of principal identity may need to be reconsidered, perhaps leading to a new definitions for authentication (*cf.* [2]).

A large open security problem in the proposed architecture appears to be the composition of more complex publications from simple ones. This composition process needs to be both secure and efficient, and may require multiple different methods depending on the nature of the more complex publication. For example, for link-local administrative streams or sensor-type even streams a protocol resembling TESLA [18] might be a suitable one. For wider-range communication and higher data rates public key cryptography combined with more traditional session keys may be more efficient. Consequently, the structure of the message and other data identifiers clearly plays a crucial security role. An ability to use self-certifying identifiers, such as ones based on hashing, hash chains, or hashes of public keys, may enable secure bootstrapping of the system without too many assumptions about external infrastructure. One potential approach here might be to tag the higher level "meta" messages explicitly with a public key [12], *i.e.*, to include the public key explicitly in the message name.

Finally, the separation between the applications and networks needs to be clarified, along with the technology challenges that are new, such as privacy of subscriptions. The resulting network properties can then lead to a deeper technology review.

Acknowledgements

We want to thank Trevor Burbridge, Dieter Gollmann, Jarno Rajahalme, and Mikko Särelä for their constructive comments to various versions of this paper. This work has been partially funded through the EU FP7 PSIRP project.

References

1. Abadi, M., Gordon, A.D.: A Calculus for Cryptographic Protocols — The Spi Calculus. Research report, SRC 149 (1998)
2. Bird, R.S., Gopal, I., Herzberg, A., Janson, P., Kutten, S., Molva, R., Yung, M.: Systematic Design of Two-Party Authentication Protocols. In: Feigenbaum, J. (ed.) CRYPTO 1991. LNCS, vol. 576, pp. 44–61. Springer, Heidelberg (1992)
3. Buttyán, L., Hubaux, J.P.: A Formal Analysis of Syverson's Rational Exchange Protocol. In: IEEE Computer Security Foundations Workshop (2002)
4. Caleiro, C., Vigano, L., Basin, D.: On the Semantics of Alice & Bob Specifications of Security Protocols. Theoretical Computer Science 367(1-2), 88–122 (2006)
5. Calvert, K.L., Griffioen, J., Sehgal, A., Wen, S.: Concast: Design and Implementation of an Active Network Service. Selected Areas in Communications 19(3), 426–437 (2001)
6. Dolev, D., Yao, A.C.: On the security of public-key protocols. IEEE Transactions on Information Theory 2(29), 198–208 (1983)
7. Eugster, G.T., Felber, P.A., Guerraoui, R., Kermarrec, A.-M.: The Many Faces of Publish/Subscribe. ACM Computing Surveys 35(2), 114–131 (2003)
8. Gollmann, D.: On the Verification of Cryptographic Protocols — A Tale of Two Committees. Electronic Notes in Theoretical Computer Science 32(1), 1–17 (2005) (revised version)
9. Haack, C., Jeffrey, A.: Pattern-matching Spi-calculus. In: FAST 2004 (173), pp. 193–205 (2004)
10. Huima A.: Efficient Infinite-State Analysis of Security Protocols. In: Workshop on Formal Methods and Security Protocols (1999)
11. Jacobson, V.: If a Clean Slate is the solution what was the problem? Stanford Clean Slate Seminar (2006)
12. Järvinen, K., Forsten, J., Skyttä, J.: FPGA Design of Self-certified Signature Verification on Koblitz Curves. In: Cryptographic Hardware and Embedded Systems, Vienna, Austria, pp. 256–271 (2007)
13. Katz, J., Yung, M.: Scalable protocols for authenticated group key exchange. Journal of Cryptology 20(1), 85–113 (2007)
14. Meadows, C.: A formal framework and evaluation method for network denial of service. In: 12th IEEE Computer Security Foundations Workshop, pp. 47–74. IEEE Computer Society Press, Los Alamitos (2001)
15. Millen, J., Shmatikov, V.: Constraint solving for bounded-process cryptographic protocol analysis. In: 8th ACM Conference on Computer and Communication Security, pp. 166–175 (2001)

16. Nisan, N., Roughgarden, T., Tardos, E., Vazirani, V.V. (eds.): Algorithmic Game Theory. Cambridge University Press, Cambridge (2007)
17. Otway, D., Rees, O.: Efficient and timely mutual authentication. ACM Operating Systems Review 21(1), 8–10 (1987)
18. Perrig, A., Song, D., Canetti, R., Tygar, J.D., Briscoe, B.: Efficient Stream Loss-Tolerant Authentication (TESLA). RFC 4082, IETF (2005)
19. Särelä, M., Rinta-aho, T., Tarkoma, S.: RTFM: Publish/Subscribe Internetworking Architecture. In: ICT Mobile Summit, Stockholm, June 10-12 (2008)
20. Scott, J., Crowcroft, J., Hui, P., Diot, C.: Haggle: a Networking Architecture Designed Around Mobile Users (2006)
21. Syverson, P., Cervesato, I.: The Logic of Authentication Protocols. In: Focardi, R., Gorrieri, R. (eds.) FOSAD 2000. LNCS, vol. 2171, pp. 63–136. Springer, Heidelberg (2001)
22. Fábrega, F.J.T., Herzog, J.C., Guttman, J.D.: Strand Spaces: Proving Security Protocols Correct. Journal of Computer Security 7, 191–230 (1999)
23. Woo, T.Y.C., Lam, S.S.: A Semantic Model for Authentication Protocols. IEEE Security and Privacy (1993)

Towards Understanding Pure Publish/Subscribe Cryptographic Protocols
(Transcript of Discussion)

Pekka Nikander

Ericsson Research NomadicLab

George Danezis: Can you relate this to the work done on peer-to-peer systems like distributed hash tables, what are the similarities in the underlying mechanisms without going into the detail?

Reply: Well to relate it to reality in networking research, you can think about the forwarding and caching systems, like MPLS or GMPLS system with added caching, so that in each of these switches you have this kind of opportunistic cache which may cache whatever it decides to cache. The protocol is something that we haven't really studied yet, and it appears that it may not be that important what we cache, maybe random caching is good enough. So we keep these distributed cache tables, but they don't seem to be that useful, and maybe replicated servers are better.

Frank Stajano: So what are the fundamental economics of this system, what is published and who pays for storage?

Reply: Right, all the messages, well actually everything is publication, so even the subscriptions are publications. Each publication is associated with a piece of metadata, which I ignore in this presentation mostly, but that piece of metadata has a field called compensation, and in a local network it's typically just an odd authentication field, saying, I am part of this community so please serve me, but in a larger setting this compensation field is assumed to create a market where you actually pay for the resources that you're using. So if I want to cache something in the network, I have to compensate the network for the caching service.

Frank Stajano: So Bob publishes and at the same time sends money along, in a sense?

Reply: In a certain sense, yes, but we don't expect it to be really money, we are speaking about multi-dimensional compensation, basically meaning that we expect there to be different kinds of compensation methods at different parts of the network.

Bruce Christianson: How does Alice know the value of ID?

Reply: It depends. For example, if we bootstrap it using linear time for our global ID for a directory, so that if I want to be part of the network I need to subscribe to a global directory, then it will send me periodic data about the rest of the directories, and so on, and from there you can bootstrap the rest.

Tuomas Aura: So then you use the same system for paying for content as for paying for the delivery?

B. Christianson et al. (Eds.): Security Protocols 2008, LNCS 6615, pp. 156–158, 2011.
© Springer-Verlag Berlin Heidelberg 2011

Reply: Yes, probably, but there are some other results from multicast, and this is a multicast like system, which mean that you can't really tell whether the publisher or the subscriber should pay for the resources, because it depends on the business situation. In a way that tentatively indicates that it depends on the contents who needs to pay for the resources in the network. But how to do that exactly, and whether we need to have a system where, for example, the publisher always pays for the resources but then the subscriber somehow compensates the publisher, or vice versa, that is an open question.

Caspar Bowden: Do you have some way of controlling who can publish to that channel?

Reply: I will come to that.

James Malcolm: I'm a bit confused, because you seemed to imply that data was long-lived, and then you seemed to be implying frames of an interactive voice conversation would be also data in this system. How do you distinguish data that you want the system to lose from data that persists?

Reply: Well that is a good question and my answer right now is that if we look at the frames in the internet, it looks like that the internet never loses anything. So maybe the right assumption is that if you publish something, like your phone call, it's not probable that this will ever disappear. Of course it depends on the caching, if you are not paying for caching your data then the network may not cache it, but on the other hand, we can't really disallow that.

Michael Roe: The whole point of forward secrecy is that it definitely does get there, even if somebody caches it, the plain text is there.

Reply: Yes, right. OK, so this is roughly where we are security wise.

One issue here, which I haven't seen modelled, is that some of the principals may be anonymous or pseudonymous. Currently when we do security protocols modelling we mostly assume that we know *a priori* who is the other party that we want to talk to. But now there may be cases that we don't know who the other party is, we just expect that there will be somebody, and we want to talk to that somebody for whatever business reasons there may be. For example, we may want to make sure that that somebody remains the same principal during the session, and so on. We may want to argue about that in terms of beliefs (like misusing BAN logic), we may want to express something like: Alice believes that there is a Bob who has at some point in the past subscribed to this particular identifier, and who wants to do something if Alice publishes on this identifier.

Then there is the question of how to model the network. Remember the network is doing more, so we can't anymore just model the network as a message-passing mechanism, and we may not be able to model the attacker as a Dolev-Yao attacker anymore because of this. It seems fairly simple to use Spi-calculus or strand spaces to model this kind of a network, it might be good some Ph.D. student. We go to the information theoretic models then, I have to say I have no clue how to model this using Dolev-Yao.

So, to summarise. We are really trying to think differently, we are trying to make the network a rough extension of the blackboard instead of a message passing mechanism. This means that, to the network, the principals have no names, only their data has tags. There seems to be a number of interesting problems in this space, some of them are outlined in the paper already (so I encourage you to read the paper), for example this is a rough formal model for Otway-Rees protocol, which doesn't really make sense in this setting because we are having multicast now. As you can see there is no Alice and Bob and Server here, as there used to be, and we need to add some identifiers to the messages so that you can actually know, or open, the channels that are used later on for delivering the messages.

Michael Roe: You still have to use AS for the subscript.

Reply: Well I tried to be as close to Otway-Rees as possible, and as close to the traditional models as possible when writing this version, but I know that this is flawed. So one of the challenges, or open questions, is how to do this the right way. It looks as though we don't need to change the protocols analysers that much. Actually Dieter had a very good anecdote about that.

Dieter Gollman: It's a reminiscence of a previous Protocols Workshop in Cambridge when Robert Morris Sr. was asked about a model for communication security. He said, you take a piece of paper, roll it on the floor, the cleaners put it in the bin, and later somebody takes it out of the bin and reads it. And that was my point to Pekka; basically we have to use this approach in modelling security quite a lot already.

Michael Roe: If we don't have physical names then maybe we shouldn't have all the fuss about authentication.

Reply: Right, although we still want to authenticate the data, we still want to know that the data has certain properties, but what those properties are, I'm not quite sure yet. Especially if I'm doing transactions, what do they mean? It seems that I am moving toward an agreement with someone, about something, for example reserving an airline ticket doesn't make much sense unless there is an airline.

Virgil Gligor: Maybe you should think of the data authentication in terms of the way we do it in say multicast emails. Essentially there you use a per-message key, and compute, for example, a MAC, and that per-message key is distributed to the subscribers using their subscription protocols, and using a public key or something you have already sent to the subscribers. So essentially, at the time of the subscription, they'll be able to reclaim this key and then check the MACs on the data published. In other words, the authentication is now an attribute, the key is an attribute of the message itself, it's a MAC of the ticket.

Reply: I agree, but I also think that there will be actors or principals there at some point of the time. My feeling is that when the network abstracts away the actors or the principals as we do here, then in order to think in terms of principals we may need to consider the reason for the protocol (which I'm calling business reason here, but of course there might be another reason for the protocol). Somehow we need to combine the previous view of doing Alice and Bob type security protocols, with this new data-centric view.

Password Authenticated Key Exchange by Juggling

Feng Hao[1,*] and Peter Y.A. Ryan[2]

[1] Center for Computational Science, University College London
[2] School of Computing Science, University of Newcastle upon Tyne

Abstract. Password-Authenticated Key Exchange (PAKE) studies how to establish secure communication between two remote parties solely based on their shared password, without requiring a Public Key Infrastructure (PKI). Despite extensive research in the past decade, this problem remains unsolved. Patent has been one of the biggest brakes in deploying PAKE solutions in practice. Besides, even for the patented schemes like EKE and SPEKE, their security is only heuristic; researchers have reported some subtle but worrying security issues.

In this paper, we propose to tackle this problem using an approach different from all past solutions. Our protocol, Password Authenticated Key Exchange by Juggling (J-PAKE), achieves mutual authentication in two steps: first, two parties send ephemeral public keys to each other; second, they encrypt the shared password by juggling the public keys in a verifiable way. The first use of such a juggling technique was seen in solving the Dining Cryptographers problem in 2006. Here, we apply it to solve the PAKE problem, and show that the protocol is zero-knowledge as it reveals nothing except one-bit information: whether the supplied passwords at two sides are the same. With clear advantages in security, our scheme has comparable efficiency to the EKE and SPEKE protocols.

Keywords: Password-Authenticated Key Exchange, EKE, SPEKE, key agreement.

1 Introduction

The username/password paradigm is the most commonly used authentication mechanism in security applications [3]. Alternative authentication factors, including tokens and biometrics, require purchasing additional hardware, which is often considered too expensive for an application.

However, passwords are low-entropy secrets, and subject to dictionary attacks [3]. Hence, they must be protected during transmission. The widely deployed method is to send passwords through SSL/TLS [36]. But, this requires a Public Key Infrastructure (PKI) in place; maintaining a PKI is expensive. In addition, using SSL/TLS is subject to man-in-the-middle attacks [3]. If a user authenticates

---

* This work was done while the authors worked on an EPSRC-funded project (EP/D051754/1).

B. Christianson et al. (Eds.): Security Protocols 2008, LNCS 6615, pp. 159–171, 2011.

himself to a phishing website by disclosing his password, the password will be stolen even though the session is fully encrypted.

Since passwords are inherently weak, one logic solution seems to replace them with strong secrets, say, cryptographically secure private keys. This approach was adopted by the UK National Grid Service (NGS) to authenticate users [4]. In the UK, anyone who applies to access the national grid computing resource must first generate a private/public key pair of his own, and then have the public key certified by NGS. The authentication procedure for the grid computing environments in the USA is similar [18]. However, developments in the past ten years reveal that users — most of them are non-computer specialists — encounter serious difficulties in managing their private keys and certificates [5]. This has greatly hindered the wider acceptance of the grid computing technology.

Hence, weak passwords are just a fact of life that we must face. Researchers have been actively exploring ways to perform password-based authentication without using PKIs or certificates — a research subject called the Password-Authenticated Key Exchange (PAKE) [9]. The first milestone came in 1992 when Bellovin and Merrit introduced the EKE protocol [13]. Despite some reported weaknesses [22, 26, 29, 32], the EKE protocol first demonstrated that the PAKE problem was at least solvable. Since then, a number of protocols have been proposed. Many of them are simply variants of EKE, instantiating the "symmetric cipher" in various ways [9]. The few techniques that claim to resist known attacks have almost all been patented — most notably, EKE was patented by Lucent Technologies [15], and SPEKE by Phoenix Technologies [24]. As a result, the scientific community and the wider security industry cannot readily benefit from the implementations of these techniques [16].

The security with the EKE and SPEKE protocols is only heuristic. Given the way the two techniques were designed, formal security proofs seem unlikely without introducing new assumptions or relaxing requirements; we will explain the details in Section 4. In the following section, we will introduce a different approach to solve the PAKE problem, and show that our solution is free from the security issues reported with the EKE and SPEKE protocols.

2   Protocol

2.1   Model

We assume the key exchange is carried out over an unsecured network. In such a network, there is no secrecy in communication, so transmitting a message is essentially no different from broadcasting it to all. Worse, the broadcast is unauthenticated. An attacker can intercept a message, change it at will, and then relay the modified message to the intended recipient.

It is perhaps surprising that we are still able to establish a private and authenticated channel in such a hostile environment solely based on a shared password — in other words, bootstrapping a *high-entropy* cryptographic key from a *low-entropy* secret. First of all, we formulate the security requirements that a PAKE protocol should fulfill.

1. **Off-line dictionary attack resistance** — It does not leak any password verification information to a passive attacker.
2. **Forward secrecy** — It produces session keys that remain secure even when the password is later disclosed.
3. **Known-key security** — It prevents a disclosed session key from affecting the security of other sessions.
4. **On-line dictionary attack resistance** — It limits an active attacker to test only one password per protocol execution.

In our threat model, we do not consider the Denial of Service (DoS) attack [3], which is rare but powerful. Since almost all PAKE protocols are built upon public key cryptography, they are naturally vulnerable to DoS attacks, in which an attacker's sole purpose is to keep a server performing expensive public key operations. When this becomes a threat in some applications, there are well-established solutions — for example, we can add a client-puzzle protocol [21] before engaging in any key exchange (also see [10]).

There are generally two types of PAKE protocols: balanced and augmented ones [34]. A balance scheme assumes two communicating parties hold symmetric secret information, which could be a password, or a hashed password. It is generic for any two-party communication, including client-client and client-server. On the other hand, an augmented scheme is more customized to the client-server case. It adds the "server compromise resistance" requirement — an attacker should not be able to impersonate users to a server after he has stolen the password verification files stored on that server, but has not performed dictionary attacks to recover the passwords [14, 23]. This is usually realized by storing extra password verification data — such as a (weak) public key derived from the password — together with a hash of the password on the server [14].

By design an augmented scheme is more complex and requires more computing power, but the added benefits are questionable. First, one may ask whether the threat of impersonating users to a *compromised* server is significantly realistic in practice [30]. More importantly, none of the augmented schemes can provide any comforting assurance once the server is indeed compromised — all passwords need to be revoked and updated anyway. Though it may be the case that some passwords are stronger than others and are more resistant to off-line dictionary attacks (as said in [23]), the "strongness" of a password is difficult to quantify, given that people often vary the same password slightly for different applications and use date of birth or pet's name as the password. If the presumption of a "strong" password turns out incorrect, the so-called "server compromise resistance" might just provide a false sense of security. To defend against the "server compromise" threat, a more proper solution is to apply a threshold scheme to distribute the password verification data among a set of servers, as suggested in [17, 31].

In this paper, we only consider the balanced case (there is a general method to convert any balanced scheme to an augmented one if needed [19]). In the following section, we will propose a balanced PAKE protocol that satisfies the outlined requirements.

2.2   Two-Step Exchange

Let G denote a subgroup of $\mathbb{Z}_p^*$ with prime order q in which the Decision Diffie-Hellman problem (DDH) is intractable [8]. Let g be a generator in G. The two communicating parties, Alice and Bob, both agree on (G, g). Let s be their shared password[1], and $s \neq 0$ for any non-empty password. Since s has low entropy, we assume the value of s falls within $[1, q - 1]$.

Alice selects two secret values x_1 and x_2 at random: $x_1 \in_R \mathbb{Z}_q$ and $x_2 \in_R \mathbb{Z}_q^*$. Similarly, Bob selects $x_3 \in_R \mathbb{Z}_q$ and $x_4 \in_R \mathbb{Z}_q^*$. Note that since q is prime, $\mathbb{Z}_q$ only differs $\mathbb{Z}_q^*$ in that the later excludes '0' [36]. Hence, $x_2, x_4 \neq 0$; the reason will be evident in security analysis.

Step 1. *Alice sends out g^{x_1}, g^{x_2} and knowledge proofs for x_1 and x_2. Similarly, Bob sends out g^{x_3}, g^{x_4} and knowledge proofs for x_3 and x_4.*

The above communication can be completed in one step as neither party depends on the other. When this step finishes, Alice and Bob verify the received knowledge proofs, and also check $g^{x_2}, g^{x_4} \neq 1$.

Step 2. *Alice sends out $\mathcal{A} = g^{(x_1+x_3+x_4)\cdot x_2 \cdot s}$ and a knowledge proof for $x_2 \cdot s$. Similarly, Bob sends out $\mathcal{B} = g^{(x_1+x_2+x_3)\cdot x_4 \cdot s}$ and a knowledge proof for $x_4 \cdot s$.*

When this step finishes, Alice computes $K = (\mathcal{B}/g^{x_2 \cdot x_4 \cdot s})^{x_2} = g^{(x_1+x_3)\cdot x_2 \cdot x_4 \cdot s}$, and Bob computes $K = (\mathcal{A}/g^{x_2 \cdot x_4 \cdot s})^{x_4} = g^{(x_1+x_3)\cdot x_2 \cdot x_4 \cdot s}$. With the same keying material K, a session key can be derived $\kappa = H(K)$, where H is a hash function. Before using the session key, Alice and Bob may perform an additional key confirmation process as follows: Alice sends $H(H(\kappa))$ to Bob, and Bob then replies $H(\kappa)$. This process is the same as in [22]. It gives explicit assurance that the two ends derived the same session key[2].

In the protocol, senders need to produce valid knowledge proofs. The necessity of the knowledge proofs is motivated by Anderson's sixth principle in designing secure protocols [2]: *"Do not assume that a message you receive has a particular form unless you can check this."* Fortunately, Zero-Knowledge Proof (ZKP) is a well-established primitive in cryptography; it can allow one to prove his knowledge of a discrete logarithm without revealing it [36].

As one example, we could use Schnorr's signature [37], which is non-interactive, and reveals nothing except the one bit information: "whether the signer knows the discrete logarithm". Let H be a secure hash function[3]. To prove the knowledge of the exponent for g^x, one sends $\{g^v, r = v - x_i h\}$ where

---

[1] Depending on the application, s could also be a hash of the shared password, so that it preserves some privacy against an honest-but-curious server administrator.

[2] Actually, the explicit key confirmation process is not essential [35]. Alice and Bob can also start using the session key straight away to encrypt data, which is called an implicit key confirmation process. In terms of security, the difference between the two approaches is insignificant.

[3] Schnorr's signature is provably secure in the random oracle model, which requires a secure hash function.

Table 1. Computational cost for Alice in J-PAKE

Item	Description	No of Exp	Time (ms)
1	Compute $\{g^{x_1}, g^{x_2}\}$ and KPs for $\{x_1, x_2\}$	4	23
2	Verify KPs for $\{x_3, x_4\}$	4	24
3	Compute $\mathcal{A}$ and KP for $\{x_2 \cdot s\}$	2	9
4	Verify KP for $\{x_4 \cdot s\}$	2	10
5	Compute κ	2	9
	Total	**14**	**75**

$v \in_R \mathbb{Z}_q$ and $h = H(g, g^v, g^x, \text{SignerID})$. This signature can be verified by the receiver through checking whether g^v and $g^r g^{xh}$ are equal. Adding the SignerID into the hash function is to prevent replaying the signature. Since Alice and Bob's SignerIDs are unique, Alice cannot replay Bob's signature back to Bob and vice versa.

In the second step of the protocol, Alice sends $\mathcal{A} = g_a^{x_2 \cdot s}$ to Bob, where $g_a = g^{x_1 + x_3 + x_4}$. Here, g_a serves as a generator. As the group G has prime order, any non-identity element is a generator [36]. So Alice could simply check $g_a \neq 1$ to ensure it is a generator. In fact, as we will explain in Section 3, $(x_1 + x_3 + x_4)$ is random over $\mathbb{Z}_q$ even in the face of active attacks. Hence, the probability for $g_a = 1$ is extremely small — on the order of 2^{-160} for 160-bit q. Symmetrically, the same argument applies to the Bob's case.

2.3   Implementation

Since our protocol involves several zero-knowledge proofs, one might concern about its cost. We now count the number of exponentiations in the protocol and evaluate its computational efficiency. Note that for Schnorr's signature, it requires one exponentiation in generation and two in verification. Hence, in our protocol, each party would need to perform 14 exponentiations in total — including 8 in the first step, 4 in the second step, and 2 in computing the session key.

To better assess the cost in real terms, we implement the protocol in Java on a 2.33-GHz laptop running Mac OS X. The modulus p is chosen 1024-bit and the subgroup order q 160-bit. The cost for Alice is summarized in Table 1; for Bob, it is the same. The results demonstrate that the protocol — executed only once in a session — runs sufficiently fast. The total computation time is merely 0.075 sec. As compared to the time that the user keys in his password, this latency is negligible at the client. However, the cost at the server may accumulate to be significant if requests are dealt with simultaneously. Therefore, the threat of Denial of Service (DoS) attacks still needs to be properly addressed in practical deployments (*e.g.*, by using [21]).

3   Security Analysis

In this section, we analyze the protocol's resistance against both passive and active attacks. First, we consider a passive attacker who eavesdrops on the communication between Alice and Bob. Alice's ciphertext $\mathcal{A}$ contains the term $(x_1 + x_3 + x_4)$ on the exponent. The following two lemmas show the security properties of $(x_1 + x_3 + x_4)$ and $\mathcal{A}$.

Lemma 1. *Under the Discrete Logarithm (DL) assumption, Bob cannot compute $(x_1 + x_3 + x_4)$.*

Proof. To obtain a contradiction, we reveal x_2 to Bob. The knowledge proofs in the protocol show that Bob knows x_3 and x_4. Hence, Bob knows $\{g^{x_1}, x_2, x_3, x_4\}$ (based on which he can compute $\mathcal{A}$, $\mathcal{B}$). Assume Bob is able to compute $(x_1 + x_3 + x_4)$. Then, he is able to compute x_1. This, however, contradicts the DL assumption [36], which states that one cannot compute x_1 from g, g^{x_1}. Therefore, even with x_2 revealed, Bob is still unable to compute $(x_1 + x_3 + x_4)$. $\square$

Lemma 2. *Under the Decision Diffie-Hellman (DDH) assumption, Bob cannot distinguish Alice's ciphertext $\mathcal{A} = g^{(x_1+x_3+x_4)\cdot x_2 \cdot s}$ from a random element in the group.*

Proof. From Lemma 1, $(x_1+x_3+x_4)$ is a random value over $\mathbb{Z}_q$, unknown to Bob. Also, $x_2 \cdot s$ is a random value over $\mathbb{Z}_q$, unknown to Bob. Based on the Decision Diffie-Hellman assumption [8], Bob cannot distinguish $\mathcal{A}$ from a random element in the group. $\square$

Based on the protocol symmetry, the above two Lemmas can be easily adapted from Alice's perspective — Alice cannot compute $(x_1 + x_2 + x_3)$, nor distinguish $\mathcal{B}$ from a random element in the group. The following theorem proves that our protocol fulfills the "off-line dictionary attack resistance" requirement (see Section 2.1).

Theorem 3 (Off-line dictionary attack resistance). *Under the DDH assumption, the ciphertexts $\mathcal{A} = g^{(x_1+x_3+x_4)\cdot x_2 \cdot s}$ and $\mathcal{B} = g^{(x_1+x_2+x_3)\cdot x_4 \cdot s}$ do not leak any information for password verification.*

Proof. Lemma 2 implies that Bob cannot computationally correlate $\mathcal{A}$ to the ciphertext he can compute: $\mathcal{B}$. From Lemma 2, even Bob cannot distinguish $\mathcal{A}$ from a random value in G. Surely, a passive attacker cannot distinguish $\mathcal{A}$ from a random value in G, nor can he computationally correlate $\mathcal{A}$ to $\mathcal{B}$. Based on the protocol symmetry, the passive attacker cannot distinguish $\mathcal{B}$ from a random value in G either. Therefore, to a passive attacker, $\mathcal{A}$ and $\mathcal{B}$ are two random and independent values; they do not leak any useful information for password verification. $\square$

While the above theorem shows that the password is secure against a passive attacker, we now show the session key is secure too. In the following theorem, we consider a stronger attacker, who knows the disclosed s.

Theorem 4 (Forward secrecy). *Under the Square Computational Diffie-Hellman (SCDH) assumption[4], the past session keys derived from the protocol remain secure even when the secret s is later disclosed.*

Proof. After knowing s, the passive attacker wants to compute $\kappa = H(K)$ given inputs: $\{g^{x_1}, g^{x_2}, g^{x_3}, g^{x_4}, g^{(x_1+x_3+x_4)\cdot x_2}, g^{(x_1+x_2+x_3)\cdot x_4}\}$.

Assume the attacker is able to compute $K = g^{(x_1+x_3)\cdot x_2\cdot x_4}$ from those inputs. For simplicity, let $x_5 = x_1 + x_3 \mod q$. The attacker behaves like an oracle — given the ordered inputs $\{g^{x_2}, g^{x_4}, g^{x_5}, g^{(x_5+x_4)\cdot x_2}, g^{(x_5+x_2)\cdot x_4}\}$, it returns $g^{x_5\cdot x_2\cdot x_4}$. This oracle can be used to solve the SCDH problem as follows. For g^x where $x \in_R \mathbb{Z}_q$, we query the oracle by supplying $\{g^{-x+a}, g^{-x+b}, g^x, g^{b\cdot(-x+a)}, g^{a\cdot(-x+b)}\}$, where a, b are arbitrary values chosen from $\mathbb{Z}_q$, and obtain $f(g^x) = g^{(-x+a)\cdot(-x+b)\cdot x} = g^{x^3-(a+b)\cdot x^2+ab\cdot x}$. In this way, we can also obtain $f(g^{x+1}) = g^{(x+1)^3-(a+b)\cdot(x+1)^2+ab\cdot(x+1)} = g^{x^3+(3-a-b)\cdot x^2+(3-2a-2b+ab)\cdot x+1-a-b+ab}$. Now we are able to compute $g^{x^2} = \left(f(g^{x+1}) \cdot f(g^x)^{-1} \cdot g^{(-3+2a+2b)\cdot x-1+a+b-ab}\right)^{1/3}$. This, however, contradicts the SCDH assumption [6], which states that one cannot compute g^{x^2} from g, g^x.   □

We now consider the case when a session key is compromised (see the "known-key security" requirement in Section 2.1). Compared with other ephemeral secrets x_i $(i = 1 \ldots 4)$ — which can be immediately erased after the key bootstrap phase — a session key lasts longer throughout the session, which might increase the likelihood of its exposure. An exposed session key should not cause any global effect on the system [36].

In our protocol, a known session key does not affect the security of either the password or other session keys. From an explicit key confirmation process, an attacker learns $H(H(\kappa)) = H(H(H(K)))$ and $H(\kappa) = H(H(K))$. It is obvious that learning $\kappa = H(K)$ does not give the attacker any additional knowledge about K, and therefore, the security of the password encrypted at that session remains intact. Also, the session key $\kappa = H(g^{(x_1+x_3)\cdot x_2\cdot x_4\cdot s})$ is determined by the (fresh) ephemeral inputs from both parties in the session. Note that $x_2, x_4 \neq 0$ by definition and $(x_1 + x_3)$ is random over $\mathbb{Z}_q$, hence the obtained session key is completely different from keys derived in other sessions. Therefore, compromising a session key has no effect on other session keys.

Finally, we study an active attacker, who directly engages in the protocol execution. Without loss of generality, we assume Alice is honest, and Bob is compromised (*i.e.*, an attacker).

In the protocol, Bob demonstrates that he knows x_4 and the exponent of g_b, where $g_b = g^{x_1+x_2+x_3}$. Therefore, the format of the ciphertext sent by Bob can be described as $\mathcal{B}' = g_b^{x_4\cdot s'}$, where s' is a value that Bob (the attacker) can choose freely.

---

[4] The SCDH assumption is provably equivalent to the Computational Diffie-Hellman (CDH) assumption — solving SCDH implies solving CDH, and vice versa [6].

Table 2. Summary of J-PAKE security properties

Modules	Security property	Attacker type	Assumptions
Schnorr signature	leak 1-bit: whether sender knows discrete logarithm	passive/active	DL and random oracle
Password encryption	indistinguishable from random	passive/active	DDH
Session key	incomputable	passive	CDH
	incomputable	passive (know s)	CDH
	incomputable	passive (know other session keys)	CDH
	incomputable	active (if $s' \neq s$)	CDH
Key confirmation	leak nothing	passive	–
	leak 1-bit: whether $s' = s$	active	CDH

Theorem 5 (On-line dictionary attack resistance). *Under the SCDH assumption, the session key cannot be computed by an active attacker if he chose a value $s' \neq s$.*

Proof. After receiving $\mathcal{B}'$, Alice computes

$$K' = (\mathcal{B}'/g^{x_2 \cdot x_4 \cdot s})^{x_2} \tag{1}$$

$$= g^{x_1 \cdot x_2 \cdot x_4 \cdot s'} \cdot g^{x_2 \cdot x_3 \cdot x_4 \cdot s'} \cdot g^{x_2^2 \cdot x_4 \cdot (s'-s)} \tag{2}$$

To obtain a contradiction, we reveal x_1 and s, and assume that the attacker is now able to compute K'. The attacker behaves as an oracle: given inputs $\{g^{x_2}, x_1, x_3, x_4, s, s'\}$, it returns K'. Note that the oracle does not need to know x_2, and it is still able to compute $\mathcal{A} = g^{(x_1+x_3+x_4)\cdot x_2 \cdot s}$ and $\mathcal{B}' = g^{(x_1+x_2+x_3)\cdot x_4 \cdot s'}$ internally. Thus, the oracle can be used to solve the Square Computational Diffie-Hellman problem by computing $g^{x_2^2} = (K'/(g^{x_1 \cdot x_2 \cdot x_4 \cdot s'} \cdot g^{x_2 \cdot x_3 \cdot x_4 \cdot s'}))^{x_4^{-1}(s'-s)^{-1}}$. Here[5], $x_4 \neq 0$ and $s' - s \neq 0$. This, however, contradicts the SCDH assumption. So, even with x_1 and s revealed, the attacker is still unable to compute K' (and hence cannot perform key confirmation later). □

The above theorem shows that our protocol is zero-knowledge. Because of the knowledge proofs, the attacker is left with the only freedom to choose an arbitrary s'. If $s' \neq s$, he is unable to derive the same session key as Alice. During the later key confirmation process, the attacker will learn one-bit information: whether s' and s are equal. This is the best that any PAKE protocol can possibly achieve, because by nature we cannot stop an imposter from trying a random guess of password. However, consecutively failed guesses can be easily detected, and thwarted accordingly. The security properties of our protocol are summarized in Table 2.

---

[5] This explains why in the protocol definition we need $x_4 \neq 0$, and symmetrically, $x_2 \neq 0$

4   Comparison

In this section, we compare our protocol with the two well-known balanced schemes: EKE and SPEKE. These two techniques have several variants, which follow very similar constructs [9]. However, it is beyond the scope of this paper to evaluate them all. Also, we will not compare with augmented schemes (*e.g.*, A-EKE, B-SPEKE, SRP, AMP and OPAKE [34]), as they have different design goals.

The design principles underlying EKE and SPEKE are similar; both protocols can be seen as a *slight* modification of the basic Diffie-Hellman (DH) key exchange protocol. However, in the protocol design, even the slightest modification could cause profound effects. The EKE and SPEKE designs are no exception, as we explain below.

Bellovin and Merrit introduced two EKE constructs: using RSA (which was later shown insecure [29]) and DH. Here, we only describe the later, which modifies a basic DH protocol by symmetrically encrypting the exchanged items. Let α be a primitive root modulo p. In the protocol, Alice sends to Bob $[\alpha^{x_a}]_s$, where $x_a \in_R \mathbb{Z}_p^*$ and $[\ldots]_s$ denotes a symmetric cipher using the password s as the key. Similarly, Bob sends to Alice $[\alpha^{x_b}]_s$, where $x_b \in_R \mathbb{Z}_p^*$. Finally, Alice and Bob compute a common key $K = \alpha^{x_a \cdot x_b}$. More details can be found in [13].

Apparently, a straightforward implementation of the above protocol is insecure [26]. Since the password is too weak to be used as a normal encryption key, the content within the symmetric cipher must be strictly random. But, for a 1024-bit number modulo p, not every bit is random. Hence, a passive attacker can rule out candidate passwords by applying them to decipher $[\alpha^{x_a}]_s$, and then checking whether the results fall within $[p, 2^{1024} - 1]$.

There are suggested countermeasures. In [13], Bellovin and Merrit recommended to transmit $[\alpha^{x_a} + r \cdot p]_s$ instead of $[\alpha^{x_a}]_s$ in the actual implementation, where $r \cdot p$ is added using a non-modular operation. The details on defining r can be found in [13]. However, this solution was explained in an ad-hoc way, and it involves changing the protocol of its existing form. Due to lack of a complete description of the final protocol, it is difficult to assess its security. Alternatively, Jaspan suggested to address this issue by choosing p as close to a power of 2 as possible [26]. This might alleviate the issue, but does not resolve it.

One implication of the above issues is that proving the security of an EKE is difficult. To address this, Bellare, Pointcheval and Rogaway introduced an "ideal-cipher model", and proved that an EKE is secure under that model [7]. However, the "ideal cipher" was not concretely defined in [7]; it was later clarified by Boyd et al. in [9]: the assumed cipher works like a random function in encryption, but must map fixed-size strings to elements of G in decryption (also see [39]). Yet, no such ciphers are readily available in practice; indeed, several proposed instantiations of such an "ideal cipher" were easily broken [39].

Another limitation with the EKE protocol is that it does not securely accommodate short exponents. The protocol definition requires α^{x_a} and α^{x_b} be uniformly distributed over the whole group $\mathbb{Z}_p^*$ [13]. Therefore, the secret keys x_a and x_b must be randomly chosen from $[1, p - 1]$, and consequently, an EKE must use 1024-bit exponents if the modulus p is chosen 1024-bit. Unlike our protocol, an EKE cannot operate in groups with distinct features, such as a subgroup with prime order — a passive attacker would then be able to trivially uncover the password by checking the order of the decrypted item. Since the cost of exponentiation is linear with the bit-length of the exponent [36], one exponentiation in an EKE is equivalent in cost to 6-7 exponentiations in a J-PAKE (for the 1024-bit p and 160-bit q setting). Hence, though an EKE only requires two exponential operations per user, the computational cost is approximately the same as that of our protocol.

Jablon proposed a different protocol, called Simple Password Exponential Key Exchange (SPEKE), by replacing a fixed generator in the basic DH protocol with a password-derived variable [22]. In the description of a fully constrained SPEKE, the protocol defines a safe prime $p = 2q + 1$, where q is also a prime. Alice sends to Bob $(s^2)^{x_a}$ where s is the shared password and $x_a \in_R \mathbb{Z}_q^*$; similarly, Bob sends to Alice $(s^2)^{x_b}$ where $x_b \in_R \mathbb{Z}_q^*$. Finally, Alice and Bob compute $K = s^{2 \cdot x_a \cdot x_b}$. The squaring operation on s is to make the protocol work within a subgroup of prime order q.

Recently, Zhang pointed out the risk of using a password-derived variable as the base [38]. Since some passwords are exponentially equivalent, an active attacker may exploit that equivalence to test multiple passwords in one go. This problem is particularly serious if a password is a Personal Identification Numbers (PIN). One countermeasure might be to hash the password before squaring, but that does not resolve the problem. Hashed passwords are still confined to a pre-defined small range. There is no guarantee that an attacker is unable to formulate exponential relationships among hashed passwords; existing hash functions were not designed for that purpose. Hence, at least in theory, this reported weakness disapproves the original claim in [22] that a SPEKE only permits one guess of password in one attempt.

Similar to the case with an EKE, a fully constrained SPEKE uses long exponents. For a 1024-bit modulus p, the key space is within $[1, q - 1]$, where q is 1023-bit. In [22], Jablon suggested to use 160-bit short exponents in a SPEKE, by choosing x_a and x_b within a dramatically smaller range $[1, 2^{160} - 1]$. But, this would give a passive attacker side information that the $1023 - 160 = 863$ most significant bits in a full-length key are all '0's. The security is not reassuring, as the author later acknowledged in [25]. Therefore, for the same reason explained earlier, the computational cost in a SPEKE is roughly the same as ours, despite that a SPEKE only requires two exponentiations per user.

To sum up, an EKE requires changing the protocol in its existing form for a secure implementation. As for a SPEKE, it has the drawback that an active attacker may test multiple passwords in one protocol execution. Furthermore, neither protocol — in the original form — accommodates short exponents securely. Finally, neither protocol is provably secure; formal security proofs seem unlikely without introducing new security assumptions [7] or relaxing security requirements [33].

We choose to solve the PAKE problem using a different approach. The novelty of our design is that we encrypt the password by juggling the public keys in a way that can be verified. As a result, our scheme is provably secure, allows flexible use of short exponents, and strictly limits an active attacker to test only one password per protocol execution. A similar use of this juggling technique was seen in solving the Dining Cryptographers problem[6] in 2006 [20]. One difference is that [20] works in a multi-party setting, while ours in a two-party one. Yet both schemes use the same technique, which we call "public key juggling" — i.e., re-arranging the public keys in a particular way, and encrypting data by introducing quadratic terms on the exponents in a verifiable way. To our best knowledge, this construct is significantly different from all past PAKE protocols. In the area of PAKE research — which has been troubled by many patent arguments surrounding existing schemes [16] — a new construct may be helpful.

5   Conclusion

In this paper, we proposed a protocol, called J-PAKE, which authenticates a password with zero-knowledge and then subsequently creates a strong session key if the password is correct. We proved that the protocol fulfills the following properties: it prevents off-line dictionary attacks; provides forward secrecy; insulates a known session key from affecting any other sessions; and strictly limits an active attacker to guess only one password per protocol execution. A Java implementation of the protocol demonstrates that the total computation time for the session-key setup is merely 75 ms. As compared to the de facto internet standard SSL/TLS, J-PAKE is more lightweight in password authentication with two notable advantages: 1). It requires no PKI deployments; 2). It protects users from leaking passwords (say to a fake bank website).

Acknowledgments

We are obliged to Ross Anderson and Piotr Zieliński for their invaluable comments.

References

1. Abdalla, M., Pointcheval, D.: Simple password-based encrypted key exchange protocols. In: Menezes, A. (ed.) CT-RSA 2005. LNCS, vol. 3376, pp. 191–208. Springer, Heidelberg (2005)
2. Anderson, R.J., Needham, R.: Robustness principles for public key protocols. In: Coppersmith, D. (ed.) CRYPTO 1995. LNCS, vol. 963, pp. 236–247. Springer, Heidelberg (1995)
3. Anderson, R.J.: Security Engineering: A Guide to Building Dependable Distributed Systems. Wiley, New York (2001)

---

[6] The Dining Cryptographers problem was first introduced by Chaum in 1988 [11].

4. The official UK National Grid Service website,
   http://www.grid-support.ac.uk/
5. Beckles, B., Welch, V., Basney, J.: Mechanisms for increasing the usability of grid security. International Journal of Human-Computer Studies 63(1-2), 74–101 (2005)
6. Bao, F., Deng, R.H., Zhu, H.: Variations of Diffie-Hellman problem. In: Qing, S., Gollmann, D., Zhou, J. (eds.) ICICS 2003. LNCS, vol. 2836, pp. 301–312. Springer, Heidelberg (2003)
7. Bellare, M., Pointcheval, D., Rogaway, P.: Authenticated key exchange secure against dictionary attacks. In: Preneel, B. (ed.) EUROCRYPT 2000. LNCS, vol. 1807, pp. 139–155. Springer, Heidelberg (2000)
8. Boneh, D.: The decision Diffie-Hellman problem. In: Buhler, J.P. (ed.) ANTS 1998. LNCS, vol. 1423, pp. 48–63. Springer, Heidelberg (1998)
9. Boyd, C., Mathuria, A.: Protocols for authentication and key establishment. Springer, Heidelberg (2003)
10. Bresson, E., Chevassut, O., Pointcheval, D.: New security results on Encrypted Key Exchange. In: Bao, F., Deng, R., Zhou, J. (eds.) PKC 2004. LNCS, vol. 2947, pp. 145–158. Springer, Heidelberg (2004)
11. Chaum, D.: The dining cryptographers problem: unconditional sender and recipient untraceability. Journal of Cryptology 1(1), 65–67 (1988)
12. Camenisch, J., Stadler, M.: Proof systems for general statements about discrete logarithms, Technical report TR 260, Department of Computer Science, ETH Zürich (March 1997)
13. Bellovin, S., Merritt, M.: Encrypted Key Exchange: password-based protocols secure against dictionary attacks. In: Proceedings of the IEEE Symposium on Research in Security and Privacy (May 1992)
14. Bellovin, S., Merritt, M.: Augmented Encrypted Key Exchange: a password-based protocol secure against dictionary attacks and password file compromise. In: Proceedings of the 1st ACM Conference on Computer and Communications Security, pp. 244–250 (November 1993)
15. Bellovin, S., Merritt, M.: Cryptographic protocol for secure communications, U.S. Patent 5,241,599,
   http://patft.uspto.gov/netacgi/nph-Parser?patentnumber=5241599
16. Ehulund, E.: Secure on-line configuration for SIP UAs, Master thesis, The Royal Institute of Technology (August 2006)
17. Ford, W., Kaliski, B.S.: Server-assisted generation of a strong secret from a password. In: Proceedings of the 9th International Workshops on Enabling Technologies, pp. 176–180. IEEE Press, Los Alamitos (2000)
18. Foster, I., Kesselman, C., Tsudik, G., Tuecke, S.: A security architecture for computational grids. In: Proceedings of the 5th ACM Conference on Computer and Communications Security, pp. 83–92 (November 1998)
19. Gentry, C., MacKenzie, P., Ramzan, Z.: A method for making password-based key exchange resilient to server compromise. In: Dwork, C. (ed.) CRYPTO 2006. LNCS, vol. 4117, pp. 142–159. Springer, Heidelberg (2006)
20. Hao, F., Zieliński, P.: A 2-round anonymous veto protocol. In: Proceedings of the 14th International Workshop on Security Protocols, SPW 2006, Cambridge, UK (May 2006)
21. Juels, J., Brainard, J.: Client Puzzles: a cryptographic countermeasure against connection depletion attacks. In: Proceedings of Networks and Distributed Security Systems, pp. 151–165 (1999)
22. Jablon, D.: Strong password-only authenticated key exchange. ACM Computer Communications Review 26(5), 5–26 (1996)

23. Jablon, D.: Extended password protocols immune to dictionary attack. In: Proceedings of the WETICE 1997 Enterprise Security Workshop, pp. 248–255 (June 1997)
24. Jablon, D.: Cryptographic methods for remote authentication, U.S. Patent 6,226,383, http://patft.uspto.gov/netacgi/nph-Parser?patentnumber=6226383
25. Jablon, D.: Password authentication using multiple servers. In: Naccache, D. (ed.) CT-RSA 2001. LNCS, vol. 2020, pp. 344–360. Springer, Heidelberg (2001)
26. Jaspan, B.: Dual-workfactor Encrypted Key Exchange: efficiently preventing password chaining and dictionary attacks. In: Proceedings of the Sixth Annual USENIX Security Conference, pp. 43–50 (July 1996)
27. Kobara, K., Imai, H.: Pretty-simple password-authenticated key-exchange under standard assumptions. IEICE Transactions E85-A(10), 2229–2237 (2002)
28. Van Oorschot, P.C., Wiener, M.J.: On Diffie-Hellman key agreement with short exponents. In: Maurer, U.M. (ed.) EUROCRYPT 1996. LNCS, vol. 1070, pp. 332–343. Springer, Heidelberg (1996)
29. Patel, S.: Number theoretic attacks on secure password schemes. In: Proceedings of the IEEE Symposium on Security and Privacy (May 1997)
30. Perlman, R., Kaufman, C.: Secure password-based protocol for downloading a private key. In: Proceedings of the Network and Distributed System Security (February 1999)
31. MacKenzie, P.D., Shrimpton, T., Jakobsson, M.: Threshold password-authenticated key exchange. In: Yung, M. (ed.) CRYPTO 2002. LNCS, vol. 2442, p. 385. Springer, Heidelberg (2002)
32. MacKenzie, P.: The PAK suite: protocols for password-authenticated key exchange, Technical Report 2002-46, DIMACS (2002)
33. MacKenzie, P.: On the Security of the SPEKE Password-Authenticated Key Exchange Protocol, Cryptology ePrint Archive: Report 057 (2001)
34. IEEE P1363 Working Group, P1363.2: Standard Specifications for Password-Based Public-Key Cryptographic Techniques. Draft available at, http://grouper.ieee.org/groups/1363/
35. Raymond, J.F., Stigic, A.: Security issues in the diffie-hellman key agreement protocol, Technical report, Zeroknowledge Inc. (September 2000)
36. Stinson, D.: Cryptography: theory and practice. 3rd edn. Chapman & Hall/CRC (2006)
37. Schnorr, C.P.: Efficient signature generation by smart cards. Journal of Cryptology 4(3), 161–174 (1991)
38. Zhang, M.: Analysis of the SPEKE password-authenticated key exchange protocol. IEEE Communications Letters 8(1), 63–65 (2004)
39. Zhao, Z., Dong, Z., Wang, Y.: Security analysis of a password-based authentication protocol proposed to IEEE 1363. Theoretical Computer Science 352(1), 280–287 (2006)

Password Authenticated Key Exchange by Juggling
(Transcript of Discussion)

Feng Hao

University College London

In today's presentation I am going to describe a password authenticated key exchange protocol. This problem is one of the central problems in cryptography. The solution to this problem has a wide range of practical applications.

This problem studies how to establish secure communications between two parties solely based on their shared password without requiring a public key infrastructure. The difficulty here is that passwords have low entropy because the human has limited ability to memorise a password, typically it has an entropy of 20 to 30 bits. On the other hand for a session key you will require a high entropy session key, typically 128 bits. Let's take one concrete example. Suppose I have a mobile phone here and I want to talk to one of the audience, say James, privately, so I use wireless communication, the data is in the air, we assume that an attacker can eavesdrop the data exchange. And we also assume that an attacker is more powerful than that, he has a jamming device, he can high-jack the session, inject 40 messages, change messages, try all kinds of wacky attacks. Also we don't trust external parties, we don't even trust network providers, so we assume the network provider will keep a copy of all the communication data, but still we want the content of communication to be private between James and me. So essentially we want to bootstrap a high entropy session key based on this low entropy secret.

This is an extremely hostile environment. In such an environment James and I share a password, which is a four digit code, so we can simply enter this code into a mobile phone. Of course you can't enter 40 digit numbers, that would be too tedious, but a four-digit code is very short, and has low entropy. So there seems a contradiction here, we need a high entropy secret, but we only have low entropy shared secret. So the first question you may ask is, is this possible? What I am going to demonstrate in the talk is that, yes, it is possible, as long as you make the right use of mathematics.

First, let's review past work in this area. In 1992 Bellovin and Merritt proposed encrypted key exchange, or EKE. This technique is widely considered a milestone in the area. In 1994 and 1996, Jablon designed Simple Password Explains your Key Exchange, or SPEKE, which is another famous solution for the problem. around that time many solutions were proposed, so people feel that research in this area is already mature, we have already had so many solutions, let's go for standardisation. So in 2000 Standardisation Association approved a special working group to review all the solutions proposed in these areas in an effort to select the best solution and to standardise it. However, it has been eight

B. Christianson et al. (Eds.): Security Protocols 2008, LNCS 6615, pp. 172–179, 2011.

years now, and as yet there is no concrete result achieved from that standardisation project.

So, we may ask, what's the problem? Well there are two problems. The first problem is patent. Many schemes are patented because the solution has commercial value. Second problem is technique. The proposed solutions have various technical issues which I am going to describe in more detail. EKE was patented by Lucent, SPEKE was patented by Phoenix, SRP was patented by Stanford, Opaque was patented by Bogmoor. As you can see, Luthan, Phoenix, Bogmoor, they are all the big network giants, they are very keen on this kind of technique because it doesn't require PKI, and the network companies appreciate the practical problems with PKI. Suppose you are an open source developer, and you want to use one of the techniques: if it is patented it automatically means you can't use it. So in practice many applications have no choice but to rely on SSL to do password authentication, but SSL requires that you need to have a public key infrastructure, so it is a heavyweight solution.

Bruce Christianson: There is a good one that doesn't use public key infrastructure that was published in this workshop a few years ago[1], and it was not subject to patent. I believe it is in use in Boston.

Michael Roe: And it's worth mentioning that we had published it as a computer lab technical report[2] several years before the version that was published in the Workshop Proceedings, to prevent it from being patented.

Reply: Yes, I am aware of this. But in this area, EKE and SPEKE are probably the two most well-known solutions. And the EKE and the SPEKE patents caused all the problems[3]. So let's study these two techniques in more detail. Both EKE and SPEKE were obtained by slightly modifying the Diffe-Hellman key exchange protocol. This is a classic protocol in cryptography, however, this protocol also has well-known limitations: it is un-authenticated so it is vulnerable to a man-in-the-middle attack. EKE tries to fix this problem by using password as a symmetric key to encrypt the exchanged items. SPEKE modifies the protocol by replacing the base g by a password-derived variable which is a hash of the password. Both protocols were designed by slightly modifying the Diffie-Hellman key exchange protocol.

However, in cryptography, designing a crypto protocol is sometimes quite tricky. A slight change but may have profound effects. We have some good examples here at this workshop. So one of the effects is that, in the original protocol you can use short exponents, but after the change you can no longer use a short exponent. First let's look at EKE.

A passive attacker can narrow down the password range. On the theoretic side, some researchers have tried to prove the security of EKE, but they couldn't do it without introducing a strong ideal cipher model. This assumption is very strong. Essentially it requires a block cipher which has an unusual property: that it works like a random function in encryption (that's fine), but it must map fixed

---

[1] See LNCS 3364 pp 190–212: Secure Sessions from Weak Secrets.
[2] See www.cl.cam.ac.uk/techreports/UCAM-CL-TR-445.pdf
[3] The patent expired in 2010.

sized strings into group elements in decryption. So by definition, it is not really a symmetric block cipher. There is no such cipher, and because there is no such cipher, these practical attacks can happen. So the practical and the theoretical results are rather consistent.

On the efficiency side, EKE uses long exponent by definition. This means that the exponentiation in the EKE protocol is expensive. Let's look at SPEKE. In 2004 Sun demonstrated one attack in which an active attacker can guess multiple passwords in one try. This result is not very surprising because three years earlier McKenzie tried to prove the security of SPEKE, and he reported that he couldn't do it without relaxing the secret requirements, in other words, you must allow an attacker to guess multiple passwords in one try. So the practical and the theoretical results are consistent. Similar to the case of EKE, SPEKE uses long exponents by definition. There are some technical reasons why they can't use short exponents because of security concerns.

Now let's move on to our new approach, public key juggling. I am sure many of you have seen juggling before. I have some juggling balls here, my juggling skills are a bit rusty so I want to stay away from my laptop. [Applause] The fascinating part about this game is that you can play juggling between two people as shown in the picture. And more than that you can actually play juggling among a group of people. There is a juggling club in Cambridge, sometimes you can see a group of people walking on Parkers Piece doing juggling together.

In 2006 my colleague, Piotr Zieliński and I proposed an efficient solution to the Dining Cryptographers problem, at this workshop[4]. Essentially we used the same juggling technique as for a group of people, for multiple party case. The Dining Cryptographers problem was first proposed by David Chaum in 1988[5], and there's been quite a few solutions proposed in the past twenty years. We demonstrated here at SPW that our solution is the most efficient in terms runtime efficiency, computation cost, and message usage. In fact we demonstrated that the efficiency is very close to the optimum you can possibly get.

This time we applied the same technique in the two party case to solve the password key exchange problem. Here is the protocol. The protocol has two rounds. In round one Alice defines two random variables, x_1 and x_2. She sends the two public keys to Bob, together with the knowledge proofs, which I will explain in more detail. Here the knowledge proof is a signature. Since Alice generates the public keys, she knows the private key, and she is able to use the private key to generate a signature to demonstrate that she knows the private key. Bob does the same thing. That round one. For round two, Alice takes the two public keys she received from Bob, and she multiplies these two public keys together with the first public key she produced, so as to get this term, $g^{x_1+x_3+x_4}$. After that she will release this result to the power of $x_2 \cdot s$, where s is the password. Since Alice knows the value of x_2, and she knows the value of s, which is the password, therefore she can produce a signature. This is the

---

[4] See LNCS 5087, pp 202–214.

[5] David Chaum (1988). "The Dining Cryptographers Problem: Unconditional Sender and Recipient Untraceability", Journal of Cryptology 1 (1): 65–75.

most important part in the protocol. Essentially Alice generates a new public key. Bob does the same thing. The protocol is completely symmetric. Now Alice and Bob do some computation each at their own side: so for Alice, she uses B divided by $g^{x_2 \cdot x_4 \cdot s}$. Since Alice knows the values of x_2 and s, she can compute the same result as Bob, since Bob knows the value of x_4 and s. And then they can take a hash and use that as a session key.

So how is this relevant to juggling? A hint is to regard each public key as a ball. Let's take another look at this protocol: in the first round Alice generates two balls, random and fresh, and she throws the two balls to Bob, and Bob does the same thing to Alice. In the second round, Alice combines all these balls together and generates a new ball, and she throws it to Bob, and Bob also generates a new ball and throws it to Alice. So you can see it's like two parties that are playing juggling games for two rounds.

In the protocol we use knowledge proofs. This is inspired by the sixth principle in designing robust protocols defined by Ross Anderson and Roger Needham: do not assume that a message you receive has a particular format unless you can check this. It's very simple, very intuitive, but it explains the majority of cases in the past ten years why protocols were broken. For example, I you have a banner and a string, and some people tell you this banner and string is in the format of A concatenate B, how do you check it's indeed in this format? And if someone claims this is the result of A times B divided by C, how do you really know this is indeed the specified format, because the attacker may give you a different format. Fortunately in cryptography there are, for certain data formats, already well-established techniques for you to check the format. For example, you can use Schnorr signature to check that the sender of the public key has the knowledge of the private key. Of course, since we use knowledge proof here, one concern would be the computation cost.

Now let's count the number of exponentiations in the protocol. The count for Alice, and for Bob, are exactly the same. Alice generates two one-time public keys, and produces two signatures, that will take four exponentiations. Also she verifies the two signatures received from Bob, so that will take another four exponentiations. In round two Alice generates a new public key and also produces a signature, so that's two exponentiations. Also she needs to verify the signature generated by Bob, that's another two. Finally it takes another two exponentiations to compute the session key. So in total it requires 14 exponentiations. At first glance this may seem a lot more than the two exponentiations in EKE and SPEKE, but note that very important, in EKE and SPEKE, the protocol only uses long exponent, typically 1024 bits, but here we allow flexible use of short exponents, 160 bits. The cost of exponentiation is proportional to the bit amounts of the exponent, in other words, one exponentiation in EKE and SPEKE is about six to seven times more expensive than in our case, so if you factor this in, the overall cost is about the same.

Bruce Christianson: You mean that the exponent in your case is much shorter than the modulus?

Reply: The modulus is the same, it's 1024 bits, but the exponent we use is short, 160 bits, because we work in the cyclic subgroup.

Bruce Christianson: And EKE cannot do that because?

Reply: By their protocol definition, they have to work on the full, free domains, they can't work on the subgroup. The intuitive explanation is that EKE uses very weak passwords to encrypt the public key, so the structure of the public key must be random.

Tuomas Aura: So for an attack against the public key, I will try to guess a password, and decrypt each of the possible public keys, and if it doesn't belong to the subgroup, I know that I guessed the wrong password[6].

Reply: Because if you use a short exponent for the public key, and work in a large subgroup, then the bit strings have structure, it's not random.

Bruce Christianson: So EKE avoids that problem by working in the full group and using long exponents so that the leakage doesn't matter. But if all I exchange is a weak encryption of g^x then the attacker can't tell whether x is long or not[7].

Reply: Yes, for the passive attack to check. So in any case, we implemented these protocols in Java. The computation time is 75 milliseconds, we didn't consider how long the user would take to key in his password, that usually takes a few seconds, so it's possible to run the protocol in the background, so that the delay is almost negligible to the end user.

Here is a breakdown for the security analysis of this protocol. Without going through the mathematics, I will just go through the important steps in the proof. First we use Schnorr signature, this is a well-established technique, it only leaks one bit whether or not the sender knows this grid logarithm. Next, password encryption: the password is inherently weak, but in our protocol design we combine the password within a public key, so it is inside this ball, and you can prove that this ball is indistinguishable from a random ball, so offline dictionary

---

[6] The idea is to avoid kangaroo attacks on the short exponent by choosing the 1024 bit modulus to be a prime of the form $q = ap + 1$ where (for a 160 bit exponent) p is a large prime of at least 320 bits. But if a has small factors then g^x leaks information about x, since whenever $b|a$ with b tractable then $g^{(q-1)/b}$ has order b so $(g^x)^{(q-1)/b} = (g^{(q-1)/b})^x \bmod q$ reveals $x \bmod b$. This is a potentially fatal problem if $q - 1$ has many tractable factors and the exponent is known to be short.

This small factor attack can be avoided by working entirely in a large subgroup of prime order p: pick g at random, if $h = g^a \bmod q \neq 1$ then h generates a subgroup of order p. Now no information is leaked about the exponent, but the fact that $(h^x)^p \bmod q = 1$ means that the attacker can tell whether or not a candidate public key is actually in the subgroup, and this leaks information about the password. See P.C. van Oorschot and M.J. Wiener, "On Diffie-Hellman Key Agreement with Short Exponents", EUROCRYPT 96, LNCS1070, pp332–343.

[7] The Secure Sessions paper (cited earlier) advocates choosing $a = g = 2$, with $p \bmod 4 = 1$. This generates the whole group and so allows a weakly superenciphered DH protocol to work with small exponents: the leakage is limited to the parity of the exponent. Pre-finding a suitable q is relatively harder, but online exponentiation is easier.

attack doesn't work. And a passive attacker cannot compute a further session key. This is a very important proof because it shows that the protocol has forward secrecy: the passive attacker, even if he knows the password, as long as he is passive he cannot break the communication. This is very desirable because at the time of communication we know that Alice and Bob share this exclusive knowledge of a long-term secret, but in the future this secret could be disclosed, so even if the long-term secret is disclosed, all the communication in the past remains secure, that is forward secrecy. The next point is, even if the passive attacker knows one session key, it doesn't help him to break other sessions. Also, consider an active attacker who doesn't know the password so he hijacks a session and engages in the communication. He can try a random guess of the password as planned, so suppose Alice is honest, Bob is an attacker, and at the end of this protocol Alice will compute a session key, and we can prove that it is infeasible for Bob, the attacker, to compute the same session key unless Bob can solve the computational Diffie-Hellman problem. Finally, key confirmation: this process gives the active attacker some feedback, he will try one password, and he will know whether this password is right or wrong, but he doesn't know anything more than that, this proof shows that the protocol has general knowledge proof feature.

So the protocol has these four properties: first, off-line dictionary attack; second, long term key security; third, forward secrecy (so if the long term secret is disclosed it doesn't help the attacker to break the communications in the past); and finally, online dictionary attack resistance (it strictly limits an active attacker to guess only one password per protocol execution). In theory it is possible that the attacker may keep trying and do the exhaustive online attack, but that kind of attack can be detected. If you see that the login attempts failed for three times then you can discontinue the communication. By comparison, EKE does not fulfil property one, and SPEKE does not fulfil property 4.

As I mentioned earlier, currently SSL is the most widely deployed solution for password authentication, mainly because of the EKE patent which expires in 2008. Let's first look at a conversation between Alice and Bob. Alice has a secret, she knows a password, and if she tries to convince Bob that she knows the secret by telling Bob the secret, in doing so she reveals her secret. If you use browser `https` for online banking, you do something similar: you contact a bank and you say, I am your customer, allow me to log onto my account, the bank will say, give me your account number and the password. So you send your password through the SSL channel to the bank, and the bank will do some verification. The question is, how do you know the bank is authentic? The current mechanism in SSL relies on the end user to carefully check the domain name on the certificate to make sure it's authentic, but this is often too much of a burden for the end user. If the end user sees a warning window pop up from the browser, there may be some problem with the certificate, do you want to accept and continue, yes or no, the chances are the user always click yes. It's not the user's fault, it's a design problem. But with J-PAKE we do something different because it is a general knowledge proof protocol. Suppose the bank wants to know whether I know the password. The bank already have a copy of my password, whether it is password or hash of password it is a shared secret, so the two parties run the protocol and at the end of the protocol the bank will know whether the two sides have the same password, this is exactly one bit of information, and neither side learns anything more than that. This is potentially much more resistant against phishing attacks. In addition, as compared to SSL/TLS, our solution doesn't require PKI. You may notice that there are three stars after this statement, which is why in this research area the patent becomes such a big problem, and why big network companies are so keen on the patent. This is the reason.

Mark Lomas: A lot of the motivation for doing this is that people are bad at remembering passwords. But if I use this protocol, I need to pick a different password for every counterparty, because otherwise I'm sharing passwords with a counterparty who can masquerade as me to the others. So the reason I'd be inclined to use a PKI is, I can use my password to get access to my key, and then I use my key to authenticate myself, which means I only need one password.

So, it is not to say I don't like the protocol, but I would suggest you ought to look for a variant where we don't use the same password for every counterparty. That is a desirable feature, but I agree, that in practice some users do use the same password.

Reply: Yes, I agree, that is the kind of scenario you can have in practice. By rights you need to have different password for different accounts, but this solution doesn't require PKI. In other words, if I want to establish a secure communication with James we don't rely on anyone else to set up a public infrastructure for us, and we don't need to pay a few hundred quid just to get a certificate; we can just do this juggling game, and we can get a strong session key. So this means that by doing away with the PKI, we save the cost of setting up PKI, and also save the cost of maintaining PKI.

Finally the summary for my talk. So I described a protocol, this protocol authenticates password with general knowledge. Essentially it does authentication like playing a juggling game. If the two parties have the same password then you will be able to complete the game, and at the end of the game each party will have a common session key, and can use a session key for communication. If the game failed then it means that the two parties have different passwords, but neither party learns anything more than that. We also explained that this follows a very different construct than EKE and SPEKE, in fact it has even better securities than EKE and SPEKE with comparable efficiency. We also compare this protocol with SSL. There are two notable advantages. The first one is it does general knowledge proof, so it prevents leaking a password to the remote site. And the second advantage is that it requires no PKI deployment.

Matthew Johnson: The first advantage will extend if you're not using the client side SSL. People use server side SSL and then send a password through the tunnel, which I would agree with you is bad, while SSL does allow the client side SSL certificates.

Reply: Yes, that is the mutual authentication, right, but not in actual reality.

Richard Clayton: One property of a system like this, is that if people compromise the server material they can steal all the passwords. I wonder if you could do it on the second phase whereby essentially having done the first bit, make sure you're talking to the right end, you then have to produce the pre-image and authenticate it. Clearly what's held on the server doesn't actually help you, you also have to supply the pre-image if you want to go on the server. Everybody gets excited about phishing, but we've no idea whether or not those thing are solved by phishing, or by monopolising servers.

Reply: Yes, I agree with you, and that's a very good question. Actually in this area there are two types of protocol. One is balanced — the one I am presenting is a balanced protocol — in which yes, the two parties have a symmetric certificate, which could be a password, or hash of password. Another one is augmented protocol, so it's not really balanced, it's more customised for the client in the server case. That would offer some kind of protection once a server is compromised. It's desirable for that reason, but there are also some problems with that approach. The augmented password key exchange essentially adds one more requirement, which is so-called server compromise resistance. This requirement says that you have, say, a hash of password stored in the server, and you should make the system secure, even if the attacker compromises that server, steals the password authentication data, but you still prevent the attacker from impersonating users to that server. There are quite a lot of papers on that, but there's a logic problem. The attacker already compromises server, and now you want to prevent the attacker from impersonating users to a compromised server, that's one issue. A second issue is that it does not security assurance, because once the attacker has the hash of password then, in theory, he can get the pre image. So I don't quite agree the notion, server compromised, because it is not clear. It's a desirable property, but server compromise, the required property is not properly defined.

Bruce Christianson: There's an argument that says a good protocol forces you to use a strong password. But protocols like the one that you're describing are still very useful even when the password is strong.

Reply: Definitely, yes.

A Real World Application of Secure Multi-party Computations
(Duplicate Bridge for Cheapskates)

Matthew Johnson and Ralph Owen

University of Cambridge
matthew.johnson@cl.cam.ac.uk, rho21@cam.ac.uk

Abstract. This paper presents a use of secure multi-party computations in duplicate bridge. A two-person computation is performed by dealing cards in a specific permutation in order to create a deal which has been pre-determined by computer. Statistical analysis is used to demonstrate that little information about the resultant hands can be derived by the participants of the computation. Experimental evidence for failure-rates and time taken to perform the operation is also presented.

1 Duplicate Bridge

To turn bridge from a game involving a lot of chance into one of skill a duplication system is used such that at least two different sets of people play with identical cards. A pair's score is then not the number of points won or lost on that hand but the difference between their score and that of the other people playing with the same cards. Thus being dealt abstractly better cards does not automatically give a better result.

There are two schemes for achieving this. The naïve approach would be to create several decks of cards sorted identically. This can be avoided using a schedule of playing multiple hands in which each set of cards are passed round between the people playing them in order. Thus, a random deal can happen at the start of the night and as long as the hands are preserved between plays the duplication is achieved.

There are circumstances where this is still not sufficient. At very large events multiple people may be required to play the same hand simultaneously. For these the duplimate system was invented. All the decks of cards are marked with barcodes so that when fed into a duplimate machine it can deal them into the right hands automatically. A computer then randomly generates sets of cards for the duplimate machine to produce.

Aside from making it possible to run large events, having computer generated hands has a number of benefits which it would also be nice to have in smaller events. Computer generated hands tend to produce more random, and hence more interesting, arrangements of the cards. It is also the custom in clubs which can afford a duplimate machine to produce a record of the hands which can be taken away and studied later. Recently, this has also been accompanied by an

B. Christianson et al. (Eds.): Security Protocols 2008, LNCS 6615, pp. 180–190, 2011.

analysis of the hands giving the contracts it should be possible to make with those cards to aid the players' reviews. There are also some competitions in which the same boards are played in clubs across the country in order to get comparisons between the players in different clubs.

Generating random hands on a computer and generating records of the hands are both simple tasks. Even analysing hands for the best contract is a solved problem, with several pieces of commercial [1] and open source [10] software implementing it and some papers [2] writing about it.

Without a duplimate machine, however, turning these into hands which can be played with actual cards is a long, tedious affair, which necessitates the person creating the hands observing them in the process and hence not able to play them. While in large events the Tournament Director is not a player, in most clubs and smaller events they will be one of the players.

2   Multi-party Computations

Ultimately the root of multi-party computations can be seen in Diffie and Hellman's seminal work introducing public key cryptography [4]. It wasn't until 1979, however, that Shamir [11] introduced the original use of multi-party computations, that of secret sharing. The Shamir scheme divides a secret between several different people such that a minimum sized subset of them must perform a shared calculation to recover the original secret. This threshold scheme was created using interpolation over a prime field.

In 1982 Yao [12] presented a general solution for any m parties calculating any function f so that the input from each party is kept secret from the others. Yao's solution used public key cryptography. A similar result using zero-knowledge protocols was achieved by Goldreich et al [5] in 1987. These were confirmed with a stronger result by Chaum et al [3] in 1988. Chaum allows the participants secure communication channels and as such does not need to rely on the trapdoor functions used in the previous protocols. In practice such channels often exist.

These protocols are, however, not sufficient for the task of duplicating cards securely. They differ in two important respects. Firstly, the computation which is carried out by the parties typically requires a computer to perform whereas in this situation the players must be able to perform it manually.

Secondly, the aim of the protocols in the literature is to produce a public result based on secret information. Here the aim is to produce a secret result. Ordinarily the model of communication used between the players results in any intermediate state which is passed between participants being known to them, which means the final result is always known by at least the last participant.

However, because these operations are being performed manually on a deck of cards it is possible for participants to receive an input, perform an operation on it and send it to the next participant without being aware of any intermediate state, as long as the cards remain face down. Thus while the first participant may know the initial state (and hence the state after their operation) it is possible to produce a scheme in which the state produced by subsequent participants (and hence the result) is unknown to all of them.

This implies a certain level of trust in the participants not to cheat by looking at the cards as they are operating on them, however, this is a level of trust which is already present in many places throughout the game.

3   Faking Duplimate

A number of years ago the notion of dealing sheets was introduced by Handley [7]. These are an alternative to a thorough shuffle before dealing used by several people in Cambridge who find it difficult or tedious to perform a well-randomising shuffle. They work similarly to one time password systems.

The user is given a sheet with a number of permutations of the string $111...222$ $...333...444...$ which are used once and then crossed out. The permutation is used to deal out a pack of cards which has been given a superficial shuffle to place them in an unknown (but not statistically random) order. The first card from the deck is place in the pile corresponding to the first number in the permutation. The second card is placed in the pile corresponding to the second number, and so on.

Because the deal is following the (randomly generated and equiprobable) permutation and not being dealt in order as is usual the shuffle does not need to provide any statistical randomness. All that is required is that the deck is put into an unknown state to begin with.

This scheme is, however, only good for producing random deals, not pre-computed ones. What is needed is a way to put the deck into a starting position known by the computer and not by the person dealing according to the dealing sheet. At first glance this seems equivalent to our original problem, however, it is possible for the state of the deck to be known to a different player, since if they don't see the dealing sheet they cannot know how the final deal ends up.

This leads neatly onto multi-party computations. If performing a deal according to a dealing sheet is considered an encryption E under a key given by the dealing sheet k then the composition of two encryptions under different keys $\{\{d\}_{E_{k_1}}\}_{E_{k_2}}$ will result in a deal which is calculable given the original deck d, and the two keys k_1 and k_2, but completely unknown to anyone who knows only two of the three.

Thus, duplication of a pre-computed set of hands is possible without any of the human participants being able to calculate the hands.

3.1   Duplication Computation Protocol

The protocol for turning dealing sheets into a multi-party computation suitable for producing duplicated boards is as follows.

1. Generate a random permutation I.
2. Apply it to the sorted deck S to get a desired target hand $T = \{S\}_{E_I}$.
3. Discard I.
4. Generate a random permutation P_1 and give it to the first dealer.

5. Generate a permutation P_2 such that $T = \{\{S\}_{E_{P_1}}\}_{E_{P_2}}$ and give it to the second dealer.
6. The first dealer applies their permutation to the sorted deck and passes it to the second dealer.
7. The second dealer applies their permutation to the deck and puts the result into the board.

There are, however, a number of issues with the scheme which has just been described. Firstly there are issues with errors, error detection and error recovery. Because the calculations are performed by humans rather than computers there is a high chance of errors creeping in. Section 3.2 covers options for error detection and recovery and section 6 gives results from a test of the system in the field.

The other, more important, issue is that because the result of each permutation is not a randomly selected element of G_{52} there is still some information which may be learnt by the people performing the operations. An analysis of this along with solutions to, or at least ameliorations of, the problems follows in Section 4.

3.2 Error Detection and Recovery

It may be the case that error detection and recovery does not matter. If a fault occurs during the dealing the result will still be a good-quality random deal (modulo an incorrect number of cards in each pile, which can be rectified before any player looks at their cards). The only problem is that it won't match the hand record. If the number of these is sufficiently small then there may be no need to do anything further.

It may well be the case that more than this is required. For error detection there are two schemes which were trialled in this research. The simplest is for one of the players to have a record of what should be in each hand. After they have played each hand the four players at that table check the record against the actual hand to spot differences. This does not allow for any correction since the board has already been played, but small errors such as exchanging a card or a suit can be noted. The hand record can then be amended for these small errors in retrospect.

In the case of large errors where no simple correction to the hand record can be made, the hand record for that deal must just be marked invalid. Players can be given a list of deals for which the hand record is incorrect. For small rates of this sort of error this solution may be acceptable.

In cases where the hands need to be exact, for example with simultaneous pairs competitions where many clubs play the same hands, any necessary corrections must be made before the first deal. When manually creating the hands for this sort of event similar error detection is needed and for this a common solution is the use of curtain cards. These are a record of what each individual hand within a deal contains which are passed with the cards, one in each pocket of the board. Players at each round (or at least the first) verify that the contents of their hand matches the curtain card.

Curtain cards detect errors before the hand has been played, so correction is possible, but there are issues with leaking information. If two players report they have one incorrect card, it will be obvious to each of them where their incorrect card ends up. In some cases this will not matter, but in others it may change the result of the play.

A solution which doesn't have this problem, but does require a non-player, is to have all the deals checked by a non-player before the event starts. This is still not as tedious as the non-player manually arranging the hands (verifying them is faster than creating them) and all the dealing work can be done by players in parallel.

4   Statistical Analysis

This scheme is designed to provide security against accidental or casual storage of information from the deal, it is not meant to be secure against a serious or organised attack. Therefore, only simple attacks are considered in this paper, and it is assumed that the two parties in the computation will not collude and that they will only use information provided to them during the algorithm (and not cheat in other ways).

4.1   Suit of First Card Dealt

Problem. Consider the knowledge of the location of the first card dealt in the second operation (hereafter P_2).

The initial deck will always be sorted identically, by suits, so that the final 13 cards dealt in P_1 are always the clubs, say. However, the first card dealt in P_2 is the last card dealt to pile 1 in P_1, so this will always be a club, unless no clubs are dealt to pile 1 in P_1.

No club will be dealt to pile 1 in P_1 with probability

$$\Delta = (39/52 \cdot 38/51 \cdot \ldots \cdot 27/40) \approx 1.27\%.$$

This is, naturally, precisely the chance of holding a club void in a given hand. The problem is that even if the first card in P_2 isn't a club, the hand receiving it might get a club later in the deal.

Without inspection of when in the rest of P_2 cards are dealt to this same hand, the probability that this hand does not hold a club can be estimated as

$$\Delta \cdot (38/51 \cdot 37/50 \cdot \ldots \cdot 27/40) = \Delta^2 \cdot 4/3 \approx 0.022\%.$$

So the hand receiving the first card in P_2 is about 58 times less likely to hold a club void than the *a priori* odds.

Generalisation. The last card dealt from P_2 produces an equivalent effect with the suit at the other end of the initial sorting, say spades. Furthermore, the cards at the ends of each pile in P_1 (i.e. dealt in positions 13, 14, 26, 27, 39, 40 in P_2) will have the same effect in either spades or clubs. [The combined effect of looking at all of these at once goes beyond the scope of this paper.]

Lesser inferences can also be drawn from cards in other positions. The second card dealt, for example, provides a much milder implication that the hand it is dealt to does not hold a club void.

Solution. The most useful solution to this problem is to randomise the initial suit order. With this modification, a single card assignment only reveals that a given hand is less likely to hold a void in an unknown suit - entirely worthless.

Initial suit order security. The initial suit order can often be determined from a look at a hand in the order it was dealt.

Because in P_1 the suits are dealt in turn, the piles at the end of P_1 will be ordered according to the initial suit order. Thus a look at the order in which cards were dealt to a hand in P_2 is very likely to allow determination of the initial suit order, which undermines the solution to the previous problem.

As this is a sub-problem of the previous problem, there is only a security issue if the person who performed P_2 is first to see the hand in question. Whilst it could be secured by arranging that this doesn't happen, a simpler solution is to add a short shuffle after the hands are dealt.

Final thoughts. The combination of several card assignments still might give some information. If a player holds a void and received a card from one of the sets of positions $\{1, 14, 27, 40\}$ and $\{13, 26, 39, 52\}$ in P_2 (i.e. the ends of piles), they may be able to conclude that their void suit was less likely to have been at either end of the initial suit order, and so that any other hand receiving a card from the same set(s) of positions as them is less likely to hold a void in each of the suits they don't hold a void in. This is pretty tenuous, however, and unlikely to be relevant to the desired level of security. Anyway, it is relieved by the solution to the next problem.

4.2   Locating High Cards

Problem. The bottoms of the piles in P_1 will generally contain high cards in the suit first in the initial suit order.

If a hand is seen to receive all four of the cards from positions $\{13, 26, 39, 52\}$ in P_2, it is certain that this hand holds the Ace of this unknown suit, there is a $3/4$ chance that it holds the King of the same suit, a $3/4 \cdot 1/2 + 1/4 \cdot 3/4 = 9/16$ chance that it holds the Queen, etc. Although the suit is unknown, it may quickly become apparent during the bidding (as there are plenty of bids which show specific cards) or play (when another hand is visible on the table). Potential results of this include:

- During the bidding, guessing that a player's partner holds, for example, the Ace and King of a suit rather than just the Ace he has shown. This may allow a better contract to be reached.

– During the play, locating a missing high card. This is often extremely valuable in deciding how to play the cards, and may result in a contract making where it would have failed, for instance.

Of course, the same applies with the suit at the other end of the initial suit order, except that these reveal the position of low cards, which are much less likely to be valuable, especially when it is difficult to determine their suit.

Even if a hand receives fewer than all four of the cards from those positions, useful inferences can be taken, especially when holding some of the missing cards.

Solution. A first solution is to modify the number of cards dealt to each pile in P_1. This needs to be done such that the three end points in the middle of the pack are independent of each other in position. However, it is also valuable to avoid having too many cards in any one pile, as this will result in a far higher than usual number of consecutive cards in this pile, which may surprise the person performing P_1 and result in insecure comments about the strangeness of the deal.

In order to make three suitably independent positions, two random numbers (r_1 and r_2) are selected and used the pile sizes r_1, r_2, $26 - r_1$ and $26 - r_2$. This results in the piles ending at positions r_1, $r_1 + r_2$, $26 + r_2$ and 52. Using even distributions between 10 and 16 for r_1 and r_2 means each pile will have between 10 and 16 cards. The middle end point will be distributed around 26 with a stronger weighting at the centre, but the outer two end points will be uniformly distributed.

This means that the ends of the piles cannot be accurately predicted, with the exception of the cards in positions 1 and 52, so it is much harder to gain useful information here.

Remaining issues. Nonetheless, when missing only one high card, it seems plausible to take the inference that the person dealt the last card in P_2 holds it. With more high cards missing, it can be inferred that this person was dealt one of them, which alters the expected distribution and might be used to choose a better line of play. In any case, this is only likely to be valuable in a slam contract.

One solution to this would be to have the person who performed P_1 (or a third person) perform a defined permutation of the hands after the completion of P_2. This is not ideal as it adds a new source of error to the process, at a guess a comparatively large one.

Also, any suggestions for a better way of distributing the number of cards in the piles in P_1 would be useful.

4.3   Further Work

It would be interesting to perform a Monte Carlo simulation to attempt to spot further patterns in the distribution of cards as this might highlight new flaws in the scheme.

5   Pescetti

The system described in this paper has been implemented in the Pescetti Pseu-doDuplimate software [8]. Pescetti is written in Java and released under the terms of the GNU GPL version 2.

The heart of Pescetti is a random permutation generator based on Knuth's shuffle [9]. This takes an array of 52 elements containing the numbers 1 through 4. For each element it is swapped with a random other element in the array. The random numbers for this are generated by the built-in Java class SecureRandom. This produces a random permutation of the cards into four piles with statistically even likelihood of any particular distribution.

To generate the desired random deal a random permutation of 13 of each number is generated and this is applied to the sorted deck, generating a perfectly random deal. This is the target hand which the permutations have to generate.

As per Section 4.1 an initial permutation of the suits is randomly generated using the Knuth shuffle on an array of the four suits. This generates an initial start deck sorted within each suit, but with the suits in a random order.

Another complete permutation is then randomly generated using the Knuth shuffle. As per Section 4.2 this starts with not 13 of each number, but at random between 10 and 16 of each number. This permutation is given as the first permutation for the players to deal, along with the initial permutation of the suits.

This permutation is applied to the deck produced by the initial permutation of the suits to generate the intermediate deck between the two permutations. Pescetti iterates over the intermediate deck, looking up each card in the target deck to produce the second permutation.

Because the first permutation and the target hand are both independently random the second permutation is also independent of the resultant hand. Pescetti generates sheets containing the permutations to be dealt. Each page contains the first permutation for two deals and the second permutation for two deals. A corresponding page contains the opposite combination for those four deals. This allows two dealers to parallelise the production of the final boards.

Pescetti calls out to a double dummy solver written by Bo Haglund [6] to produce hand records containing double-dummy results.

6   Case Study

Pescetti was tested at the Cambridge University Bridge Club in two test periods, firstly in November 2007 and secondly January to March 2008. These trials were used to discover what problems there were with the human part of the system. and what improvements could be made.

6.1   Time

One of the pre-requisites of this system being acceptable is that it can be completed in a reasonable length of time. The two comparisons for this scheme are:

shuffling and dealing random boards with no hand record and manually arranging hands into a pre-dealt set of hands. The former is the normal operation for
any club without a duplimate machine and should be regarded as an ideal target
time. Taking longer may be acceptable given the extras which are provided by
this system. Getting close to that time would make it a plausible system for use
each week.

If the system takes too long for that, but is still faster than manually sorting
hands then it may still be usable on the occasions that this is required. There
is also the added improvement that a non-player is not required to setup the
boards.

Timing results. In the trial there were typically between two and four pairs
of people dealing the boards. Each had two or three sets of four boards to deal
between them for a total of around twenty four, depending on the movement
and number of pairs playing. The first couple of weeks took around twenty five
minutes, but this has reduced to around fifteen minutes fairly consistently.

This compares favourably to shuffling and dealing randomly. It is not as good
(typically around ten minutes to shuffle and deal), but most people do not spend
long enough shuffling the cards to get completely random hands.

At the end of the night every player was asked to sort one board which only
took a couple of minutes for the whole set to be sorted ready for dealing in
subsequent weeks.

For comparison it takes fifteen to twenty minutes to put a set of boards
through a mechanical duplimate machine. The method described here is therefore very similar in terms of time to other methods of computer dealing.

6.2   Error Rates

Since there are a number of failure modes which cannot be detected during the
dealing process some errors will be present in the final deal. High error rates will
diminish the usefulness of the process and therefore to be successful it needs to
be shown that they are sufficiently small.

Error results. For the first week curtain cards were provided for all the hands
and players asked to check the first time they were played. It proved impractical
to fix the errors during play and so for subsequent weeks they were checked by
the director as the boards passed his table.

The error rates did not decline through the first test period as hoped, ranging
from nine on the first night through to six on the final night out of twenty four
to twenty eight boards. However, it was observed that a number of the failures
coincided with certain people dealing them. On the one occasion where only two
pairs who were experience at using the dealing sheets produced the boards there
were only four errors. In the second test period there were generally between
two and four errors and on one occasion all the deals were perfect.

The errors varied from single cards or entire suits being swapped, through
multiple single-card mistakes to some hands where all or most of the cards were

Table 1. Errors in each session

Session	Failures	Recoverable Errors
14/03/08	1	3
07/03/08	2	3
22/02/08	0	0
15/02/08	2	2
07/02/08	3	4
31/02/08	4	2
30/11/07	5	2
16/11/07	7	1
01/11/07	4	1

incorrect. None of these can be corrected in play, but some are very easy to correct if a non-player with the desired hand records checks the hands. Table 1 gives a break-down by session of the recoverable and non-recoverable errors which were encountered.

Some of the dealing mistakes were caught during the dealing process and caused re-deals. This happened typically once or twice per week. In addition there was usually one board which was discovered at the start of play containing an incorrect number of cards in each hand. This could be discovered during dealing by counting the cards into each hand after dealing, but sorting and re-dealing is quite time consuming.

An interesting type of error is that when an entire suits is swapped. Caused by a failure in the initial ordering of the suits, these errors don't affect the analysis of the hands: the reader need just swap the analysis of the suits as well. It may affect calculation of par scores.

6.3   Further Work

The case study performed here was quite informal. A more rigorous and extensive trial would provide better evidence over the efficacy of this system.

Before the system could have widespread adoption there also needs to be a general acceptance of the security in the bridge playing community. Any further work in this area should consider ways in which it can be presented to the community at large.

7   Conclusion

This method of producing duplicated boards is at least partially successful. It does not take too long to be feasible and the error-rate is around 10–20%. For applications such as a club night which would otherwise just have random boards it does provide added value and better quality hands. With experience of those using the dealing system it should be possible to keep error rates in the 0–10% region.

In terms of security, the statistical analysis shows that the information leakage to the dealers is very small. It is unlikely that any of the dealers would be able to correlate the information they have without the aid of a computer in order to influence the game in anyway. Certainly it is secure against accidental discovery of information by an otherwise honest party, which is the main goal of this technique.

For applications where this is not feasible it would be possible to have the hands checked by a non-player before the game and re-deal those which fail. This is time consuming, but less than having non-players create all the hands from scratch (a process which is not error-free either). In the absence of a duplimate machine, this is the best available solution when all hands must be accurate.

Acknowledgements

The authors wish to thank all the members of the Cambridge University Bridge Club for their patience when trying out new dealing methods and for those who had useful comments about how to improve the system.

References

1. Bailey, W., Goldberg, E., Ford, B., Kucera, G.: Deep Finesse,
   http://www.deepfinesse.com/
2. Chang, M.S.: Building a Fast Double-Dummy Bridge Solver. Tech. Rep. TR1996-725, New York University Computer Science (August 1996),
   http://cs.nyu.edu/web/Research/TechReports/TR1996-725/TR1996-725.pdf
3. Chaum, D., Crépeau, C., Damgård, I.: Multiparty Unconditionally Secure Protocols. In: 20th Annual Symposium on Theory of Computing, pp. 11–19. ACM, New York (1988), http://portal.acm.org/citation.cfm?id=62214
4. Diffie, W., Hellman, M.E.: New Directions in Cryptography. IEEE Transactions on Information Theory IT-22(6), 644–654 (1976)
5. Goldriech, O., Micali, S., Wigderson, A.: How to Play Any Mental Game. In: 19th Annual Conference on Theory of Computing, pp. 218–219. ACM, New York (1987)
6. Haglund, B.: DDD, http://web.telia.com/~u88910365/
7. Handley, B.: Dealing Sheets. Personal Communication
8. Johnson, M.: Pescetti—Pseudo-Duplimate Generator,
   http://www.matthew.ath.cx/projects/pescetti/
9. Knuth, D.E.: The Art of Computer Programming. Seminumerical algorithms, vol. 2, ch. 3, pp. 124–125. Addison-Wesley, Reading (1969)
10. Richardson, B.: DDS, http://www.bridge-captain.com/downloadDD.html
11. Shamir, A.: How to Share a Secret. Communications of the ACM 22(11), 612–613 (1979), http://portal.acm.org/citation.cfm?id=359176
12. Yao, A.C.: Protocols for Secure Computation (extended abstract). In: 23rd Annual Symposium on Foundations of Computer Science, pp. 160–164. IEEE, Los Alamitos (1982)

A Real World Application of Secure Multi-party Computations
(Transcript of Discussion)

Matthew Johnson

University of Cambridge

We start with a deck of cards, which is sorted in order, in suits. Two dealers each get given a key, and these numbers here represent a series of piles, and the order into which they deal the cards into the piles. The sequence is randomly generated by the computer in advance. For the second dealer, there's another permutation that looks the same. This is also random, although it is actually a mapping between the intermediate state and the desired hand we need at the end. But since those are both randomly generated, it's also random. Each dealer only sees one of the keys.

For those people who don't know, bridge is a partnership trick taking game. You typically play with four people around a table, and the people opposite each other are playing together either to try and take a number of tricks they've contracted for, or to prevent the opposition from taking that many tricks. This obviously depends a lot on the cards that you're given, so in order to turn this into a game of skill rather than a game of chance, duplicate bridge was invented. In this form of the game you have more than one table of four players playing with these cards, and so instead of scoring the number of points you get to the number of tricks you take, you get some function of the difference between your score and the scores of people playing with exactly the same cards somewhere else. And in this way it turns into a game of skill.

Now obviously you need some way of having multiple hands the same. A simple way of doing this that doesn't require having multiple decks which are identical, is have a scheme of movement by which you have one copy of the boards, you deal them at the start, and you pass them around in order, and they're played by various people as they go round the room. However, for large events you can't do this because there's no scheme that works for that number of people without multiple decks of cards, and there are actually other reasons that you might want to have your cards generated in advance by computer. There are some forms of competition where everybody in the country plays the same sets of hands, which are sent in electronic form to the club in advance.

This paper presents a method by which you can produce hands which you've generated beforehand on a computer. Now there does already exist a way of doing this, the duplimate system[1] was invented for doing this, it involves a piece of hardware which can read the face of the cards (they actually have bar-codes written on them) and then put them into the correct pockets in the board for

---

[1] `http://www.duplimate.com/`

B. Christianson et al. (Eds.): Security Protocols 2008, LNCS 6615, pp. 191–197, 2011.
© Springer-Verlag Berlin Heidelberg 2011

you. These tend to cost several thousands pounds for the machine, even second-hand, so I developed this protocol for the University bridge club, which doesn't have thousands of pounds, in order to do this somewhat more cheaply.

The traditional multi-party protocols, which were introduced by Shamir and Yao, have a shared known result which we're generating, but the inputs from each person are secret, and the computations are done on a computer. However, here we're aiming for a result that is secret to the participants, we know what the inputs are because we know we're putting in a sorted deck in at the start, and the computations, such as they are, aren't performed by computer servers, so there's a large restriction on what you can actually do. The advantage that we have here is that the intermediate state, when it's passed between the two dealers, can be secret.

I should also comment here about the attacker model we're using. There are a lot of ways to cheat at this game, and if you just deal the hand randomly then obviously people can look at the cards. So we're going to assume for the moment that they aren't going to cheat in ways like that, because most players are inherently trustworthy. The problem is that the bridge players know enough about the game that if they get some small amount of information, even inadvertently, they can use this within the game.

So we want to ensure that neither of the two dealers having seen their keys can deduce much about the hands, even after they've seen one of them. They shouldn't be able to deduce any more than they would normally about the other three players at the table.

Frank Stajano: You say having seen one of the hands, but you weren't seeing anything when you did the shuffle were you?

Reply: I wasn't seeing anything then, but next I'm going to play the hand. When I pick up one of the hands I will gain some information about what's in that hand. If I can remember the key that I was given to deal from, and see one of the hands, that shouldn't allow me to deduce more information about the other players.

Frank Stajano: In terms of the modelling the attacker, would the attacker remember all these magic numbers and stuff?

Reply: We're assuming that they will be able to remember these. As I'll explain later, there are still some small things where you can say some of the probabilities will change slightly, but most of these require a computer to be able to work out, so we're not too worried about them. We assume that you won't be able to take this lot and run it through a computer. But any suggestions for enhancing the security that we get out of this are certainly very well accepted.

James Malcolm: Is this is only for the times when you're not playing the game remotely?

Reply: The assumption is that you're playing the game in person, you have actual cards, you want to sit down at a table with real people, and have cards which you can play normally. But for whatever reason you want the hands that you're playing to be predetermined by the computer, whether this is so that it matches what everybody else in the country is playing, or simply so that you can have interesting hands — maybe you want to have a night where all of the hands fit some sort of pattern — or just so you can have a copy afterwards that you can look at and say, you should have made ten tricks, you only took nine, maybe you should think about what you should have done differently.

James Malcolm: So it's a secure way of generating hands from a sorted deck.

Reply: It's a way of taking a sorted deck and producing the hands which are predetermined by the computer. The protocol you saw works like this: on the computer you generate a random permutation, and this is used to take the sorted deck and turn it into the target deck, this is basically a random deal. I was introduced to these permutations by Ian Jackson, who used them for people who find shuffling rather tedious. They use them essentially as a one-time pad, you have a sheet full of these, you give the pack a quick shuffle to an unknown state then follow the sheet and cross this off. That obviously isn't any good for producing anything other than random hands, because the initial shuffle means that you can't tell what state you're going to end up in. We generate a random permutation, which gives us the target hand PF that we want to get. Alternatively you can do something here to produce specific hands, or you can just load hands which you were given, but we generate random hands. So then we generate PI, which is the initial suit ordering, and a complete permutation, P1. Then you calculate P2, so that it is a mapping from the intermediate position given by encrypting PI under P1, to the desired target state. This is a fairly simple operation to do, but P2 will be random because both the intermediate and the target state are random. Then we give the first permutation to the first dealer, the second one to the second one, and then we have this operation you can see here. Obviously the two permutations do each need to be kept secret from the other dealer because if you can see the whole sequences it's possible to work out what the result is.

Frank Stajano: These permutations are a specific type of permutation, not the random permutation of any card from anywhere?

Reply: This looks like a very secure protocol, the reason it isn't is because actually these things are not randomly chosen elements from $^{52}P_{52}$, they are restricted in that we're going through the pile in order and dealing into four piles. So there will be some residual order from the original deck in the remaining piles.

Frank Stajano: So the question was, is it possible to reach any random permutation you can devise?

Reply: This protocol will allow you to produce any set of four hands, but it won't allow you to produce the contents of those hands in any order[2] and I shall talk next about some of the fixes we had to make to the protocol because of the obvious information that you could get.

---

[2] The first permutation can produce any four hands, each in canonically sorted order. Ironically, it is the need to use two successive random permutations that introduces the residual information problems.

George Danezis: A key point is that dealer 1 and dealer 2 are both going to play in the game?

Reply: Yes. If they aren't the obvious way of doing this is in one permutation, which is actually faster than sitting down to create all the decks by looking at the cards and putting them in the right place.

If we always start with the deck in the same order, say the last 13 cards that you deal will all be clubs, it's very likely that the last 13 numbers of permutation 2 will contain a number 1 at some point, and this means that the top card in the first pile is going to be a club, which means that the top card at the start of the second deal is also going to be club. Now because there is also the added probability of being dealt a club later in the deal, it turns out that the first hand you deal to from permutation 2 is 58 times less likely to have a club void than in a random deal. The obvious fix to this is to randomise the order that we start the suits in (which you say with the suit order permutation), because this now means that you know that there is a suit in which P2 doesn't have a void, which is self-evident, and not a useful piece of information any more, because you don't know what the suit is. Although there's a caveat that you have to shuffle the hands after dealing the second time, before putting them into the board, otherwise if the dealer plays that hand first, then from the order that they're in, the board will allow you to produce the original order.

George Danezis: So the inference in my mind is that the first permutation is done with the four piles, and that we all receive the same number of cards, is that right or not?

Reply: It changes the probability only slightly if you have a different number of cards in each pile.

George Danezis: But it's not a necessary condition because you are going to go through a second phase and balance the hands?

Reply: Correct, and actually to fix this problem I'm going to change that.

Bruce Christianson: You shuffle the hands at the end of the second permutation?

Frank Stajano: Because otherwise they can infer something from the order of the cards in their hand, you shuffle them before they see the hands.

Reply: Yes, sure, to pass the cards around you have what's called a board, which is essentially a plastic square thing with four holes in it, which you put the hands in and you give them to people to play, they play them, shuffle each hand separately, put them back again, and pass them around. So they are used to doing that shuffle.

OK, so regardless of what order the suits are in, the top card will be an Ace, and at the end of P1 this Ace is guaranteed to be on the bottom of one of the piles because it's dealt first: you don't know which pile but it will be on the bottom of one of them. This gives us four positions in the intermediate deck, one of which will contain an Ace. So if the second dealer looks at these four positions, and if they were all given to the same hand, you know that hand has an Ace, and in fact if any two are given to the same hand, then the probability has changed to the a priori one, that hand is more likely to hold an Ace. This result also holds for the other high cards although not as strongly because you have eight possible positions for the second card and so on. The solution is to not have 13 cards in each pile in the first permutation, because this isn't required. However if nearly everything is dealt to the same pile, then this doesn't alter the hands enough, you get too many long runs of consecutive cards and then the second dealer can infer that if their permutation also has long runs of consecutive cards that probably corresponds to actual card sequences. So we chose a range between 10 and 16 rather than fixing 13. There's still a certain probability distribution around the four points where the first card is likely to be dealt to, but it increases the numbers sufficiently that it's now unlikely to give you much utility.

We tried this out at the University club, we've been using it for the last two terms, I was particularly interested in not just the abstract security of the thing, but how well it worked in practice, what issues there are with it being dealt by humans, and there being possible errors in doing it, ways of recovery from it, and whether it is actually suitable, does it take too long. So we tried this out in two trials. There were three sessions in each trial. We tended to have around six dealers who would deal in pairs so they could each have the corresponding permutations for a set of boards and pass them between each other, separated into pairs. Generally it took between 10 and 15 minutes to deal around 28 boards, which is fairly comparable to how long it takes to shuffle and deal with that many people, and also the town club here has a duplimate machine and they say it takes about 20 minutes to put a full set of boards through, so it's fairly comparable to the other solutions. The observed error rate was higher than I would have liked, on only one occasion were all of the hands perfect, and there were generally between four and six boards with errors. Having said that, there did seem to be some correlation between some of the dealers and a large number of errors, so you could probably reduce this by some amount of training and some careful selection. And, as you'll see in a minute, some of these errors are not as severe as others.

Errors generally correspond to having cards swapped in the wrong positions, and that's a fairly common problem when doing this. One thing that people often get wrong is when you have to deal two cards off the same pile, do you do 1, 2, or do you just take two cards and put them straight down. Those errors are fairly easy to correct, either beforehand if it matters, or afterwards. Sometimes we get amusing errors such as entire suits being swapped, where they've got the initial permutation wrong, and actually this doesn't affect the analysis of the hand at all, you can just swap the suits around in the analysis as well.

Richard Clayton: Is it possible to do that without affecting the bidding?

Reply: It will affect bidding, so you can't compare it to other people playing who didn't swap, but if you look at an analysis showing how many tricks you should make in each suit, you can just swap those suits as well[3].

There are a few options for error detection correction. The first one is to ignore errors completely. Given that the alternative was to have a night where everything was randomly dealt anyway then — as long as the error rate isn't too

---

[3] Depending on what ended up as trumps.

high — that's probably acceptable. Sure on some of the boards your hand record afterwards would be incorrect, but the alternative to that is just not having one. And you will still get a good quality of randomness, even when it's gone wrong. An obvious improvement to this is to note which of the hands is wrong, and this is the solution we use at the University club. When I send out a copy of the results I note which few boards are incorrect and the rest are all fine. I have a copy of what hands should have been dealt, and after I've played them I will check to see whether they're correct. And unless you're playing in some sort of national duplicate where it matters exactly what the hands are, this system works very well.

If you do want to do correction, the system that's commonly used is curtain cards where you have a copy of every individual hand written down, and before people play them they check against the paper copy whether the actual cards match. The disadvantage with this is that correcting them generally leaks a lot of information: if two players say, oh, I've got this extra card and I don't have that missing card, and another player does have it, then after it's been fixed you know who now has the extra card that you had. For a small card this might not matter, but if it's the Ace of spades then it might make quite a difference to the play. Another option is having a non-player checking beforehand. Although if you have a non-player they could just sort all the cards out beforehand, this approach does allow some parallelisation, and verifying that a hand is correct does not take as long as sorting all of the cards out and putting them in the right place.

Richard Clayton: You check the hands before you play them, can you not check after you play them? Essentially what you then get is an incomplete movement, which you may get anyway.

Reply: Yes, one possibility is that for the first round some people didn't actually play the correct hands, but check them afterwards, make any appropriate corrections and then pass them on. Generally it's desirable to have a full movement because then everybody plays everybody else, and it's fully compared. But certainly you could have everybody check the board after the first round. Generally when most of the errors are single card swaps I tend to check them afterwards, update the hand records before sending them out, and then people, for the majority of hands, get the correct result.

There are some more things that would be useful to do in this area, the first one being more rigorous trials. I was trying to avoid disrupting the University club who had a lot of forbearance with me trying out these new crazy things anyway, but more rigorous trials collecting more specific data on how well people can manage to deal these things, timings and error rates, would improve this a lot. Another interesting thing would be to do some Monte Carlo simulations to try and see if there are any extra patterns coming up that we might not have noticed, which could leak information.

Finally, I recently discussed this with some people including Ian Jackson, who suggested that if we had a different primitive in the first permutation, that mixes the cards in a different fashion, this might provide better security. Obviously there's little that can be done in the second permutation because you do need to get them into the four piles, however, some sort of permutation which is designed to move large blocks of cards long distances might improve things somewhat.

So to finish off, we think the security is sufficient. There is not a lot that can be learnt by either dealer without a good deal of mathematical processing. Even then you're just altering some of the *a priori* probabilities by a small amount, which at high level play might make a difference, but generally speaking at club level isn't going to matter. It doesn't take too long. And whilst the error rate isn't zero, it's generally good enough, and there are ways that you can work around it.

Frank Stajano: With the parallelism you mentioned earlier, how do you ensure that the hands are identical at each table?

Reply: Yes, when you're comparing outcomes you do need the hands to be identical. Generally within one club you only need one copy of each hand, so even if it doesn't match what your ideal deal was, at least all your scoring works, it just wasn't the hand you thought you were going to have. Most clubs don't have multiple copies of the same hand, I will play the hand with my table, then I'll pass it to your table and you'll play it, and it will be the same cards.

Frank Stajano: So you mean the exact same cards are used again? Won't the other tables know what happened and play the same way again?

Reply: Yes, exactly the same. We don't mix the cards in the middle as we are playing them, when you play a card you put it down in front of you, and then afterwards you pick your cards up, you shuffle them, you put them back in the board, and they get to the next table in a sufficiently random order. The tables are a fair distance apart, you try not to look at them. There's quite a lot of trust in this game anyway.

Does anybody have any ideas of how to improve this, particularly any ideas of other mixing strategies we could use in the first half.

Richard Clayton: You could mix in some red cards and some blue cards, and then take out all the blue cards at the end and check that they're in the order that they should be.

Reply: OK, that would work.

Mark Lomas: It's not an improvement to the protocol, but can I recommend reading "The King of Clubs" by Agatha Christie, because in that story, Poirot is able to identify all the conspirators in a murder just because a bridge hand was misdealt.

Reply: Yes, I have read it although it was some time ago. Great, thank you.

Covert Communications Despite Traffic Data Retention

George Danezis

Microsoft Research,
Cambridge, UK
gdane@microsoft.com

Abstract. We show that Alice and Bob can communicate covertly and anonymously, despite Eve having access to the traffic data of most machines on the Internet. Our protocols take advantage of small amounts of shared state that exist in many TCP/IP stacks, and use them to construct a covert channel. Techniques inspired from Direct Sequence Spread Spectrum (DSSS) are used to make sure that the communication is covert and resistant to noise. We implement a prototype based on ICMP Echo (ping) to illustrate the practicality of our approach and discuss how a more complex protocol would modulate information through the use of TCP features to make communication detection very difficult. The feasibility of covert communications despite stringent traffic data retention, has far reaching policy consequences.

1 Introduction

This work contributes to the understanding of covert communications on deployed networks such as the Internet. We show that if any shared state can be accessed and influenced by two parties they can use it to communicate indirectly, making it hard for observers to correlate senders and receivers of messages. We also present a very common feature of the IP protocol [1,2], based on the IPID packet field, that can be used to implement such covert communications. As a result our scheme does not require a dedicated infrastructure (as mix networks do), but uses any of the large number of deployed machines to relay messages.

We further show that the 'noise' produced by other, innocuous users, can be used to enhance covertness — given the observer does not know the shared key it becomes difficult to assess whether there is a communication at all. To achieve this we are inspired by techniques close to DSSS, that allow for low power signals to be hidden and uncovered from high noise environment. Finally we note that our scheme allows for covert communication despite, even stringent, data retention. This is partly due to the low level mechanisms we rely on (raw IP packets) and the very low signal power that would require prolonged, very costly, observation to allow the identification of a communication.

We first introduce in Section 3 the requirements of a cover communication systems, and discuss why established technologies only partially satisfy them. In Section 4 we present the basic TCP/IP mechanisms on which we shall build two

B. Christianson et al. (Eds.): Security Protocols 2008, LNCS 6615, pp. 198–214, 2011.
© Springer-Verlag Berlin Heidelberg 2011

systems: a basic one based on ICMP Echo requests (Section 4.2) and a second, more covert one, based on TCP circuits (Section 4.3). We discuss extensions and open issues in Section 5 and present our conclusions in Section 6.

2   Background and Related Work

Covert and jamming resistant communications are a well studied discipline in the field of military and civilian radio communications. *Low probability of intercept and position fix* techniques like frequency hopping and Direct Sequence Spread Spectrum (DSSS) have been developed to force an adversary to spend a lot of power to jam a signal, as well as to hide altogether the existence of a communication from those that do not know a shared key [3]. Such technologies have been deployed in military tactical radios, but have also become part of civilian communications with frequency hopping being used in GSM phones, and CDMA (a variant of DSSS that uses orthogonal codes) being used in mobile communications and high-speed modems.

Yet relatively little attention has been directly payed to the *covertness* of communication in the context of the Internet. The field of anonymous communications, as started by David Chaum's [4] proposal for mixes and mix networks, attempts to provide unlinkability of senders and receiver. These anonymity properties fall short of full covertness, in that an observer is in a position to determine that some form of communication is taking place. Jamming resistance is also difficult to achieve, since the anonymous communication infrastructure in deployed systems [5,6,7], can easily be targeted and rendered inoperable by a powerful adversary. A peer-to-peer approach [8,9] to providing anonymity may change this, but so far no such system was found to provide strong anonymity properties.

Steganography [10], the embedding of ciphertext into innocuous data, also provides some form of covertness. An adversary observing a communication cannot determine its content with certainty, and messages can be transferred under the cover of 'normal' traffic. Yet steganography does not hide the acts of communication themselves, or the communicating parties. Therefore traffic analysis techniques that map social structures [11,12] to extract information would still be able to uncover information. Such techniques often ignore content and are unlikely (in the absence of cover traffic — which would bring us back to anonymous communications) to be affected by steganographic techniques.

Despite the little attention payed to covertness properties, traceability of communications has become a policy hot topic. National legislatures, often after terrorist incidents, have imposed 'traffic data retention' requirements on the telecommunications and Internet service provider industries [13,14,15], forcing them to log call, information access and location data (not content). At a European level EU Directive 2002/58/EC [16] (Directive on Privacy and Electronic Communications) and its December 2005 amendment [17] respectively allowing and making retention mandatory, replaced Dir. 1995/46/EC [18] (Data Protection Directive) and Dir. 97/66/EC [19] (Telecommunications Privacy Directive) that prohibited such practices. The granularity of the retained data is variable, and the directives and laws often refer to communications in an abstract manner to allow for technology independence. As a rule of thumb for this work we shall assume that everything that is routinely logged in deployed systems shall be available for inspection. This requirement is much more stringent than the most draconian data retention schemes proposed, that usually only require logging high (application) level communication events and user identification events (when the user is authenticating to an ISP). Relaxing the attacker models would make covert communication more efficient, yet the principles to achieve a secure scheme would be the same as presented in this paper.

There exist other, simpler, approaches to circumvent traffic data retention and achieve covert communications in practice. The simplest approach would be to use one of the many open relays documented in the SORBS list, for anti-spam purposes. These include SMTP (email) and SOCKS (any TCP stream) relays that would allow two parties to get in contact and talk. Another more ambitious solution would be to establish a bot-net, composed of many compromised machines, and deploy a parallel communication infrastructure that does not log anything. These solutions rely on the assumption that the relays are not observed by the adversary, which is most probably true. The solutions we propose on the other hand allow covert communication even when under some forms of surveillance. In this sense our techniques take advantage of the fundamental limits of traceability versus covertness, and raise significantly the cost of surveillance.

3   Covert Communication Requirements

Alice and Bob would like to communicate without Eve, the adversary, being able to observe them. They share a symmetric key K, unknown to Eve, and can use established cryptography techniques to protect the secrecy and integrity of exchanged messages. In addition to this they would like the mere act of communication to be unobservable to Eve: Eve should not learn that Alice or Bob are communicating with each other, or engaging in an act of covert communication.

Hiding the fact that Alice and Bob are communicating with each other could be achieved using anonymous communication protocols [4,6,5,7]. Yet these protocols (like encryption itself) are very easy to detect, therefore jeopardising covertness. They use standard handshakes, fixed message sizes and formats, a more or less fixed and public infrastructure. As a result, it is easy for Eve to determine that Alice and Bob (along with many others) are taking part in an anonymous communication protocol — which in many cases would give rise to suspicion. Due to their dependence on mixing infrastructure such systems may also be prone to legal compulsion (to log or reveal keys), targeted denial of service attacks or blocking.

The straight forward composition of steganography and anonymous communications comes also short of providing both anonymity and covertness. A message, that possibly contains steganographic embedded information, that is transported anonymously is already very suspicious, and a clear indication that the sender and the receiver (although not linked) are taking part in some covert communication. On the other hand a mere steganographic message might provide covertness of content, in that the true message is not revealed to Eve, but also provides a clear link between Alice and Bob.

We therefore propose that covert communication mechanisms should have certain characteristics.

Definition: *A covert communication system has to make use of unintended features of commonly used protocols, in a way that does not arise suspicion, in order to unobservably relay messages between two users.*

The use of common communication protocols is essential in not arousing suspicion, since any deviation from the norm may indicate an act of covert communication. The challenge is to find generic enough features of common protocols that allows messages to be relayed through third party machines. Any direct communication between Alice and Bob would create a link between them, that may in the eyes of Eve contain a covert channel or steganographically embedded information. On the other hand the use of an intended communication channel provided by a third party can be subject to logging and interception. As a result the only option for implementing covert communications is to use unintended features that allow relaying of messages. Furthermore these features should be exploitable without giving rise to suspicion to an observer (which again would jeopardize covertness).

Given all these requirements it is surprising that such features, not only exist in deployed communication protocols, but they are abundant.

The security of any covert communication scheme is dependent on the observation capabilities of the adversary. We wish to mostly consider an adversary that observes the world through retained traffic data. Furthermore, we would ideally want to provide security against a global passive observer, that has access to any information transiting on the network. We present a spectrum of systems, protecting Alice and Bob from an Eve with increasing surveillance capabilities. As we expect the more we bound and reduce Eve's capabilities the more efficient our systems can be, while still remaining covert.

There are also inherent advantages to finding and exploiting low level network mechanisms to provide covert communications. First low level mechanisms are likely to be used in a variety of ways, depending on the protocols that are stacked on them. This adds variance to the network behavior that would allow communications to be more effectively hidden. Secondly, low level mechanisms are also more abundant — more machines run vanilla TCP/IP than a particular version of a web-service. This allows for more choice when it comes to finding a relay, which in turn increases the cost of an adversary that has to observe all potential hosts for communication. Finally low level protocols produce high granularity traffic data, the storage of which is orders of magnitude more costly than storing high level network events — compare the cost of storing web access logs versus the cost of storing the header of every single IP packet traversing a network.

In the next sections we concentrate on a particular feature of many Internet Protocol (IP) implementations, namely sequential IPID values, that is low level and exhibits all the necessary characteristics to facilitate covert communications.

4   A Covert Communications System

Our key contribution is to show that there is a ubiquitous feature of deployed IP networks that allows for covert communication. The Internet is a collection of networks that 'talk' the same Internet Protocol (IP) [2] to exchange packets containing information. Each packet starts with a header that contains routing information, but also a special identification IPID field. The IPID field is 16 bits long, and is used to detect duplicate packets and perform fragmentation and reassembly of IP packets in the network. The creator of the IP packet sets its identification field to "a value that must be unique for that source-destination pair and protocol for the time the datagram will be active in the Internet system." [2]

Many deployed operating systems and TCP/IP stacks use a simple counter to set the value of the IPID field on outgoing packets. This feature has been used in the past to perform security sensitive monitoring in a manner of ways. Steven Bellovin uses the serial nature of the IPID field to monitor the number of different machines behind a Network Address Translation (NAT) gateway [20]. The IPID can be determined either by a global or a 'per-host' counter. The availability of some machines with global counter makes possible a techniques known as 'idle scan' or 'dump scan' [21], that determines which TCP [1] ports a machine is listening to, without sending any direct traffic to it. This technique is implemented in the Nmap [22] network scanner. Applications of serial IPID fields to remote monitoring and traffic analysis have also been proposed [23,24,25].

We are going to use the serial nature of IPID fields of many Internet connected computers in order to allow for covert communications. We explain how to implement covert communications using an intermediary that uses a global IPID counter.

Alice wants to talk to Bob, with whom she shares a key K, over an intermediary called Charlie. Charlie implements an IP stack that selects IPID values using a global counter. Note that if Alice an Bob can force Charlie to emit packets, and if they are able to observe any packet from charlie they will be able to communicate. More concretely, Alice will at each time $2t_i$ force Charlie to emit n packets, while Bob will observe a packet from Charlie at times $2t_i + 1$ to retrieve n. The number of packets n is the information that has been transferred between Alice and Bob. By repeating this process Alice can transmit to Bob arbitrary messages.

The first question that arises is: how can Alice and Bob force Charlie to emit packets, and receive packets from him. We shall present two ways in which this is possible based on ICMP Echo [26] and TCP [1], in subsections 4.2 and 4.3.

A second worry is that Charlie will also be generating traffic with third parties, incrementing the IPID counter, and adding noise to the observation of Bob. We note that this is a great opportunity for cover traffic: if Alice and Bob were the only parties that Bob would be receiving and sending information to, they may be linked easily by an observer. On the other hand if Charlie is engaging in multiple conversation, including with Alice and Bob, it is difficult for even a direct observer to establish who may be communicating with whom. Furthermore we shall make it difficult for other clients to establish that there is any signal in the IPID data, by using the shared key K to allow Alice and Bob to communicate over that noisy channel.

4.1   Transmission over a Noisy IPID Counter

Assume that Alice and Bob want to communicate the binary symbols $n_0 = 0$ or $n_1 = 1$, over the channel. They use their secret key K in order to produce two pseudo-random traffic patterns v_0 and v_1 of length l corresponding to each symbols n_0 and n_1 respectively:

$$v_{0i} = H(0, i, K), \forall i \in [0, l-1] \tag{1}$$
$$v_{1i} = H(1, i, K), \forall i \in [0, l-1] \tag{2}$$

We assume that H is a good hash function that takes bit strings and produces uniform values in the interval $[0, 2\mu]$. As a result each symbol is mapped into a traffic pattern, which is a sequence of l values in the interval $[0, 2\mu]$[1]. Alice sends in each round the number of packets specified in the sequence of the symbol she wishes to emit one value at each time period time. For example to transmit the string '0110', the sequence v_0, v_1, v_1, v_0 should transmitted, which would take $4 \cdot l$ time periods.

Bob observes packets from Charlie with IPID increments, from one time period to the next, of u_i for $i \in [0, l-1]$. How does Bob determine the symbol sent by Alice? Based on the knowledge of K, Bob can construct a filter to determine if the traffic pattern v_0 or v_1 is embedded in the noise. To differentiate between the two symbols Bob calculates the values r_0 and r_1, for each candidate symbol:

$$r_j = \sum_{i \in [0, l-1]} v_{ji} u_i, \quad j \in \{0, 1\} \tag{3}$$

The difference between the value of r associated with the correct symbol, versus the value of r associated with other symbols grows linearly with the length of l. It can be shown (full derivation in Appendix A) that, if the selection of traffic levels v follows a probability distribution D (in our example the uniform distribution $D = U(0, 2\mu)$), this difference is:

$$\mathbb{E}(\Delta r) = \mathbb{E}(r_{\text{correct}} - r_{\text{incorrect}}) = l \cdot \mathbb{V}(D) \tag{4}$$

---

[1] We will see that the hash function H should produce values indistinguishable from any distribution D, that is a good model of 'typical' traffic (given the information known to the adversary). The uniform distribution, used as an example here, is not such a distribution, and is therefore insecure against an adversary that logs ICMP Echo packets and events. Such events are considered too low level to be subject to retention at the moment.

The function $\mathbb{V}$ denotes the variance of the distribution D.

It is therefore clear that, if the key K is known, Bob can reconstruct the appropriate traffic patterns v to extract the correct symbols from the IPID in the long run, despite any noise. Furthermore by increasing the length l of the traffic pattern we can afford to keep the additional traffic injected by Alice low and make it difficult for an observer to detect that any communication is taking place.

Our results hold for any distribution D, and therefore we are also free to use a traffic distribution that looks realistic *i.e.* that mimics the characteristics of some type of innocuous traffic. In fact the covertness our this scheme depends on the adversary's ability to distinguish between the distribution D used and 'normal' traffic, not containing any covert information.

4.2   An ICMP Echo Realization

We have established that if Alice can force Charlie to emit any packets, and Bob can receive any packets from Charlie, Alice and Bob can communicate through Charlie using information encoded in the IPID field. The simplest way for Alice and Bob of achieving this is using the ICMP Echo [26] protocol, often referred to as 'ping', that must be implemented by a compliant TCP/IP stack (although some firewalls block it). ICMP Echo allows a host to send a packet to a destination address, which in turn echos it back to the original sender. Alice can therefore send 'ping' messages to force Charlie to increment his counter since responding increases the counter by one. Bob can use the same facility to receive messages from Charlie and determine the state of his IPID field.

This simple minded approach provides surprisingly good results, yet has some security shortcomings as we shall see. Figures 1, 2 and 3 illustrate a single run of our prototype in a low noise environment. For this experiment we used 30 second long traffic patterns of length 30 (which indicates a time interval of at which Bob must observe the counter of one second) from a uniform distribution $U(0, 100)$, to transmit one symbol out of an 8 bit alphabet.

We first collect the data sent by Alice (figure 1). This data is likely to contain some low frequency noise, that can be filtered out, since it is not likely to contain any useful information. To eliminate its effects we calculate the predictors r using a randomly generated traffic pattern, and use this as the baseline for detection (this is equivalent to subtracting from $r_{correct}$ a random $r_{incorrect}$ providing us the result we expected). The values of $r_{incorrect}$ for all times are shown in figure 2. Note some patterns emerging, that are due to the traffic patterns not being orthogonal. These might represent a security problem since they leak the message content and their regularity would leak the existence of a message. We shall discuss how to avoid them in the discussion section.

Finally we calculate values of r for three candidate symbols in figure 3. The value of r for 'H', 'E' and 'A' is denoted by '+', '*' and 'o' respectively. A spike detection filter is also applied. The transmitted string can easily be extracted by choosing the symbol with the highest peak at a 30 second interval. Furthermore

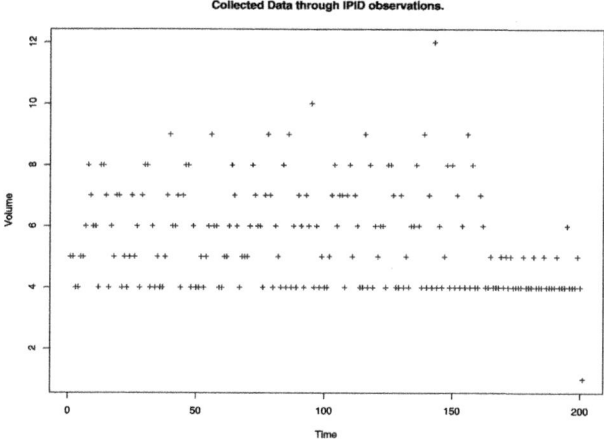

Fig. 1. Raw data as collected using the ICMP Echo method

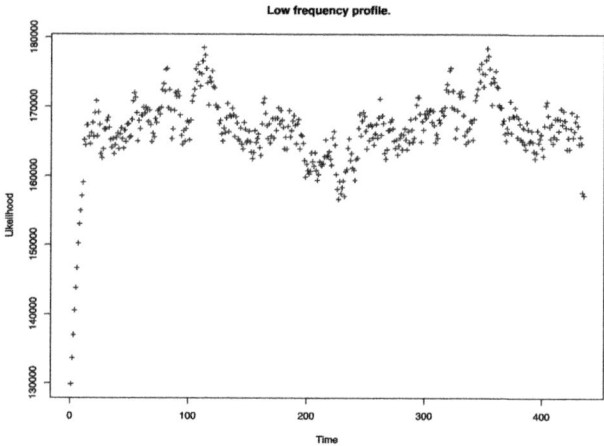

Fig. 2. The low frequency profile of the collected data

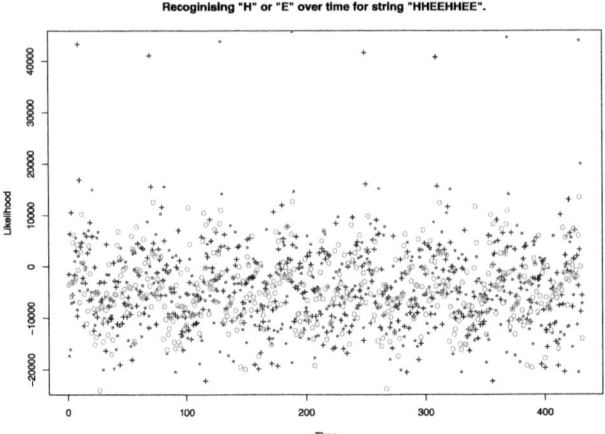

Fig. 3. Recognition of two different symbols

we can see that there is little danger of losing synchronization, as long as the difference between a correct and an incorrect symbol is large enough.

The key drawback of the ICMP Echo based technique is that large volumes of ICMP traffic from legitimate users is not common. Such traffic is often the precursor of an attack, and indicative of hostile intentions. As a result standard intrusion detection systems, such as SNORT [27] log information about high rate of ping packets. To keep under the radar of such detection systems we would need to limit ourselves to the transmission of a very low volume of ping packets in time. As a result the variance of the distribution D would be lower, and the rate at which we could transmit and correct for noise would be greatly reduced.

As a proof-of-concept ICMP Echo shows we can engineer covert communications using deployed mechanisms. Yet triggering intrusion detection systems, let alone provoking logging, is not compatible with our requirements for covertness, and the low rates that Alice would have to suffer to evade detection force us to look for a different solution.

4.3   A TCP Based Realization

The Transmission Control Protocol (TCP) [1], provides multiplexed, reliable and bidirectional stream communication between two Internet hosts. A session is established between two hosts using a 3 way handshake, and then further data can be exchanged in both directions between the hosts. TCP also provides facilities for rate and congestion control, that we shall make use to provide covert communications.

Two key concepts in TCP congestion control are *acknowledgments* and *windows*. Each TCP packet contains a serial number, and an acknowledgment number.

The acknowledgment number is set by the sender to be the serial number of the last TCP packet received, which is part of a continuous sequence from the beginning of the transmission. Conceptually this means that all previous packets, with smaller sequence number, have already been received. Packets that are not acknowledged are re-sent at intervals according to some set algorithms [28,29] (with exponential increase of the delay and linear reduction, to slow down when there is congestion).

Each host also provides a hint about the amount of data it can hold in its buffers at any time, which is called the window size, also included in each TCP packet sent. The window size indicates the maximum number of unacknowledged bytes that can be sent to that host. Using this mechanism the receiver has control over the rate at which data is reaching him or her.

Alice and Bob, that want to communicate covertly, can use the congestion control features of TCP to modulate a global IPID counter. To do this Alice establishes a TCP session with a third party, Charlie (that implements an IP stack with serial IPID values), and so does Bob. An HTTP (web) request would be perfectly adequate. During the setup of the TCP connection they both negotiate a suitably small maximal payload size (using the Maximum Segment Size option in TCP) to ensure that even if small amounts of data are transmitted many IP packets are generated. Alice can control the rate at which the intermediary's IPID counter is increased by modulating the window size, and by only acknowledging packets when more packet transmission is desirable. As a result Alice can lead Charlie to transmit a set number of packets pet unit time, and increase the IPID field by the amount dictated by the traffic pattern of the codeword she wishes to transmit. Bob on his side keeps the windows very small, and only acknowledges a packet at a time, forcing Charlie to only send one packet per unit time. This allows Bob to read Charlie's IPID counter contained in the TCP packet, without adding too much noise, and recovering the codeword embedded by Alice.

It is important to note that, even genuine, TCP traffic has quite a large variance, and as a result the information encoded by Alice can be extracted by Bob, despite shorter keywords and higher levels of traffic, without compromising covertness. The degree to which the TCP traffic characteristics have to perfectly match a typical TCP connection depends on the level of surveillance expected. In case each and every packet is logged, it would be important to stick to the degrees of freedom provided by standard TCP congestion control algorithms that regulate traffic. This should make cover traffic indistinguishable from 'normal' traffic, but would reduce the bandwidth of the channel — the only parameters of the traffic distribution that Alice could control are the random back-offs, simulated congestion in links, full buffers, *etc.* On the other hand if we only expect the connection establishment to be logged, and maybe even the content of the stream, but not the packets themselves, Alice can modulate at will all the window, acknowledgment and Maximum Segment Size parameters to maximize the bandwidth of the channel.

5   Evaluation and Discussion

So far we have provided an overall framework within which Alice and Bob can communicate covertly if they can modulate and read a shared counter. Yet, as for most real-world security systems, the devil is in the details, and a lot of details have to be carefully considered before such systems can be considered secure.

5.1   Auto-correlation and Synchronization

The first problem with our simple-minded traffic pattern design is illustrated in figure 2, where an adversary can observe a traffic pattern forming (the different parts of the message look the same). The reason for this is that we use the same traffic pattern to transmit the same symbol. As a result an adversary auto-correlating the traffic volume should be able to extract the full traffic code book, and recover (or at least detect) signal transmitted. The solution to this is to never use the same traffic pattern again. To do this we can include in the generation of the traffic pattern the time, or sequence number of the symbol (denoted t), and include this in the random generation of the traffic pattern for each symbol:

$$v_{0it} = H(0, i, t, K), \forall i \in [0, l-1] \tag{5}$$
$$v_{1it} = H(1, i, t, K), \forall i \in [0, l-1] \tag{6}$$

This means that 0s and 1s will be represented with different traffic patterns according to the time, or their position in the ciphertext.

The new approach for generating traffic patterns to encode symbols is secure, but imposes an additional requirement on Alice and Bob to have some way of synchronizing their clocks or their transmission. Off-the-shelf technology, like GPS, can make this easier, and even cruder Network Time (NTP) based protocols should be able to provide an appropriate time resolution to synchronize the traffic pattern code books. The design of self-synchronizing yet secure codes would be an interesting potential avenue of research, which is beyond the scope of this work.

5.2   Identification of Intermediate Hosts and Incentives

Alice and Bob need to find an intermediate host that implements its IPID using a global counter to be able to use our techniques. During our experiments we scanned our local sub-net (a /24 section of the global address space), and discovered 50 machines responding to ICMP Echo requests. Out of those about 30 used a counter to determine the IPID values of IP packet. About 5 of these used a global counter shared amongst all destinations, the others using only a per-destination counter. An estimate of one machine in ten exhibiting this feature gives hope that finding an appropriate host should not be too difficult.

The simplest approach would be for Alice and Bob to determine an appropriate host ahead of time, and use that for communication. This may not be possible, and they may need to determine a host 'on-the-fly'. A simple-minded approach would be for Alice and Bob to seed a random number generator using their shared key K and test random Internet hosts until they find the first one that exhibits the right characteristics. The number of hosts that they will have to try follows a geometric distribution, and if one in ten hosts is appropriate, then we expect about ten hosts to be tested before finding a good one.

Sadly the simple-minded approach described above is not very covert. In case the adversary controls even a small fraction of the Internet she will be able to observe two parties attempting to connect to the controlled hosts simultaneously. The probability this happens repeatedly becomes quickly very small (the probability of Alice and Bob both accessing l random hosts by chance becomes $\mathcal{O}(2^{-32 \cdot (l-1)})$), and after even two observations the adversary can determine that Alice and Bob are trying to find a good relay to talk to each other. This is far from being merely a theoretical threat: large organizations control class A IP address spaces (including MIT and IBM) and large portions of unused address space is connected to Honey Nets [30] to detect automatic scanners — these real world entities and projects would most definitely detect Alice and Bob.

Strategies to avoid detection while identifying appropriate intermediaries would have to masquerade, once again, as legitimate traffic patterns. This might include a random query to a search engine for a relatively common term, and then using the shared key to select candidate hosts from the retrieved results. Alice and Bob selecting hosts using a random (but popular) walk over web-sites may also decrease the likelihood of suspicion or interception.

It is worth noting that unless a host in controlled by the adversary it has very few incentives to stop providing a service as an intermediary. No security properties of the intermediary host are affected at all by our scheme. Alice and Bob communicating, particularly under low noise conditions, is only imposing a very small burden (a few packets a second) — hardly noticeable for current networking infrastructures. Logging such activity in comparison would be much more expensive than bearing the cost of the transmission, and changing operating system or applying a patch that changes the IPID behavior would not be worth the inconvenience. As a result we do not expect this behavior to change any time soon.

5.3   Reducing Noise and Adaptive Codes

It is clear from our constructions that both Alice and Bob can affect Charlie's IPID counter, and they can both observe it. This can prove invaluable for Alice as she can determine the amount of noise present on Charlie and adjust the 'traffic strength' she uses to encode its symbols accordingly. This would involve applying a set multiplicative factor to all the traffic patterns she induces so that they are still detectable despite the noise.

Since she is receiving feedback, to the same degree as Bob, she can also assess whether the pattern induced are easily detectable and vary their lengths accordingly. This approach favors covertness, since the traffic strength induced can be used by an adversary to detect the covert communication.

More efficient coding techniques may be developed to take into account all the information that Alice and Bob are aware off, that will be undoubtedly more efficient than our simple minded scheme. These are beyond the scope of this work. At the same time our scheme has the advantage that it allows for very simple interactions, where Alice induces the increase of Charlie's counter, and Bob only observes it, to be turned into a full covert communication medium.

5.4   One-Sided Covertness and Firewall Piercing

There is a body of literature concerned with censorship resistance [31,32], and in particular communication across a filtering firewall, that has a particular type of covertness requirement. In this setting only one partner needs to remain hidden, the one inside the firewall, and has to acquire a small amount of information to communicate with the outside world. This information is usually a 'fresh' address for an anonymizing proxy through which further unfiltered communication is possible. This can be compared to a 'bootstrapping' problem for censorship resistant technologies.

We note that our approach would be extremely effective in providing such information through the firewall. Bob, who is inside the firewall, chooses hosts outside in a pseudo-random way, according to some pre-determined key, until an appropriate host is found to allow for covert communication. Then Alice sends a small message (about 32 bits) that is the fresh address of a proxy, that is not yet on the blacklist of the firewall. Bob retrieves the fresh address and can communicate further through the proxy.

In this scenario we can optimize considerably our algorithms without fear of compromise, since both Alice and Charlie are on the trusted side of the firewall, and not subject to surveillance. The advantage that the covert communication protocol offers to Alice is the ability to modulate the network address that Bob has to access, so that the firewall cannot block the initial communication.

5.5   High Level Events and Counters

For most of this work we have concentrated on low level events, since they are unlikely to be the subject of logging and traffic data retention. Yet our techniques maintain some covertness despite observation and logging (as long as the traffic distribution that carries the covert message is indistinguishable from genuine traffic). We can therefore consider using high level protocols to communicate covertly.

The first approach is to use high level events to increment the IPID counter, instead of low level ICMP Echo packets or TCP features. In this case Alice and Bob find a suitable Web Server, with a global counter determining the IPID, and simply perform a set of web requests, according to a common distribution sampled using a pseudo-random number generator seeded with their shared key. This will result in the IPID counter increasing, and (in the long run) information flowing from Alice to Bob.

A second possibility is to ignore altogether low level counters such as IPIDs and only use high level counters such as counters measuring the number of accesses to particular web pages, that many web-sites incorporate. It is clear that

Alice can influence the counter (by performing requests) and Bob can simply read it, and as a result covert communication is possible. Shared counters can also be found in abundance in on-line multi-player games. All the same algorithms for transmission and error correction would also apply to these cases.

6   Conclusions

We have shown that covert communications, that allow Alice and Bob to communicate indirectly and covertly are possible despite widespread traffic data, or even content retention. The bit rates we achieved easily with our prototypes are of the order of 16 bits a second, but can be effortlessly increased using more symbols of the same length. We expect a mature covert communication system to be able to carry a few hundred characters in a few seconds, an amount comparable to contemporary text messaging on mobile phones.

The covertness properties we provide are based on a key assumption: that Alice and Bob are able to generate traffic out of a distribution that looks realistic to the adversary. Very much like steganography and steganalysis relies on very good models of what images 'look like', it is likely that the field of covert communications on the Internet will have to spend more time studying traffic models, and finding efficient ways to tell apart real and synthetic traffic. Such models exist, in the network measurements literature, but have not been designed or used for such security purposes yet.

The model of the world of that adversary is crucially linked to the amount and kind of traffic data retained — the less data, the more uncertainty the adversary will have about the true distribution of the traffic, and higher rate covert communications are possible. If all data transiting in the network are available, then the inherent uncertainty of network traffic behavior can still be used to achieve low rate covert communications. Widening the traffic data to be retained would, of course, considerably raise the cost of the retention scheme.

Finally we can only hope that this study informs the debate about traffic data retention, as to its effectiveness in tracing determined adversaries that wish to communicate covertly. Many simple 'hacks' are possible to evade proposed retention, yet we have demonstrated that there are fundamental limits to the ability to trace, and well grounded ways to evade it. Widening the net of retention to detect those would require logging at the IP level, with limited success, which would make the policy even more expensive, for even lower returns in terms of intelligence product.

Acknowledgments

Many thanks to Nick Feamster for suggesting having a look at the IPID mechanisms in IP. Klaus Kursawe suggested using shared state in on-line games for covert communications. Richard Clayton has provided valuable early feedback.

References

1. Postel, J.: Transmission Control Protocol. RFC 793 (Standard) (1981) Updated by RFC 3168
2. Postel, J.: Internet Protocol. RFC 791 (Standard) (1981) Updated by RFC 1349
3. Anderson, R.: Security engineering. Wiley, Chichester (2001)
4. Chaum, D.: Untraceable electronic mail, return addresses, and digital pseudonyms. Communications of the ACM 24(2), 84–88 (1981)
5. Danezis, G., Dingledine, R., Mathewson, N.: Mixminion: Design of a Type III Anonymous Remailer Protocol. In: IEEE Symposium on Security and Privacy, Berkeley, CA (2003)
6. Moeller, U., Cottrell, L., Palfrader, P., Sassaman, L.: Mixmaster protocol version 2. Technical report, Network Working Group (2004) (Internet-Draft)
7. Dingledine, R., Mathewson, N., Syverson, P.: Tor: The second-generation onion router. In: Proceedings of the 13th USENIX Security Symposium (2004)
8. Freedman, M.J., Morris, R.: Tarzan: A peer-to-peer anonymizing network layer. In: Atluri, V. (ed.) ACM Conference on Computer and Communications Security (CCS 2002), pp. 193–206. ACM, Washington, DC (2002)
9. Rennhard, M., Plattner, B.: Introducing MorphMix: Peer-to-Peer based Anonymous Internet Usage with Collusion Detection. In: Workshop on Privacy in the Electronic Society (WPES 2002), Washington, DC, USA (2002)
10. Anderson, R.J.: Stretching the limits of steganography. In: Anderson, R. (ed.) IH 1996. LNCS, vol. 1174, pp. 39–48. Springer, Heidelberg (1996)
11. Sparrow, M.K.: The application of network analysis to criminal intelligence: An assessment of the prospects. Social Networks (13) (1991)
12. Klerks, P.: The network paradigm applied to criminal organisations. Connections 24(3) (2001)
13. Center, E.P.I.: Data retention (2006), http://www.epic.org/privacy/intl/data_retention.html
14. International, P.: Data retention (2006), http://www.privacyinternational.org/category/free-tags/data-retention
15. Observatory, S.: The surveillance of telecommunications in the eu (2006), http://www.statewatch.org/eu-data-retention.htm
16. Directive on privacy and electronic communications (2002/58/EC). Official Journal of the European Communities (2002)
17. Final data retention directive (COM(2005) 438 Final). Commission of the European Communities (2005)
18. Data protection directive (1995/46/EC). Official Journal of the European Communities (1995)
19. The data protection telecommunications directive (1997/66/EC). Official Journal of the European Communities (1997)
20. Bellovin, S.M.: A technique for counting natted hosts. In: Internet Measurement Workshop, pp. 267–272. ACM, New York (2002)
21. "antirez" Sanfilippo, S.: Dumbscan. Personal communication (1998), http://www.kyuzz.org/antirez/papers/dumbscan.html
22. Fyodor: (Nmap – free security scanner for network exploitation and security audit.), http://www.insecure.org/nmap/
23. "antirez" Sanfilippo, S.: about the ip header id. Personal communication (1998), http://www.kyuzz.org/antirez/papers/ipid.html

24. "antirez" Sanfilippo, S.: How to learn firewalling relations using the ip id increment. Personal communication (1999), http://www.kyuzz.org/antirez/papers/moreipid.html
25. Paxson, V.: About the ip header id. Personal communication (1998), http://www.kyuzz.org/antirez/papers/ipid.html
26. Postel, J.: Internet Control Message Protocol. RFC 792 (Standard) (1981) Updated by RFC 950
27. team, S.: (Snort) http://www.snort.org/
28. Braden, R.: Requirements for Internet Hosts - Communication Layers. RFC 1122 (Standard) (1989) Updated by RFC 1349
29. Floyd, S., Henderson, T.: The NewReno Modification to TCP's Fast Recovery Algorithm. RFC 2582 (Experimental) (1999) Obsoleted by RFC 3782
30. Sudaharan, S., Dhammalapati, S., Rai, S., Wijesekera, D.: Honeynet clusters as an early warning system for production networks. In: Fernández-Medina, E., Hernández, J.C., García, L.J. (eds.) WOSIS, pp. 77–83. INSTICC Press (2005)
31. Feamster, N., Balazinska, M., Harfst, G., Balakrishnan, H., Karger, D.: Infranet: Circumventing web censorship and surveillance. In: Proceedings of the 11th USENIX Security Symposium (2002)
32. Köpsell, S., Hilling, U.: How to achieve blocking resistance for existing systems enabling anonymous web surfing. In: Proceedings of the Workshop on Privacy in the Electronic Society (WPES 2004), Washington, DC, USA (2004)

A   Derivations

Here we prove that we can efficiently extract the symbols transmitted over a noisy IPID counter (equation 4). We have defined the values r as:

$$r_j = \sum_{i \in [0, l-1]} v_{ji} u_i, \quad j \in 0, 1 \tag{7}$$

The variable v denotes Bob's guess about the traffic pattern used by Alice, and the variable u the traffic pattern observed by Bob. We assume that Bob's observation contains some noise at each time $i \in [0, l-1]$ denoted n_i^*. So we can rewrite $u_i = s_i + n_i^*$, where s_i is the hidden traffic pattern actually used by Alice, and n_i^* is the noise.

We want to calculate how well r differentiates between correct symbols, and incorrect symbols. Therefore we define $r_{\text{correct}} = r_j$ if $v_j = s_i$ (meaning the equality of the traffic patterns), and $r_{\text{incorrect}} = r_j$ if $v_j \neq s_i$ (meaning the Independence of symbols at each time i).

We now calculate the expected value for r_{correct} (we use extensively the linearity of a distribution's expectation $\mathbb{E}$).

$$\mathbb{E}(r | n_i^*, \forall i.v_j i = s_i) = \mathbb{E}\left(\sum_{i \in [0, l-1]} v_{ji} u_i | n_i^*, \forall i.v_j i = s_i \right) \tag{8}$$

$$= \mathbb{E}\left(\sum_{i \in [0, l-1]} v_{ji}(s_i + n_i^*) | n_i^*, \forall i.v_j i = s_i \right) \tag{9}$$

$$= \sum_{i \in [0, l-1]} \mathbb{E}(v_{ji}(s_i + n_i^*) | n_i^*, \forall i.v_j i = s_i) \tag{10}$$

$$= l(\mathbb{E}(v_{ji} s_i | n_i^*, \forall i.v_j i = s_i) + \mathbb{E}(v_{ji} n_i^* | n_i^*, \forall i.v_j i = s_i)) \tag{11}$$

$$= l(\mathbb{E}(v_{ji}^2) + \mathbb{E}(v_{ji}) n_i^*) \tag{12}$$

Similarly for $r_{\text{incorrect}}$:

$$\mathbb{E}(r | n_i^*) = \sum_{i \in [0, l-1]} \mathbb{E}(v_{ji}(s_i + n_i^*) | n_i^*) \tag{13}$$

$$= l(\mathbb{E}(v_{ji} s_i | n_i^*, \forall i.v_j i = s_i) + \mathbb{E}(v_{ji} n_i^* | n_i^*, \forall i.v_j i = s_i)) \tag{14}$$

$$= l(\mathbb{E}(v_{ji})^2 + \mathbb{E}(v_{ji}) n_i^*) \tag{15}$$

From the above two expressions we can show equation 4:

$$\mathbb{E}(\Delta r) = \mathbb{E}(r_{\text{correct}} - r_{\text{incorrect}}) \tag{16}$$

$$= l(\mathbb{E}(v_{ji}^2) + \mathbb{E}(v_{ji})\mathbb{E}(n_i^*)) - l(\mathbb{E}(v_{ji})^2 + \mathbb{E}(v_{ji})\mathbb{E}(n_i^*)) \tag{17}$$

$$= l(\mathbb{E}(v_{ji}^2) - \mathbb{E}(v_{ji})^2) \tag{18}$$

$$= l\mathbb{V}(v_{ji}) \tag{19}$$

Covert Communications Despite Traffic Data Retention
(Transcript of Discussion)

George Danezis

Microsoft Research

Frank Stajano: You're making a hierarchy where the adversaries can do less and less to snoop on everything. You can have another classification where they can still do everything, but just more and more localised.

Reply: Yes indeed, and I think in realistic scenarios, given the traffic data legislation, this is the case. This legislation works at a national level, or at a European level, or at a US/European level, yes.

Richard Clayton: In Denmark they thought it would be a jolly good idea to meet all their data retention requirements by doing sampling: running sampled netflows on their main Internet exchange, then keeping those ones for six months.

Reply: OK, it can be geographically located, and you get all the data within a geographic location, or you get a sample from a wider set. We will see that the protocols actually degrade gracefully, with the more information the adversary has. The objective of the adversary will be to use these logs in order to distinguish between a normal communication, and a not so normal communication. The less information they have about what's going on, the more difficult this process effectively is, because some information is totally invisible, and the rest of the information might be giving a misleading idea. We are trying actually to provide security for covert communications, despite everything being logged at the limit, but of course that will make the situation quite inefficient, and the secure communication rates will be quite low.

The key thesis of this paper is that covertness is possible. It is possible to achieve covert communications, even if everything is logged in the network, but there are some conditions that have to be met. And luckily many of these conditions are actually met in today's information networks.

There is a relation between covertness and censorship resistance. Alice and Bob want to communicate, but Alice is behind a firewall, and the firewall maintains a list of proxies that Alice may be using in order to access Bob. Bob is of course blocked, and all these proxies are blocked. So how is it possible for Alice to find the address of the fresh proxy that she could use in order to communicate to Bob? It's an interesting problem, because you only need to transmit to Alice a very small amount of information, effectively 32 bits, an IP address, that she will then be able to use as a proxy to break out of the firewall into the open Internet, and communicate with Bob. And if you think about it, the covert communication solution is quite applicable here, because Alice and Bob can share a key, and then Alice inside the firewall, and Bob, somehow have to use this key in order to choose a common service that is outside (this is not a proxy, this is just

B. Christianson et al. (Eds.): Security Protocols 2008, LNCS 6615, pp. 215–219, 2011.

a service that allows them to communicate covertly). Then they modulate their communication in order for Bob to transmit to Alice these 32 bits, that Alice can then use as a proxy to achieve high bandwidth communication to bypass the firewall. And covertness here is key, because you don't want the firewall to be able to block this communication just because it has certain characteristics.

Frank Stajano: In this situation, you are using your trick to get through the firewall. Are you still covert once you talk to the proxy, or are you giving away the fact that you and Bob are talking to one another?

Reply: That's a very good question, that is beyond the end of the protocol here. In the case of Tor, the adversary model is very specific that you will be discovering proxies, and then it will take some amount of time for these proxies to be blocked. So effectively you get a fresh address through some covert communication, or some other medium, and then you use that address, and eventually get discovered and blocked, and then you need a fresh one again, and this game continues.

Frank Stajano: That's the game for the availability, not the game for not going to jail.

Reply: Yes, sometimes you will end up in jail, and that's OK.

Steven Murdoch: Also Tor traffic as of version 0.2 looks very much like SSL, not perfect, but a lot closer than it used to be.

Reply: The content, yes, the timing of course might not.

I hope I have convinced you that even if the adversary sees every single packet in the network, it is still possible to convey some information from Alice to Bob if they're collaborating, without the adversary being able to tell the difference from innocuous communications with a third party. Now this is very inefficient, I have a demo that transmits about five to twelve bits a second from Alice to Bob, using our old secretary's printer as a medium. The printer has this feature of these IPID fields being just a counter, and therefore I was able to communicate through it at a very low rate. Now this is already quite dangerous if we're talking about trying to deny communications to groups like terrorists, because you can send an SMS sized message in a few minutes, which could be enough to wake up a sleeper cell to perform an operation, or something like that. So the prospects of denying communication to motivated groups that only need very low bandwidth communications to coordinate, is pretty bleak under these circumstances. Even more bleak is trying to deny the ability to have covert communications if you don't log everything, because if the logging happens at a particular granularity the adversary will always have the ability to communicate just below that granularity, where there is effectively no logging, and to use high bandwidth channels at that level in order to communicate. The thing that makes it slightly more difficult is that these high bandwidth channels will also have to be able to modulate some shared resource that is not logged, and so forth, in order to achieve both anonymous and covert communication.

Ross Anderson: So long as the communications content isn't logged that gives you the big bandwidth opportunity. You can find a remote resource, and the state can be modulated by your message content.

Reply: Yes, indeed, and I think that the mind twist here is that you need both: you need both a communication channel that is high bandwidth, but you also need a shared resource that you can modulate at a high bandwidth. I think the second part is slightly harder than the first, because of course you can send a lot of TCP packets, or IP packets, that are not logged, except if you trigger some IDS system, but for them actually to have an effect that is plausible on the third party service that can then be read is not a trivial matter, I couldn't think of many such resources.

So to some extent traffic data retention is effective in denying communications between wicked people and good people if the wicked don't want to be traced. The second thing is that the more stringent the regime the lower the bit rates, and that by itself I think is of some value to law enforcement: to effectively reduce the bandwidth at which wicked people can talk with each other can be seen as already a small victory. And the main reason why all of this research is totally pointless is, that there are so many better ad hoc ways to achieve covert communications using compromised machines, and so forth, on the Internet. So if you assume that the bad guys are bad, and they're happy to do things that are illegal, it is so much easier to just, as well as doing drug trafficking or terrorism, do some computer crime in order to achieve covert communication.

Frank Stajano: I really liked the slide that you had quite a bit earlier, where you were listing things like anonymity, and then steganography, and all that stuff. The problem that you pose, I think, seems to me solved by the combination of two things that you had on those slides. One is the steganography, and one is breaking it up, not talking directly from one to the other. But once you do that you have so many possibilities that are open which you haven't all described (it would be impossible to describe them all) and which don't have to involve doing illegal things: it could just be posting to Usenet and doing something very innocuous like reading a certain Usenet group that everybody reads, like `alt.sex`, and how could you stop people from doing that?

Reply: I think that the Usenet example is the typical one, because it falls exactly in this framework that I said. You have a high bandwidth channel to it that you can plausibly use, and that you can embed information within, and you have a shared state, which is the Usenet server that is effectively a huge bulletin board.

Frank Stanjano: So long as the co-conspirators are happy to go to a lower bandwidth, there's no way you can stop them, because they can always embed something with higher steganography and more noise.

Virgil Gligor: What about false positives on covert communications? Suppose that Alice and Bob don't know each other, and they happen to use the same service. They would appear to actually use covert communication with each other.

Reply: Yes, and this is key to achieving true anonymity with covertness, because if we see only Alice and Bob communicating with the service, and Alice and Bob want to talk to each other, then it might be possible for an adversary observing this to gain some evidence that Alice might be talking with Bob. But if also Charlie and Deborah, and all these other people, are also interacting with this service, then it is much more difficult to draw this inference.

Virgil Gligor: Yes, that's true, but actually my point is different. Suppose that only Alice and Bob use the service and they don't know each other, here they could be communicating.

Reply: To a third party, yes.

Virgil Gligor: If you look at work done on auditing the use of covert channels since 1990, you'll find that this is a common case. Even if you identify all the variables in the shared service which could be used as channels, you'll never know which channel Alice and Bob actually used, because there are multiple sets of variables. Sure, there is communication, there is information passed, but you won't know on which variable it was done. So the upshot is that it's extremely difficult to figure out covert communication between Alice and Bob using a shared service.

Reply: Extremely difficult, yes. Probably I have restated several things that were previously invented, and investigated in secure multi-level systems.

Virgil Gligor: Right, but the reason that was done was because there was a requirement at that time that use of covert channels above a certain number of bits per second should be audited, so people were trying to see what you can get out of audit trails. And it turns out that it is very difficult to tell which channel Alice and Bob are using, if any. Yet even when they didn't know each other, when in fact there was no deliberate covert communications, covert communications still appeared in the log.

Reply: There was still a leakage of information, yes.

Mark Lomas: You realise it's possible for Alice to communicate with Bob, even if Bob never uses the shared service. I use Google Alert to look out for things that may be of interest to me, for instance one of the terms I've set up is data protection, so if Google ever adds something to its index to do with data protection then I get an alert. Let's imagine that you want to communicate with me covertly, and we've agreed in advance to use Google Alerts to look up data protection. You now go to any old website, one that I never visit, and you insert your message, but you embed the term data protection within it. When Google finds it, it tells me, and since there are thousands of people who legitimately ask to have those messages delivered, nobody by analysing will have any idea that I deliberately targeted that message.

Reply: I think this particular proposal is very interesting, because it effectively creates a kind of two-hop anonymisation network. What we have been discussing here is a single service acting as a wall between Alice and Bob, not to be seen to be communicating, but here I think there are two hops, because Alice is talking first to a website, let's say changing a page to create an index term, and then Google looks at this website and grabs that information, and then Google sends the email to Bob, who finally receives the message. So you have two intermediary services working together to disentangle this communication.

Mark Lomas: The reason that I think that's a good approach is this. Let's imagine that the authorities do suspect Alice, and they've been monitoring her very carefully, and they're certain she's conspiring with someone, so they're going to track absolutely everything, we're going to distrust everything she proposes, they'll never have any reason to suspect that I'm the person that's receiving it.

Reply: Indeed.

Richard Clayton: You can see exactly the same system being useful for phishing, whereby people put an unusual word onto a phishing website and wait for Google to index it, and then they send out URLs which are Google with directions, or "I'm feeling lucky", essentially, so that it goes to the top of the search. The point of doing that is that the Google URLs go straight through the spam filters because they're not seen as being wicked.

Reply: Very nice. OK, so what we should take home from this talk (and I think some of you already have been doing this) is that there is a fun new game to play now every time you look at a computer system or network. The game is to identify shared state in shared services, and find out how you can modulate the shared state in order to achieve covert communication. And if you want to get a bit more scientific about it, you have to do what Virgil suggests, and what is described in the light pink book, of actually finding out the capacities of these channels, and what the possibilities for false positives are, and so forth.

Now you should not be afraid of noise when you look for these shared services. Noise is your friend, noise means that other people are also modulating this channel, and therefore your interaction with the service is all the more plausible. And you should probably have a look at the contents of the paper to find out how to overcome this noise and still achieve some rate of communications over noisy channels, and I'm sure there are more advanced coding techniques to achieve that.

So in conclusion, combining anonymity and steganography is not as simple as just taking a steganographic system and an anonymity system, and plugging them together. They don't compose trivially, and from the point of view of the Protocols Workshop, I think this is the interesting observation. You actually need to have a different mindset in order to achieve both properties at the same time. In particular, you need to kind of abuse common services in order to use them as communication channels. The second point to remember is that traffic data retention cannot really eliminate covert communications between collaborating parties, so the idea that somehow traffic data retention is going to prevent wicked conspirators from organising their wicked conspiracy, is a fallacy. That's not going to happen. It might help us catch dumb criminals, or people who send abusive letters to victims, but that's as far as it's going to go. The third point is to explore further this relation between covertness and availability. It's a bit questionable in my mind how these two notions relate, do you need availability to achieve covertness, do you need covertness to achieve availability, no-one has looked at this in a principled way, and I haven't here.

What Next after Anonymity?

Ross Anderson and Steven J. Murdoch

University of Cambridge Computer Laboratory

Abstract

In recent years, interest has shifted from protecting the confidentiality of data to protecting the confidentiality of metadata. The police often learn more from traffic analysis than from content interception; thus anonymity becomes more important than confidentiality in the classical sense. Many researchers have been working with systems such as remailers and Tor in order to provide anonymity of various kinds against various threats.

In this note we argue that it's often not enough to protect the confidentiality of metadata; we may have to protect its authenticity, availability and other properties as well.

The call for papers talked about time travel. This immediately brought to mind struggles with backup and recovery systems. It's convenient if you can let users recover their own files, rather than having to call a sysadmin — but how do you protect information assets from a time traveller? One system familiar to us allows users to recover any file or directory in their filespace, which has the effect of overriding any revocation that may have taken place in the meantime. Worse, a recovery system may give the user access to directories that were always closed to him, by combining ACLs on pathnames. And what if the recovery functionality is buried in an application to which he needs access in order to do his job? This is an example of an example of technological development suddenly providing an extra dimension to the access control space of which sysadmins must be aware; but it may also be seen as system designers paying insufficient care to protecting the authenticity of file metadata.

Backups cause further problems. Suppose you're a human-rights activist in Russia. Two of the many problems you face, and which may become pressing when the police raid you and look at your computers, are that they will find out who you've been talking to — and that they will take your computers to stop you doing useful work. To protect against the second threat you need to keep backups. However, if the cops get hold of your backups, they can compare them with the current disk image, and see that unallocated random data have changed. TrueCrypt is much the same (though perhaps slightly better than StegFS as it's actually used by real businesses for 'normal' file encryption). In this case the metadata property we want to protect isn't authenticity or availability but deniability. A purist might argue about whether the content of the random "unallocated" data is really metadata, but the filesize certainly is.

These points have not been entirely unknown to previous writers. For example, the MLS pioneers in the 1980s remarked that although in theory it might seem

B. Christianson et al. (Eds.): Security Protocols 2008, LNCS 6615, pp. 220–222, 2011.

possible to build a minimal TCB for a multilevel secure system, in practice one ended up with a substantial part of the operating system having to be trusted once one considered things like backup and recovery in detail. Even further back in the history of security, an example of metadata manipulation might be a soldier putting on a false badge of rank to do something he shouldn't.

How does this affect protocols?

Given that the great majority of real-world crypto failures result from poor implementation rather than from weak crypto or (one hopes, after sixteen years of these workshops) protocol design, we suggest that protocol designers should start to think about how we can minimise the risks that result from tampering with key material. Papers on API security have shown how a protocol suite that contains several individual protocols, implemented on a single device, can be attacked by substituting unexpected keys into invocations of particular protocols. They have concluded that strong, consistent typing systems can go a long way to mitigating these risks.

Other attacks we ought to consider are where a dishonest principal uses time travel to swap new keys with old, and perhaps (where CBC is used) to swap parts of keys by swapping blocks.

It's already known that the classified world obsesses much more than the open one about the destruction of old keys; in December, at the Chaos Communication Congress, someone who'd reverse-engineered the Xbox 360 announced that Microsoft had invested serious money in hardware to ensure that the device could not be rolled back to an old version of the hypervisor. Propagating hard revocation is not as easy as it looks; even given a number of trusted devices with one-way counters, how can we ensure that revocations aren't rolled back, perhaps by some quorum of conspirators? Doing all this robustly may be an interesting research problem.

The second theme for the protocol research community may be how "normal" metadata are dealt with. Traditionally, protocol researchers ignored stuff like email headers: only the contents of the curly brackets mattered. But the world moves on. Remailers may scrub (or encrypt) headers, while Torbutton goes to great lengths to close down as many side channels as possible. DKIM - formerly Yahoo's domain key antispam system — signs email headers, in order to verify the ISP of origin. As a result, it's trusted by the Tor bridge autoresponder, which allocates bridge relay nodes to enquirers. If an opponent could spam this, he could exhaust the pool of relay nodes, or get Tor to spam Gmail or Yahoo, causing it to be blacklisted.

A third theme, and perhaps a more traditional one, is the difficulty of telling what's data and what's metadata. Suppose for example a boss sends an employee a PGP-signed message saying "You're fired!" The victim can simply forward this to someone else, as (by default at least) PGP authenticates only the sender, not the recipient. Of course a thoughtful boss can write "Dear Fred, You're fired!" but this is less than optimal as it breaks a level of abstraction. This is a much more common problem than one might think, as a name at one layer in the stack might be an address at the next, and so on. It's also hard to solve in the general case: PGP, for example, is usually applied somewhere short of the mail server. In theory, one might have a policy of always encrypting as well as signing, and there are indeed technical mechanisms one might use to prevent a recipient combining an old signature with a new encryption. But this is not entirely satisfactory because of the growing complexity.

To sum up: the metadata matter, and not just their confidentiality. It might be useful if we had some systematic thinking about this.

What Next After Anonymity?
(Transcript of Discussion)

Ross Anderson

University of Cambridge

We've been doing anonymity for seven or eight years now, and the call for this workshop asked about time travel. Here's the wide mouth frog protocol, which I discussed at this workshop fifteen years ago. The idea here is very simple, Alice says to Sam, I'm Alice, I want to speak with Bob, and here's my timestamp, and there should be a key in there, this is K_{AB} that Alice wants to send to Bob. Sam then says to Bob, Alice wants to talk to Bob, and here is the current time T_S, and here is the key K_{AB}. So Alice simply acts as a key translation service.

The vulnerability is that Sam updates the timestamp, so if you've got a Dolev-Yao opponent who controls Alice's link to Sam, and Bob's link to Sam, then this opponent can re-send to Sam these successive packets, and get the timestamp continually updated. This means that the timestamp can be kept live forever. An example of when that is a bad idea is that if the secret police have seen that Alice is trying to communicate with Bob, so they keep the key alive while they get round there in their truck and break Alice's door down or whatever, and get hold of the key. So that was an example of time travel from a Protocols Workshop fifteen years ago. What do we have more recently?

This particular one was pointed out by Martyn Johnson. At the Lab we use a NetApp filer, basically a log-structured filestore which does automatic backup very efficiently, and allows users to recover deleted files themselves. In the old days much of what of what the system administrator did was recovering files from backup for people who had typed rm* in the wrong directory, and so if you go to any directory and type list .snapshot, it shows you weekly backups taken of that particular directory. It's very convenient, it means that you almost never have to go to the system administrator with a request for backup, but the problem is that this enables you to travel back in time through access controls as well. The filer simply displays, and acts, on the access control list that was in the directory you're currently looking at, at the time you're looking back to. So you may never have had access to files in the directory /foo/bar, for example, but if there was access to foo a week ago, but not to bar, and access to bar a month ago, but not to foo, then by doing the necessary list .snapshot, go back a week, list .snapshot, go back three weeks, you can get access to material that you never ever had access to. This is an interesting new type of vulnerability I think; we didn't think about that kind of thing before. It's about metadata. This is people not thinking through the security properties of metadata, and how you can change these: in this case, by time travel; in the previous case, by using Sam as an oracle to update a timestamp in a message that otherwise remained the same.

B. Christianson et al. (Eds.): Security Protocols 2008, LNCS 6615, pp. 223–231, 2011.
© Springer-Verlag Berlin Heidelberg 2011

What are the wider implications? We've been talking about applications that aren't so much concerned about confidentiality of data, but of metadata. Anonymity systems are a good example. And the NetApp case suggests that the integrity of metadata may also over time become a growing problem, because as people move from passive attacks to active attacks, tweaking the context is often a way to break stuff. This is nothing enormously new. Think of reputation attacks. I spent the earlier part of this week in Istanbul at EuroCrypt, and reading history books of the city threw up that an awful lot of skulduggery went on both in Byzantine times and in Ottoman times. If you were the finance minister and you wanted the Grand Vizier executed so you could become the Grand Vizier, you would set out to blacken his good name with the Emperor or later with the Sultan, and the entire history of that city is tied up with attacks on people's metadata by conspirators at court, and in the harem too, because the women in the harem were trying to get all the other women's sons executed so that their sons would become the next Sultan. So there's historical precedent. How does it become more complex in information systems? Well, data at one level can be metadata at the second, and context at a third, and as systems evolve, the context becomes metadata, and the metadata becomes data, and of course the security engineer, the security architect is always running along ten years behind trying to keep up.

Here's another example. This is the Denning Sacco protocol. Alice says to Bob, here is a certificate, and then she signs a key and a timestamp under her key, and encrypts it under Bob's key. Famously the attack on that is that Bob, having decrypted Alice's message, then encrypts it under Charlie's key, and then can masquerade as Alice to Charlie. And one application after another makes this mistake. PGP, for example, by default authenticates the sender of the message but not the recipient. If you want to authenticate the intended recipient, then that is left up to something being put in the message content: in other words, it's application syntax. It's flexible, people upgrade it, they mess it up.

So the conclusion that we drew from all this, at Protocols '94 I think, is that when it comes to protocols, the robustness is provided by explicitness, you should put in everything that you can think of. Stuff fails because the protocol designer didn't put in Alice's name and Bob's name here, in the actual key packet, and I'll come back to that later. Another lesson we missed is that we have tended in this community to view time as a freshness bit. We have thought for many years about freshness in terms of: does this message come from the current protocol run, or does it come from a previous run of the protocol? And I think the first example I showed you should convince you that this isn't always appropriate. The wide mouth frog protocol basically failed because time can be incrementally updated, and unless you design Sam so that he won't let the same packet be continually refreshed, you can then parlay a perhaps ten second lifetime for a protocol into perhaps a one hour lifetime for the truck to get round and break Alice's door down. Another example that should illustrate this is the NetApp attack, which happens because time in real life is complex, NetApp shows you a dozen or 20 different default times to which you can travel back, and by combining data from these different times, it's possible to do bad things.

This leads us to ask whether time travel can be used to swap new keys for old, the Aladdin attack you might call this. This could apply not just to whole keys, but perhaps even to parts of keys. How do we go about this? Existing crypto APIs mostly have keys in large equivalence classes, as we've discussed at previous Security Protocols Workshops when we looked at API attacks. Your Visa security module, for example, has all PIN keys, and terminal master keys, in the equivalence class defined by encryption by two particular device master keys. So what can we do about this? We're given a limited amount of resource. For example, if trusted computing ever happens, TPMs have one-way counters, so the question then is, do you use these to try and design out certain kinds of time travel, or is that too complex? Some devices, like the XBox 360, go to some trouble. According to people who have reverse-engineered them, and reported this at the Chaos Computer Club Congress in December[1], Microsoft went to some trouble to ensure that people couldn't roll back the XBox 360 operating system to a previous version, because presumably the previous version is the one that has been rooted so that people can now go and buy lots and lots of XBoxes and use them to factor numbers or whatever. So there's a research challenge for the community here, can we come up with something better? Do we need a framework for managing secure time that does a little bit more than say just, this is from the current run of the protocol, or, this is from a stale run of the protocol. Is there some useful secure service here that might be offered?

Now it's not just the internal users who rely on metadata. Other people rely on the metadata. Sometimes these third parties are attackers, and at other times they are more neutral third parties. Another example that comes to mind is working on projects such as ONI and Tor, we've been worrying about what happens to human rights workers in places like Russia and Vietnam, where the local secret police are a bit stroppy. People in such countries are often using a bundle of tools such as TrueCrypt, Skype, Tor, and so on, to try and keep some of the contents of their laptops away from the boys in blue. Now crypto is fairly good nowadays, thanks in part, I hope, to the previous workshops here and elsewhere, so the police use things like shotgun mics, and root kits, and key loggers, and compulsory key disclosure (in the UK that's RIP, elsewhere it might be even more brutal). Incidentally, a curious thing happened since the last Protocols Workshop, I got phoned up by some chap who was desperate for advice because he had been served the first key production order under RIP, and this chap was none other than an animal rights terrorist, and you know, I'd been one of the people that these guys were going for two or three years ago when the University was thinking of building an animal house, and there was a week in which they spammed the Computer Lab, and tried to persuade all my colleagues that I was wicked person because I was torturing monkeys. So there's an interesting little bit of history. Compulsory key disclosure does

---

[1] Michael Steil and Felix Domke,
   see http://events.ccc.de/congress/2007/Fahrplan/events/2279.en.html

happen even in countries like Britain. And if you are a policeman, and you want to get an order for a key disclosure, you presumably need some lawful cause, because otherwise the lawyers will challenge it, and that lawful cause might be the scientist with unallocated random data in a file system. So if the policeman can show that you are actually running a hidden container in TrueCrypt, he can say gotcha.

Richard Claydon: I was going to point out that in fact the police were trying to get the keys for communications which had occurred before the Act came into force, because they were still stored on the disk after the Act came into force, so there's a time travel there.

Reply: Yes, that is interesting. The point that I was about to come to is backup versus deletion. Perhaps the animal liberation front were dumb in keeping their old data backed up, but the same kind of problem affects trade unionists in Vietnam, because there are two bad things can happen when the people's security police come round. The first is that they can take your computers away to stop you doing any useful work, because everybody nowadays needs computers, you can't live without computers, it doesn't matter whether you're a good guy or a bad guy. And the second bad thing is that the police can examine the computers they took to see if you've been doing particular types of work. And the dilemma here is that you need backups because of (1) and the backups place you at risk of (2). Is there a nice way of dealing with this dilemma? Well, to return to the main theme of this talk, it's about the metadata. The key metadata property here is deniability, as George Danezis was remarking in the previous talk.

In addition to opponents, such as secret policemen, using your metadata, and all the related questions about whether you can change it, whether they can change it, whether you can obscure it, and so forth (I've no doubt these questions will come up as the arms race here evolves), there's a question of relying on other people's mechanisms. Now we have all known for years in the protocols community that this is a bad thing, we've all heard of the chosen protocol attack[2], and yet these lessons are widely disregarded in real life. A very interesting example is an attack that occurred last year on Ubuntu, a charitable foundation in South Africa that spends Mark Shuttleworth's millions on worthy causes like child health. The South African banks were the first to introduce for online banking a two channel authentication scheme. How this basically works is that when you go to your browser and say, pay $100,000 to somebody or other, you get a text message which says, hi, this is Standard Bank, if you really want us to pay $100,000 to so and so, then please key in 4612 as the authentication code in your browser now. From many points of view, this is a really good way to do authentication, it's better than most types of two factor authentication, everybody's got a phone nowadays, and although it's possible for somebody close to you to do an attack, it's not possible for the average Russian phishing gang to simultaneously compromise PCs and mobile phones in a sufficiently correlated way for this to be a problem.

---

[2] See LNCS 1361, pp 91–104.

So how was this attacked? Well, somebody phoned up MTN, one of South Africa's big phone companies, and said, hello, I am the secretary of the Treasurer of the Ubuntu Foundation, Mrs So and So, who is far too important and busy to speak to you on the telephone. She has lost her mobile phone, will you please post her another SIM card. All right, said the helpful phone company, that's at 123 Acacia Avenue isn't it? No, they said, she's actually moved, it's 456 Another Street. So the phone company helpfully posted a new SIM to the attackers, and they went in and helped themselves to a bundle of Mark Shuttleworth's charitable money. This has led to a huge dispute between the phone company and Standard Bank about who's liable. Standard Bank has offered to pay half of it, *ex gratia*, to make the whole thing go away, but they declaim all liability. The phone company say, we're not in the business of banking, it's not our problem, different threat model, go away, and I expect that this one will run and run.

Here's another metadata example. DKIM, which is Yahoo's old domain key anti-spam system, is used to sign emails to verify an ISP of origin. A number of large email service providers use this, and the Tor bridge autoresponder trusts DKIM signatures when it's allocating bridge relay nodes, because at least then you know which ISP things came from. The problem here is that if a bad guy gets hold of several thousand email accounts, he could then spam the autoresponder, exhaust the pool, and undermine the anonymity that's given by this particular means of accessing hidden services. What one can do about this is not altogether clear. The council of perfection that everybody in this community has known for at least ten years, is that you should never use other people's security mechanisms, but in the real world that doesn't work. Infrastructure costs money, and one of the main reasons that the software world is so much more lively, and so much more innovative, than the world of steel or the world of potatoes, is that you can build software on to the other people's infrastructure. The Internet's already been built, hundreds of millions of people already have PCs, you've got a bright idea, you can write some code, you can ship it, and within a year a hundred million people can be using it, and you can have a company like YouTube, or whatever, that you sell for a zillion, that's the attraction. The downside is, people are necessarily in this world forever sharing infrastructure, and that means relying on other people's security mechanisms.

What are the system implications of this? Virgil Gligor was making some comments earlier on the early MLS systems, and back in those days people aimed at a minimal trusted computing base. And if you read the papers, and talk to the veterans from the early 1980s when this work was being done, people usually failed. By the time the developers had put in all the machinery to deal with all the real world things that a real system needs, like backup and recovery, the TCB ends up being a fair proportion of the operating system. I'm sure our guests from places like Microsoft have these scars all over their backs as well. So if you try to get all the metadata managed properly, and think through all the implications, you end up with a complex system that is so rigid, and so difficult to evolve, that your MLS system stays stubbornly several years behind the technology curve, and they remain a niche player.

Back in 94 when I wrote my thesis[3], it was around the theme that robustness is explicitness. I was at conference in Kyoto two years ago where Kitano, who's the director of the Computer Science Laboratories at Sony, and was the founder of systems biology, was explaining his thesis about bio-informatics, which is that robustness is evolvability. Living things, in order to survive in the long term, have got to be able to evolve, because environments change, predators improve, and so on. If you had a very simplistic organism in which one gene coded for one protein, and all proteins were necessary for life, then it would be toast, because any mutation would be fatal because all of a sudden there's a necessary protein which you don't have, and so the organisation isn't viable. And this insight has spawned this whole field of systems biology where people look at, for example, how organisms have got multiple copies of similar genes, so these act as a kind of evolutionary capacitor, that store up the ability to a change in the future[4].

Did I simply get it wrong by saying that robustness is about explicitness? Certainly now we're moving into a world of big, complex, socio-technical systems, things like Facebook, for example, where they're changing the system every week in response to pressure from users, and from advertisers, and where each change brings in new bugs, which results in further pressure, and the whole thing evolves constantly, just like a living organism. So we're moving towards a more biological type of world. How do we go about modelling this? How do we reconcile this with protocols? Again, the theme is that new stuff constantly seeps in, often first as implicit context, something that's not even in the prospectus of the system designers, it's just something that the users of the system share as a concept. Then it becomes metadata, and then finally it becomes a trusted state. How do you manage an evolving world in which unexpected stuff migrates in and becomes part of your trusted base?

I've been trying to think about this a bit, and in the second edition of Security Engineering, which was out two weeks ago[5], one of the arguments I make is that evolvable secure systems are about managing the evolution of APIs. It's more or less agreed that APIs are equal to architecture, and at previous Protocols Workshops[6] we've seen that APIs really are critical for security, because they are in a sense a generalisation of the concept of a protocol. So, the thesis I'm making here, and in the book, is that controlling the API is the security architect's job, and if this is right, then the question for the security engineering and research community is, what sort of tools should be forged for him.

In conclusion, metadata matter in all sorts of ways. It's not just the anonymity, and it's not just the covertness of metadata, it's their integrity, deniability, and other properties that we haven't really got a proper grip on yet. Now that we've

---

[3] Anderson, Ross John. Robust computer security. University of Cambridge: Ph.D. Dissertation.

[4] For an even earlier account based on information theory see Lila Lee Gatlin, Information Theory and the Living System, Columbia University Press, 1972.

[5] This shameless plug refers to Security Engineering: A Guide to Building Dependable Distributed Systems; 2nd Edition (Wiley, April 2008)., a must for every home.

[6] See LNCS 3364, pp 288–300 also LNCS 5087, pp 40–51 and LNCS 5964, pp 147–151 and 171–177.

started thinking about metadata in the context of anonymity, we have to expand that. And so this leads us to a couple of research challenges. First, we need better ways for protocols to cope. I discussed as an example earlier that we need better ways of coping with time, time isn't just the freshness bits, it can sometimes be a lot more subtle, sometimes it's incremental change with no backward change, other times it can have non-monotonic properties, as happened with net app. And there's another broad research challenge which is to understand evolvability better. Further large complex systems will evolve, how do we see to it that they evolve in a secure way? And my thesis is that this is about controlling the APIs.

Mark Lomas: H G Wells gave a beautiful example of how to get past a locked door, he said, all you need is a time machine, go back to before the door was put there, drag your time machine a few yards, and then go forward in time again. He wrote that more than a hundred years ago, but maybe he was at the back listening to your talk Ross.

Richard Clayton: Some of these ideas are really difficult because you can't patent them. When you go to the patent office with your mark 3, the patent officer will tell you there was a man in with mark 5 in a couple of hours earlier. A lot of real world protocols break because of time travel. One of the better art forgers over the last decade or so made some very good paintings, the trouble is that the art world depends heavily on provenance, so he managed to get into the bowels of the Victoria and Albert Museum where he managed to replace some catalogues on the shelves there, with ones which included his paintings. Then when he then presented them, and people said, oh, this doesn't look quite like this artist, he said, well it was bought about 1959, you might be able to find some proof of that, so they went off all by themselves to the Victoria and Albert Museum, and found the catalogue, and said, oh yes, it's in there, and gave him lots of money.

Reply: Well I suppose Mr Google may be helping to solve this problem by digitising all the catalogues, so you've got a window of maybe ten years or so to exploit time travel art frauds.

Robert Watson: Protocols in APIs have another time travel problem, which is that as you include your protocols in the API and change the API in response to vulnerabilities, you have to deal with all the implementations which still exist, so a frequent problem fixing security vulnerabilities in operating systems is that by changing the behaviour of the operating system but trying to keep compatibility of all applications, you may actually introduce vulnerabilities in applications that weren't there before.

Reply: Well indeed, this is the huge problem, and I think it's made an awful lot worse by the fact that in many development projects there isn't sufficiently vicious control of the API, in that somebody who wants a file read routine that uses four parameters rather than three just goes and writes one, and that becomes part of your vast legacy base.

Robert Watson: You can never rid of it once it's in there.

Reply: Exactly, so people should simply not be allowed to manufacture such stuff. If you think of the conflict theory work we were doing in the security economics context, we came to the conclusion there that if you have defence being the sum of efforts, that's best; defence being the efforts of an individual champion, that's second best; and if defence is the effort of the weakest link, that's worst of all. Now coding is the weakest link, so you should have as few programmers as possible, and as good as possible. Bug finding is the sum of efforts, so you should have many testers working in parallel. But the security architecture of the task is an issue of the champion, the knight who goes out in front of the host in order to do battle with the champion from the other side, so the security architect should be the highest paid guy in the company, and he should have absolutely dictatorial powers to stop some coding monkey introducing a new API. So that's how this fits with the security economics analysis.

Pekka Nikander: If we think about the boundary between the system and the environment, that is changing all the time. So essentially part of the environment is, in a way, regularly getting into and becoming part of the system, and that is what causes this pressure to the rest of system to evolve in order to cope with this. How to change the system boundary and still remain the desired properties of the system, even though part of the system has changed?

Bruce Christianson: There is a point that you introduced there, that a good way of protecting protocols is to include as much as possible of the shared context between parties. For example, hash it all and XOR it with the message to be sent, and that forces the other side to check that their shared context really does match yours: they think they're running the same protocol, so they should think they're getting the same message. If they can't decrypt the message then some of the context is wrong. The problem that you identify now is exactly that that shared context is often in a state of random change, and it's therefore not at all clear what should be included in that hash and what shouldn't. How do you get agreement between the two ends about what's in and out if you're talking to a legacy system?

Ross Anderson: Well this was a 1994 idea, you just hash everything in sight — grandmother's maiden name, size of kitchen sink, the works — and stick that in all your protocols, and with a little bit of luck that will keep you safe for a few years. We're beginning to realise now that that's not enough, and Kitano's point about evolvability is one that strikes more and more accord. In Microsoft, for example, they built a hundred million line operating system, which they can only do because they've got a sixty million line operating system to start off with. Other systems at the application level, your Facebooks, and MySpaces, and so on, are playing the same game. So can you come up with a neat way of extending this to legacy? Well of course there's a formal way of doing it, which is to say that you have got a grandmother's kitchen sink hash at the beginning of every protocol, and each version of the protocol has got a list of all the items that go in granny's kitchen sink, and then you have the basis of a manageable process whereby version n goes to n+1, part of the specification is new items for granny's kitchen sink, and around that you can perhaps build more or less formal mechanisms which will manage the upgrade cleanly. Commercial realities may stop this, but you could then say, application software that runs on version n will not be guaranteed to run on version n+2, or you could even say, application software that runs on version n will be guaranteed to never work on version n+2 or later.

George Danezis: Catastrophe theory applies to evolution, right, you need extinction events to leave room for a new species to form. To some extent it is a good thing that catastrophe events like the Y2K bug happen, so that all the legacy code was pulled out. Maybe we need more of those in software.

Robert Watson: Maybe we shouldn't be making things possible, because by doing that we extend their timeline.

Reply: Yes, death to the Neanderthals.

Virgil Gligor: They certainly tried, but look how many MVS operating systems we still have around.

Reply: I presume some still exist.

Pekka Nikander: Does this really mean that when we are designing protocols we should not make them truly crypto-agile, instead we should firmly fix the crypto they're in. We know that every crypto algorithm sooner or later will be broken, so if we don't make the protocols crypto agile, then we know the protocol is going be broken sooner or later, and that forces us to go for the next one.

Robert Watson: It's good for software builders too.

Reply: But then there are some aspects of systems that are owned, like Windows, and there are some aspects that aren't owned, like the Internet, or protocols such as TLS, and clearly different mechanisms are appropriate in each case. If you develop the idea of evolvability over time, you might find that different incentives call for different mechanisms. I'm just pointing out here that this is a bundle of issues that should be thought about together, and the particular way in which the protocols community needs to perhaps start thinking more in systems terms than in formal terms.

Remodelling the Attacker in Voting Protocols

Peter Y.A. Ryan

University of Luxembourg

Introduction

There have been significant advances in recent years in the development of high-assurance voting systems [1,2,3,4]. However, despite formal proofs of the technical core of such protocols, wider analysis continues to throw up a remarkable array of threats and attacks against voting systems, many non-technical [5,6]. To properly understand these threats we need to better understand the capabilities of attackers. Furthermore, we observe that in many of these attacks, the users (*i.e.* voting officials and even the voters) become extensions of the attacker's capabilities. Thus to fully model the attackers and the threat environment we need to include the behaviour of the voters, including their perception of the system's security.

In this paper, we outline a number of known attacks to illustrate this theme and will also explore the problem of determining the security requirements for voting systems. There is to date no consensus on this, even leaving aside the differences due to different jurisdictions *etc*. We argue that to a large extent, the security requirements are driven by the perceived threats. Thus, requirements and threat models go hand in hand.

Threats to Verifiable Elections

For the purposes of this paper we will concentrate on threats to the secrecy of the ballot. Such threats give rise to dangers of vote buying or coercion and illustrate our theme particularly clearly. Furthermore, we will concentrate on attacks that utilize capabilities or perceptions of the voters.

The Evolution of Secrecy Requirements and Threats for Voting Systems

Originally, ballot secrecy was not recognized as a requirement for voting systems and early elections were conducted *viva voce*. As the threats of vote buying and coercion were recognized as means to deflect voters from freely expressing their democratic intent, the requirement for ballot secrecy was recognized.

More recently, as people started to explore cryptographic voting protocols, it was recognized that the original notion of ballot secrecy needs to be strengthened to take account of the more active rôles of the attackers and of the voters. Now we observe the possibility that voters may have the capability to construct a proof of

B. Christianson et al. (Eds.): Security Protocols 2008, LNCS 6615, pp. 232–234, 2011.

the way they voted from secret information they may hold along with information generated in the course of the protocol. A number of early protocols, *e.g.* FOO [7], are vulnerable to the possibility that voters could open their encrypted ballots by handing over keys or randomization factors to the coercer. The recognition of such threats leads to the requirement of *receipt-freeness*: there should be no way for a voter to construct a proof that would be convincing to a third party of the way they voted. We can capture the notion of receipt-freeness formally in terms of opacity modelled in the trace model [8].

The notion of receipt-freeness is concerned with the possibility of the voter constructing a proof (*i.e.* receipt) for their vote after the execution of the voting protocol. It was later recognizing that a coercer may be proactive during the unfolding of a cryptographic voting protocol and this leads to further threats: a coercer may observe and influence steps of the protocol as they unfold. This leads us to the stronger notion of *coercion resistance*: a voting protocol is coercion resistant if, even where the coercer is able to observe certain steps of the protocol as they unfold and control the voter's actions, it is still not possible for the coercer to be sure as to how the vote was cast. This requirement can be formalised in terms of opacity in the testing equivalence model [8]. Note that coercion resistance is similar to the notion of resistance to adaptive chosen plaintext attacks, generally regarded as the acid test of a crypto primitive.

Psychological Attacks

Even if we assume that all the technical challenges described above have been addressed and suitable counter-measures identified, it is still possible that voter-verifiable schemes may be subject to forms of psychological attack. Such an attack might take the form of a coercer succeeding in persuading a significant part of the electorate that the secrecy of their vote is not in fact protected by the encryption in their receipt. Note that it is not necessary for the adversary to have a way to extract the vote, just the ability to persuade the voters that he does. In this sense, the perceptions of the voters become part of the threat model and impact the security of the scheme.

Countering such threats is difficult. A campaign of public information may help but is unlikely to eliminate all fears. Note that, unless the scheme provides unconditional privacy, voter's fears may have some substance: advances in computation and cryptanalysis (*e.g.* quantum computers) may lead to algorithms hitherto regarded as secure being broken in the future. Is the fear that your vote may be exposed 20 years hence enough to coerce a voter? Even if the scheme provides unconditional privacy, the voters still need to be convinced. The Farnel mechanism [9], in which voters get randomly selected receipts corresponding to voters cast by other voters, might help address this problem. Implementing the Farnel concept in a fully satisfactory fashion remains a challenge however.

Other styles of attack have been devised against voting systems, not necessarily cryptographic, such as chain voting, the so-called Italian attacks *etc.* that depend on some degree of acquiescence of the voters. These attacks would all be very difficult to identify without a suitable understanding of the rôle of the voters and their psychology. The challenge then is to find ways to model in a more systematic way the rôle of voters and their perceptions. In this talk I will explore these and other threats and discuss ways that we might model the entire system more effectively and achieve a higher degree of coverage of system vulnerabilities.

References

1. Chaum, D.: Secret-ballot receipts: True voter-verifiable elections. IEEE Security and Privacy 2, 38–47 (2004)
2. Neff, A.: Practical high certainty intent verification for encrypted votes (2004), http://www.votehere.net/documentation/vhti
3. Ryan, P.Y.A.: A variant of the Chaum voting scheme. Technical Report CS-TR-864, University of Newcastle (2004)
4. Chaum, D., Ryan, P.Y.A., Schneider, S.: A practical voter-verifiable election scheme. In: di Vimercati, S.d.C., Syverson, P.F., Gollmann, D. (eds.) ESORICS 2005. LNCS, vol. 3679, pp. 118–139. Springer, Heidelberg (2005)
5. Karlof, C., Sastry, N., Wagner, D.: Cryptographic Voting Protocols: A systems perspective. In: USENIX Security Symposium (2005)
6. Ryan, P.Y.A., Peacock, T.: Prêt à voter: a systems perspective. Technical Report CS-TR-929, University of Newcastle (2005)
7. Fujioka, A., Okamoto, T., Ohta, K.: A Practical Secret Voting Scheme for Large Scale Elections. In: Workshop on the Theory and Application of Cryptographic Techniques: Advances in Cryptology, pp. 244–251. ACM, New York (1992)
8. Bryans, J.W., Koutny, M., Mazaré, L., Ryan, P.Y.A.: Opacity generalised to transition systems. International Journal of Information Security 7(6), 421–435 (2008)
9. Araújo, R., Custódio, R.F., van de Graaf, J.: A verifiable voting protocol based on Farnel. In: IAVoSS Workshop On Trustworthy Elections, WOTE 2007 (June 2007)

Remodelling the Attacker in Voting Protocols
(Transcript of Discussion)

Peter Y.A. Ryan

University of Luxembourg

Frank Stajano: When you said that you wanted the voters to able to verify, they verify only the first step?

Reply: Well yes, in effect, the voters can only verify that their receipt appears accurately on the web bulletin board.

Frank Stajano: But they can't verify that it's really theirs can they?

Reply: Well all of these steps are done on the web bulletin board. We have various tellers who take this batch of receipts, they do re-encryptions or whatever on them, and post the intermediate steps on a web bulletin board. Those become committed to the web bulletin board, and then a phase of decryption is done, probably threshold decryption, so partial decryptions. But all of these are published and auditable in some way, for example, using partial random checking.

Frank Stajano: Can I tell at the end of the whole exercise that a particular secret was really mine?

Reply: No.

Frank Stajano: Or that it was someone who voted like me?

Reply: No, you can't trace your own vote down to here. For example, there's no way you can directly confirm that, yes, my vote for Kerry has appeared here.

Michael Roe: But can't you confirm that what comes out of the end is genuinely a permutation of what went in, as part of the protocol?

Reply: Precisely, that's exactly what I was trying to come to, yes. There are various universally verifiable checking audits that go on on the information that's posted on the web bulletin board, to check first of all that all of these shuffles are genuine permutations, so no plaintext has changed, and then that all the decryptions are performed correctly, with zero knowledge proofs or something. (I gather zero knowledge is not very well viewed in this part of the woods, but I actually think they're rather cool.) Those checks are done by auditors, but are universally visible and verifiable by anyone. In a sense this is all maths, this part of the process, and the cryptographic techniques for doing it, are well understood. The tricky bit is really how you get the votes encoded in a trustworthy way, I think that's the really delicate part with all these systems, and I'm not sure anybody's really achieved that in an entirely satisfactory way. Because of course it's crucial that voters are convinced that their vote is accurately encoded here, but now I'm getting slightly off-track from what I was planning to say.

So there are three parts to the argument. First of all you have to be convinced that your vote gets correctly encoded here, that it's correctly shuffled here, and that it's correctly decrypted here. And if you believe those three steps — and there are mechanisms to check that they're all done correctly — then you should

B. Christianson et al. (Eds.): Security Protocols 2008, LNCS 6615, pp. 235–240, 2011.
© Springer-Verlag Berlin Heidelberg 2011

be confident, as long as you check that your receipt goes into the tabulation, that it comes out here, but you can't directly trace it.

Ross Anderson: Would it be useful to slot the attacks into two types? The first is where you coerce or bribe the voter, and the second is where you cheat by monkeying with the mechanism. If you look at the Russian attack at the election that was coerced, civil servants were told, vote for Putin or you'll be fired, and so people were happy with the result. However, in Kenya and in Zimbabwe, the election was basically cheated and people were not happy with the result. So in real political terms, there's a big difference between the two: voters who are coerced, or bullied or bribed, will likely not go out into the streets and protest the results of the election afterwards, because they have been suborned by the process of bullying or corruption, whereas a purely technical attack does in fact risk the president being strung up from a lamppost. Very different in terms of their effect in the real world.

Reply: That might well be an interesting way to cut things up. Another issue, which I wasn't planning to talk about today is the taxonomy of these attacks, and we have thought about that, and there is a paper which takes a stab at that[1]. We can categorise them in the first instance as attacks against a particular security property, whether it's integrity or secrecy, and so on, but you can also break it down in other ways, and that's one way of slicing it.

The chain voting attack many of you already know. It more or less works with the UK system, for example. The coercer somehow gets a blank ballot form out of the polling station, marks it with the candidate he wants to push, and intercepts a voter who is entering the polling station, gives this marked ballot to the voter, and says, if you come out with a blank ballot you'll get ten pounds. And you can see that the processes of the UK voting system favour this kind of attack because you're given a ballot form, you go off privately, supposedly to mark it, then the polling clerk is supposed to make sure that you put it in a box before you leave, and so if the voter does emerge with a fresh blank ballot, that's a fairly strong indication to the coercer that he actually cast the marked one he was presented with.

Frank Stajano: With the chain voting attack, the coercer is able to get hold of a blank ballot. If someone else can do the same, they can just resell that to the coercer and pretend that they cast their vote the way the coercer wanted.

Reply: Yes, chain voting is not a flawless attack, but it kind of works with the current UK system. However it's a very virulent attack if you've got a voter verifiable system, because the coercer can note the crypto serial number if you like, and see that it gets posted to the web bulletin board, so he gets a direct confirmation that the voter really did cast the marked-up ballot.

Virgil Gligor: Alternatively the voter could be coerced to go in and not vote at all, and come out with a blank ballot paper.

Sandy Clark: But then there wouldn't be any receipt.

Virgil Gligor: There wouldn't be any receipt, but ... ah! so that's where the verifiability comes.

---

[1] Tjøstheim *et al.*, LNCS 5964, pp 114–132.

Reply: Yes, so voter verifiability, which in one sense seems to be a very desirable property, is actually extremely dangerous here. So that's one example. What I'm trying to do here I guess is give you some examples of attacks which have been identified, but not by any systematic way, as far as I am aware. And it's not clear to me how we would actually get to them in a systematic way, that's the message I'm getting to. The chain attack is perhaps not so difficult because in a sense it's clearly a chain of custody type of issue that information about what should be secret (in the case of a voter verifiable scheme), and only visible to the voter, has leaked out to the coercer. So perhaps that one is not so difficult to catch in a systematic way, but some of the others I think get increasingly difficult.

For example, the Italian attack is a somewhat surprising one, I'm not sure what sort of formal analyses it would drop out of automatically, and apparently it was really used, I think in Sicily. The idea is, you've got some kind of system where there's in fact a large number of possible ways you can mark a ballot, compared to the number of voters. For example, if you've got a single transferable vote so you can mark rankings against the candidates, and you've got a reasonable number of candidates, then clearly you can get a large number of possibilities. The coercer's trick is to say, well you must in effect identify your ballot by using some particular sort of distinctive pattern in the low rankings. (Of course for the high rankings, you put his candidates.) And again, this is particularly virulent in a voter verifiable scheme, because all this stuff gets posted so the coercer can check that the uniquely identified ballot appears with the correct candidate ranked top. So that's pretty nasty, and again, it's not very clear to me how you'd find this attack systematically. I suppose a systematic analysis of all the information that's legitimately available through the protocol might perhaps spot something like this eventually, but it's quite tricky it seems to me.

Michael Roe: You can try and do some information flow in observation schemes to discover there's an obvious leak in that the results leaked how somebody voted. The fact that their candidate got a non-zero number of votes and at least one person voted for them, isn't an information leak, but if you have leaking information out of an individual vote, then you see the bandwidth of this channel is much higher.

Ross Anderson: There's another analogy in the US, there was an anonymity scheme to make threats and promises, by encoding, for example, zip codes in the least significant digits of the ballot options. And the web-based election at Oxford, for example, was . . .

Reply: OK, there's a whole bunch. I guess they were on my list of subliminal channels, and cryptographic channels for encoding information in ways which will appear subliminally on publicly posted information.

Matt Blaze: It seems like this is just classically a subliminal channel.

Reply: Yes, I suppose perhaps it is. So arguably if you didn't know this in advance you might find it by an analysis of the information flow and stuff, yes, but it wasn't found that way historically.

Matt Blaze: It's interesting that I've never heard a requirement for a voting protocol of freedom from subliminal channel.

George Danezis: But isn't the transferable vote just an example of a paper based election system that is, effectively, broken. I mean, we being technical people say that moving voting schemes to computers introduces vulnerabilities, but in fact the single transferable vote system itself should have a very simple output, which is who wins. But in order to get that output you have to expose intermediate results, namely the permutation of the preferences of anonymous voters, which allows you to link them back to the votes. So it is basically a technical shortcoming of STV, that you cannot get results without leaking that intermediate information, in the same way as computer mediated voting sometimes has such shortcomings.

Reply: Right, yes. I guess in a conventional election all the processing stages of the STV would be done privately, and only the final result would be announced. But if you do this naively of course ...

Frank Stajano: Aren't there election monitors?

Reply: Well I guess there will be, but I suppose you can argue that the amount of information they can extract from observing is fairly limited.

Ross Anderson: But this is a case where the election monitor is a bad thing because each party can have a monitor who can do the attack.

Reply: Well there are dangers in monitors as well, yes, but if you do this kind of thing naively in a voter verifiable scheme with all the intermediate steps posted in an auditable way on a web bulletin board, then it's disastrous. Now there are countermeasures, that's one of the things I should have stressed, to all these attacks that I've been mentioning. For example, James Heather's got a nice notion of lazy decryption, where you just decrypt the highest rank at each stage of the STV process, you just reveal the top ranked candidate, which is all you need to do the next step, and so you can actually conceal a lot of the information which would be dangerous. But that's a whole talk in itself.

Frank Stajano: I didn't know this was called the Italian attack, they probably do it everywhere [laughter], but some details are different from what actually happened, it wasn't really single transferable, it was just a list of preferences. But anyway, the thing that may be significant in terms of modelling the attackers, it was not virulent with voters, it was that the Mafia had someone who volunteered to count votes, they had to drag people from the general public as those who run the election, and you always ensure you have one of yours there to do this dreadful job of being counter, and then they verified that someone had in fact done it.

Reply: Yes, in the conventional hand counted system, that's the way it's done.

Frank Stajano: You should not assume that the thing runs in a black box and you only see the official output, because you have an observer inside if you are doing that kind of scam.

Reply: I agree, that's the way it was done with a conventional system. The point I was trying to make is that if you transfer this into the context of voter verifiable systems naively then you run into big problems, because it's visible to everyone. And I think this is where we really get into tricky territory when we start talking about the psychological attacks, and where the coercer is actually exploiting, for example, the voters perception of the security of the system to try and coerce them. An instance of this might be, if you can persuade a significant number of the electorate that in fact the crypto doesn't conceal their vote, then, even if that's not technically true, if they're persuaded of it they will still probably be coerced, so that's turning the voters' psychology against the system. And of course if in some sense it's not unconditional privacy, which quite a lot of these schemes aren't — we give unconditional integrity guarantees, but maybe 20 years hence when RSA is broken, your vote will be revealed, so you're not getting unconditional privacy — then there may be some truth in this, and maybe that prospect is enough to coerce some people, and maybe this is where we need time machines again.

Another instance of this, there have been proposals to try and make remote voting, Internet voting, for example, coercion resistant, by using a notion of tokens. I think Juels, Jakobsson and Catalano came up with this originally[2]. The tokens are random-looking strings which have a valid token, in a precise sense, encrypted in them, so the system ultimately can tell if a token is valid. If you have been coerced you can just slightly corrupt your token, and use that to cast in the presence of the coercer, and then subsequently you recast using the valid token. Technically that's quite a nice idea, but clearly it needs quite a lot of understanding, and confidence, and belief in the minds of the voters for it to be genuinely coercion-resistant. Even if it's technically coercion resistant, if people don't believe it, it won't be actually coercion resistant, people will still be vulnerable. So these are interesting attacks, and this is I think where we're getting into very difficult territory in terms of trying to systematically model the adversary when the adversary starts to exploit these aspects of the voters' beliefs.

Michael Roe: In the same way the voters must believe in the voting system, you must believe that the published the result actually is the right result.

Reply: Quite, yes. That's why I tried to stress this notion of demonstrable accuracy, but of course, with a voter verifiable system, the underlying arguments that demonstrate the count was accurate are really quite difficult, and how many of the stakeholders and electorate would buy into those kind of arguments is not clear. But again, that's a whole other issue.

I guess I'm claiming that the adversary models in the voting system are particularly rich, and we need in some sense to enrich our ways of trying to model them. So, as I hope I've illustrated, in particularly the users may become an extension of the adversary capabilities, and in particular their perception of security may be exploited by the adversary to undermine the system. I haven't

---

[2] A. Juels, D. Catalano, and M. Jakobsson. Coercion-Resistant Electronic Elections. Cryptology ePrint Archive, Report 2002/165, 2002. A. Juels, D. Catalano, and M. Jakobsson. Coercion-resistant electronic elections. In WPES '05: Proceedings of the 2005 ACM workshop on Privacy in the electronic society, pages 61–70, New York, NY, USA, 2005. ACM. See also http://www.rsa.com/rsalabs/node.asp?id=2860

really gone into it, but typically these systems are vulnerable to various fairly complex patterns of collusion. There still is no consensus about what are the correct requirements, or correct models, for voting systems. I suspect we'll never come up with an entirely systematic method which will, identify all attacks, that's probably just impossible, but at least we can reach a point where we have a higher degree of assurance that we've caught most of the significant attacks. There are lots of nice formal analyses of the cryptographic core of these systems, and that's just great, but the system may still be widen open because of these kind of socio-technical attacks, so in line I guess with Ross' thing about why crypto systems fail, it's often not the crypto, it's the surrounding system.

Ross Anderson: Well there may be psychology and politics aspects of security as well. In the UK, for example, polls tend to understate Conservative support and overstate Labour support by several percent because it's considered to be unfashionable to admit that you're going to vote Tory. Therefore, following this train of thought, the Labour government will have less incentive to secure a ballot than a Conservative government, because if there is doubt about privacy of ballots, some people may vote Labour who would otherwise have voted Conservative.

Michael Roe: The party in power always got put in power by the current system, which may mean that they don't have incentives to change it.

Ross Anderson: It's not entirely clear.

Bruce Christianson: Until it looks as if that system is going to put another party in power.

Bridging the Gap between Vulnerabilities and Threats in Electronic Voting
Abstract

Matt Blaze and Sandy Clark

University of Pennsylvania

1 Introduction

Several recent studies[1] have reported substantial vulnerabilities throughout the designs and implementations of current commercially available optical scan and DRE electronic voting system used in the United States. Every system examined by the security research community (from four major vendors) was found to have software flaws and architectural failures that, under some circumstances, could allow an attacker to take control over precinct hardware, alter or fabricate recorded results, or install and virally propagate malicious software and firmware throughout the entire system. These systems suffer from basic cryptographic and key management errors, buffer overflows in modules that accept input from untrusted sources, easily circumvented access controls, backdoor debugging modes, and feature interaction and configuration vulnerabilities. In some cases, system-wide viruses can be introduced by a single individual voter or temporary precinct poll worker.

The high stakes of many elections in the US creates substantial incentives for sophisticated attackers, and so the current vulnerable systems appear to expose the integrity of elections (and public faith in them) to grave risk. That serious technical security problems are pervasive across the electronic voting landscape is now widely recognized, having been confirmed in virtually every independent examination of e-voting source code and hardware.

And yet, actual technical attacks against electronic voting systems have been, apparently, extremely rare, at least so far. This seems surprising. If software of similar quality were deployed in consumer, financial, or Internet products (e.g., in PC operating systems, bank audit systems, or web browsers), we would expect attackers to take control through viruses, malicious users, or the network soon after the systems became live. Of course, it is possible that successful e-voting attacks are indeed occurring but are simply never detected. But it seems

---

[1] Several academic teams and others examined the election procedures, equipment and source code used in Ohio http://www.sos.state.oh.us/SOS/elections/voterInformation/equipment/VotingSystemReviewFindings/EVERESTtestingReports.aspx and in California http://www.sos.ca.gov/elections/elections_vsr.htm, with the aim of identifying any problems that might render elections vulnerable to tampering under operational conditions.

B. Christianson et al. (Eds.): Security Protocols 2008, LNCS 6615, pp. 241–243, 2011.

implausible that, given the incentive (and propensity) for losing candidates to investigate irregularities, the occasional attempted attack would not be at least occasionally discovered if these systems were indeed being routinely targeted.

If the systems are insecure and yet attacks are not occurring, several possible conclusions come to mind. An optimistic one is that the security of these systems, even if imperfect, is adequate for the threat; if so, the security community is idealistically and unrealistically demanding in raising concerns about weaknesses that may be harder to exploit than we credit under the operational conditions. A more pessimistic conclusion is that, as in the early days of the Internet, the attackers have simply not caught up to the opportunity yet, but when they inevitably do, the landscape will irrevocably change, tipping the balance into chaos.

How do we determine which conclusion is correct? Unfortunately, while the security community has reasonably good tools for modelling an ideal attacker (who has full access to source code, can control every interface to which she has access, is as smart as we are, and plays every hand dealt according to an optimal strategy), we are less successful in characterizing how real attackers can be expected to behave, especially in newly-deployed systems. While an idealized attacker is a very useful model for conservatively analyzing software, protocols and cryptosystems, the threat of an army of perfectly performing adversaries is less convincing when held up as a reason not to deploy otherwise useful systems or to allocate budget to repairing security problems that have not yet been exploited.

2   Toward Convincing Attacker Models

In a previous paper, we advocated the study of various human scale security systems, such as non-electronic physical security mechanisms, financial transaction protocols, and so on. Such systems have several useful and inherently self-correcting properties not found in most modern software and communications security protocols.

First, human-scale are generally introduced over a gradually increasing user base, allowing security flaws to be discovered (by attackers or others) and implementations corrected or abandoned before an entire society depends on them. Second, they are generally much simpler than fully functional general purpose software systems, allowing users interested in protecting their best interests to make relatively informed decisions about their security and to customize their features according to their requirements and tolerance for risk.

Computerized electronic voting systems as deployed today, of course, have neither of these protective properties, but they do enjoy a few natural defenses that have more in common with physical systems than with general-purpose Internet computers. They are used only rarely a few times a year and so the attackers learning curves are inhibited by limited access, at least to live systems. The systems are not generally networked, although the back-end election management systems may provide a vector for attacks over the Internet in some cases. The systems in use in any jurisdiction may change between elections (although as the systems mature we might expect them to become more stable). And attacks must generally involve physical access to election hardware entailing exposure and the risk of being significant criminal liability.

We propose that, while it seems inevitable that attackers will eventually exploit these system, to potentially catas- trophic effect, these systems present a rare opportunity for a research program in the life cycle of the security arms race.

What are the economics of attacking and defending such systems? How long will it take before attacks start occurring? How will vendors, election officials, and the public respond after attacks are discovered? Will the next generation systems be more effective against attack? How can we model the attackers economic and technical decisions? Can we use such a model to predict how long we can get by with insecure software, protocols, and procedures in newly deployed systems? Does our experience with Internet security have and relevance here?

This talk will ask some of these questions, and lay out a the beginnings of a research agenda in the security arms race.

Bridging the Gap between Vulnerabilities and Threats in Electronic Voting (Transcript of Discussion)

Matt Blaze

University of Pennsylvania

First of all, I apologise for having a talk on the theme (remodelling the attacker), which I never do, but I'm making up for that by not actually having any answers, only some questions. This is joint work with Sandy Clark, who's here. As designers and implementers, we would probably agree in practice that in spite of our best efforts, it's easier to deploy insecure systems, and design insecure protocols, or build horribly insecure cryptosystem algorithms, than it is to build secure ones. That's what history seems to suggest, even if we think we're very smart, in practice what we deploy first tends to be really horrible in retrospect. But there is at least some lag between the time that we give attackers an opportunity to attack us, and the time that they realise that this is the case. We tend to deploy an insecure system and then add the security later. So one question that seems relevant to the practice of security is precisely how long this honeymoon period lasts, between the time we throw out a terribly insecure system, and the time we are going to be required by the attackers to fix it. How long do we get to get away with the insecurity, what does this curve look like.

I'm going to talk about this in the context of voting, and particularly electronic voting in the US, partly because for the last year I've been sucked into working in this area, and also because I think it provides an interesting laboratory for us. I'm going to be speaking about a very different kind of electronic voting from what Peter Ryan was talking about in that the systems that I'm going to talk about are just demonstrably, absolutely horrible. Even the worst of the problems that Peter was describing would be an improvement over what I'm going to be talking about right now. In the United States we have very high stakes for elections, and there's a lot of money spent attempting to influence the outcome of an election, in particular, the money spent to influence the election on conducting a campaign and advertising, greatly outstrips the amount of money spent in conducting the election itself. So we could quadruple the spending on conducting the polling, and it wouldn't make a dent in the overall economic cost of conducting an election in the United States. There may be political difficulties in doing that, but overall this is a very high stakes environment. Since 2000 the US has been rushing to deploy what, by any metric you could apply from the computer security world, are horribly insecure, hastily deployed, essentially first generation computerised voting systems, and in fact these have been mandated by law. These have been use now for at least one presidential election, and several national elections, and countless local elections, and it also appears to be the

B. Christianson et al. (Eds.): Security Protocols 2008, LNCS 6615, pp. 244–255, 2011.
© Springer-Verlag Berlin Heidelberg 2011

case that these systems are not being exploited by attackers in practice, which seems surprising in some sense.

Elections in the United States are a highly decentralised process. The Federal Government is not involved, except to set very broad standards. Each State has its own very specific rules, there are 50 States in the US. Within the States the elections are almost always operated by counties, there are three thousand counties throughout the US, that is to say, there are three thousand customers of voting machines and voting technology throughout the United States. Voting within each county tends to take place within local neighbourhood precincts, so each county may have a hundred, or more, polling places that are intended to be within walking distance of the voters. Elections in the United States are much more complex than in most countries, we don't have preferential voting in most places in the US, but we make up for that by having large numbers of races, it's not at all unusual for there to be fifty choices that a voter has to make in any given election. Even within a precinct there may be several different ballots that voters have to get, depending on where they precisely live, which party they're affiliated with, and so on, there may be differences in some of the races that they make decisions on. So we have this really strong incentive, because of the complexity, to mechanise this process, but there's enormous pressure in the United States, perhaps more so than in other places, to use some sort of information processing technology to calculate the results of this large number of races.

Those of you who are old enough to remember the 2000 election in the United States, may remember this famous photograph, a fellow looking at a punch card ballot in Florida, trying to determine what the intent of the voter was in this manual punch card system. This photo was emblematic of what was wrong with voting technology, this antiquated, non-computerised voting technology that the United States, a backward third world country with respectable democracy, was still relying on, and this is a horrible embarrassment that we could be reduced to having somebody examine ballots to find out what they mean. And there was a great controversy about what the outcome of the 2000 election was supposed to have been, and so this picture was regarded as a horrible weakness: we have to do away with the poor man with the glasses squinting to look at this ballot, and replace him with something more modern.

So the United States passed the Help America Vote Act after the 2000 election, it was passed with very broad bi-partisan support. The Act was basically a funded mandate that required that States, in order to receive the funding (of which there was a great deal), switch to disabled accessible voting technology. This was effectively interpreted to mean Direct Recording Electronic (DRE), or at least touch screen machines with the capability to have other interfaces added to them. The off-the-shelf technology that existed in 2000 were touch screen voting machines primarily of the direct recording variety, although that's not specifically required by the Help America Vote Act. So vendors filled the void to produce products that would comply with the Help America Vote Act, for which there were suddenly three thousand customers with a giant pile of money. These systems were hurriedly produced.

The kinds of technology that the Help America Vote Act allows, and that's used now in most of the US, include either direct recording electronic voting machines, or optical scan precinct counted ballots, with a ballot marking device available to the disabled for people who can't operate the pencil and paper interface. So there are still paper ballots available in some places, but they are precinct counted so it confirms that your ballot isn't spoiled before you leave the polling place, and there has to be a ballot-marking device available. There's also absentee voting by mail, by postal voting, which is in most places primarily for voters who aren't able to get to the precinct.

Now, we know that these electronic voting machines are really computers, we know that the security of computers depends partly on the security of software, and we know that we don't know how to deploy secure software, or design secure protocols in practice the first time around. I won't go into the potential vulnerabilities of these machines in any detail because Peter Ryan gave an excellent overview of some of the threats in these systems, but in particular you'll note that the voting machines are no longer independent entities. Because these voting machines are essentially producing an electronic output, even in a paper ballot system, the precincts have counting machines that then produce output that's taken to the county central office. The direct recording machines produce electronic output that goes to the county office. These systems are basically part of a big distributed system.

Ross Anderson: You're actually talking about a different family of attacks from Peter, he was talking about vote coercion, you're talking about vote stealing. As I remarked earlier, these are in practice quite different beasts.

Reply: They share some properties, and they have differences as well. In particular, one of the properties of a distributed system with a centralised back-end is that the compromise of the back-end is catastrophic, and in the case of a system that's communicating, it is possible that the compromise of one of the edges of the system can have consequences far beyond the output of that particular edge machine. So, for example, if I can do something to tamper with one of the precinct voting machines, I may not only affect my own vote, I may be able to affect all the votes in that precinct, and when it's counted I may be able to affect all of the votes in the county by exploiting some vulnerability in the interaction between the precinct machine and the back-end when it communicates in whatever way it communicates.

Now there are a number of safeguards that are intended to make sure that these machines are faithful, to make sure that the vendors can't put in hidden back-doors, to make sure that there aren't horribly insecure voting vulnerabilities. Among them, the most important is certification of the machines, you have to get a seal of approval thing that somebody has looked at your code, looked at your system, and confirmed that there are no vulnerabilities in it. You can imagine how well that works. Occasionally States asked for an independent review outside of the certification process, that's relatively new, it's almost always wildly opposed by the vendors and the county officials who have already bought the equipment. The concept of the voter verified paper audit trail, which is used in many places in the US, is different from the web bulletin board model. Here the electronic voting machine has a continuous paper tape in which you can see a printout of how the machine thinks you voted, and then that scrolls back and is stored in a secure place. In the event of a recount, the printout can be counted rather than the electronic record, and assuming that the voters check to see that the thing on the printout matched what their entry was, then this should reflect the will of the voter. In some places there are mandatory audit recounts.

Jan Martina: In this verified paper audit trail, do you know for the paper and the electronic vote which one is correct?

Reply: It varies by State. In some States the rule is that electronic record counts, in which case what's the point of the paper record, in other States the rule is the paper record counts, and other States don't have a rule.

Sandy Clark: The paper ballot is only countable (even when we look at it) if there's some sort of recount.

Reply: Right, or there's an audit. So in some States there is also a sampling of precincts in which you have to do this checking to see if there is a discrepancy, even if a discrepancy hasn't been raised. The numbers should match. There's also this concept of parallel testing, to prevent voting machines from acting one way when they're being tested, and acting a different way under live election conditions, in some States some of the machines are taken out of service on the election morning and run through a simulated election, and the output of those machines should be correct, that way the machines can't have code in them that triggers differently on election day than it would before election day.

Bruce Christianson: And that output is very carefully not put back.

Reply: And that output is carefully not included in the real election, yes.

Richard Clayton: And that leads to the really difficult question of how you're going to simulate an election just like the real one.

Reply: That's right, there's a difficult problem of making it indistinguishable, and again, this is intended to prevent the problem of malicious code from the vendor, or malicious code from somebody who has gotten hold of the machines in advance of election day, rather than bugs in the software.

OK, so in the Untied States there are four vendors that have risen to the challenge and performed a great public service by accepting the large amounts of money that the Congress allocated for producing these voting machines. A lot of people are worried about the security of these systems, to say the least. There have been many questions raised about their security. In particular the hardware and software is a trade secret, so anybody can't go and just look at the code and confirm how they operate, even an aggrieved candidate who wants a recount has no general recourse to examine the source code.

Sandy Clark: Why is that? I would have thought that the technology here with all of the building of proxies, making them robust, so they can be operated by real people who aren't experts and so forth... Why do they consider the software to be a trade secret?

Reply: Because they sell it. Basically Congress said, come up with some voting systems and we'll buy it, and the companies produced it, and made the code a trade secret, and that hasn't been challenged, so it seems unfortunate.

Peter Ryan: It seems strange that that's where the expertise is, or where the lack of expertise is?

Reply: Well, there's some sort of expertise, they've been successful, they're quite expert at selling them.

I did two independent evaluations, two of the largest comprehensive independent evaluations on voting technology. The State of California and the State of Ohio, which use between them all four of the different vendors systems, contracted with various academic computer security specialists, of which I was one in each study, to look at different voting machines, with access to the source code provided by the vendors, and access to the systems, to find out whether or not there were any problems. I'm going to talk specifically about one which is kind of a representative sample. Don't take that as singling out that particular vendor in any way, because all of the systems have similar problems of various sorts, this will just give you a flavour of what the current practice in voting is. I think you'll appreciate the insignificance of the vulnerabilities that Peter was talking about a little more when you see what some of these are.

The parameters of this project were the result of a very painful negotiation process intended to ensure our independence. The bottom line is that we ultimately came out with the ability to issue an unedited report that could not be seen by the vendors before publication. And we would pre-redact out anything that directly revealed a trade secret, that is, we didn't include any lines of source code in our published report, but the judgement as to whether or not we would report vulnerabilities rested exclusively with us, and that was essentially the sticking point. We only had ten weeks to go from delivery of the source code and equipment to production of the report, so this was a very hurried project. In theory this should be easy, right? In theory somewhere inside these voting machines is a line of code that says, `Vote[this_candidate]+=1`. Verifying that the voting machine works correctly should be not much more difficult than grepping for `+=1` throughout the code, and making sure that it is in fact there and executed when the button is pressed, and making sure that it isn't, for example, `+=2` or `-=1`, that should certainly raise a red flag. So this should be a simple process, in theory. In theory, theory and practice are the same, in practice they're different.

Mark Lomas: You're revealing intellectual property here?

Reply: No, because that line didn't actually appear in any of the systems. In practice of course, these carry with them all the problems, not merely of addition by 1, but the problems of managing any kind of complex distributed system. In particular the interaction between the machines that collect the votes, and the machines that count the votes, is as critical as ensuring that the machines will correctly maintain the internal tallies.

In fact many of the likely vulnerabilities in these machines can only be uncovered by looking at the flow of data, and at the interfaces between the voting machines and the back-end system. I won't go into attacks against voting, the bottom line is that we decided to focus only on particularly serious ones, that is, attacks that might have a catastrophic result rather than a local result: attacks that can affect the entire outcome of the election, rather than changing the votes by a little bit; attacks that might have the potential to virally propagate from one machine to another, or from a machine to the back-end; attacks that compromise both the primary data and the audit data; and attacks in particular that are practical for a voter or a poll worker to actually carry out under operational conditions. So we ignored large numbers of attacks that would be interesting in an academic context — we didn't even search for attacks that we'd be able to publish at a conference — in favour of attacks that might be simpler but would be a real threat in practice, that we thought we could actually carry out as relatively unprivileged people, either voters or as poll workers, which is a pretty easy job to get in the United States, because of course there are thousands of them.

Nobody had looked at the entire system including its back-end before, so that was a nice opportunity. So what did we do? The first observation is that we had 700,000 lines of code to look at, more than six languages, and the system was not designed for analysis, this is not a system that was defined with code verification being one of its primary objectives. So basically standard high assurance software methodology would say, this system cannot be analysed, therefore it should be assumed not to be secure, but that would be unsatisfying. So instead we looked at this from the perspective of the attacker, we said, alright, we've been presented with one of these things, I want to be president, how do I do it? So we split the modules up, looked at things where we thought there might be vulnerabilities, and tried to find them.

Sandy Clark: We threw darts.

Reply: We basically threw darts. We had to, because of the proprietary nature of this, we had to do everything in a secure room, we couldn't use our own computers, and login from home, we had laptops with the source code on which we locked in a safe at the end of the night.

So what did we find? These results mirror the results that the people who looked at the other systems found. We found that virtually every component of the system was vulnerable to practical attacks that you could carry out under operational conditions based on the procedures that they have. We found it was possible to alter the results from a precinct if you could touch any of the hardware at a precinct. You could alter the software, the firmware running in that equipment if you could touch the equipment, and of course a voter touches the equipment. You could erase or tamper with the audit records. You could use altered precinct data to attack the back-end system: if you can get hold of the media that's sent back at the end of the election day, then you can use that to exploit vulnerabilities in the back-end system and load arbitrary code on the counting machine for the entire county. And that these attacks could virally propagate to the entire system, even across platforms, between elections. We only looked at things that could be done by an individual, a poll worker or a voter. None of the vulnerabilities we found had any easy procedural fixes, you'd have to actually fix the software in order to prevent some of these things, unless you add a requirement that the voter is not allowed to interact with the voting equipment.

The back-end system has exploitable buffer overflows in every single module that accepts input from precincts. So a single compromised result from a single machine, can load arbitrary code on the back-end and run it, and of course that back-end system is used to tally the entire county's results, and also to provision the machines in the next election.

It's worth pointing out that these vulnerabilities were equally present in the optical scan and the paper ballot system, and in the DRE system. DREs have this reputation of being inherently more insecure, but we found that both were implemented so badly. A simple attack was that a little combination of button pushes allows you to put the machine into touch screen re-calibration mode. If you do that in a particular clever way you can deny access to particular parts of real estate on the screen and prevent ballots for certain candidates from being cast. This is interesting because it was very simple, it arose directly from the user interface, and it matches behaviour that voters had actually complained about with this hardware. So it's possible that this attack was being carried out, and we were not the first to discover it. It's possible to disable the logging of records, or to add new records to the voter verified paper audit trail because of the RS232 connector: the printer is on top of the machine and not actually even protected by any screws, so you can just unplug it, plug your palm pilot in and add paper audit trail records to your heart's content. This is also the stable storage audit record for things like, "the screen has been put into re-calibration mode", but if you just unplug the printer it never gets logged. We found that it was possible to emulate the supervisor device (called a Personal Electronic Ballot, PEB) with a palm pilot and a magnet, and we built an emulator for it, and that worked very quickly. And we were able to figure out the protocols to do this simply by analysing the infrared protocol, we didn't actually need the source code to figure out how to do that. That was just representative. We were able to exploit every component of the system, and the people who looked at the other systems were able to exploit every component of theirs. And we used the standard of, only report the things that can be exploited in practice.

We published our report. Voting is one of those areas where lots of people are unhappy with the outcome of the previous election, and would love to be able to claim that it was the fault of the equipment, so it acts as a kind of kook magnet for people who want to use your result as evidence that the machines actually were attacked. But of course we don't know whether they were attacked. The official response from the vendors, and also a lot of the county officials who bought the equipment, was first of all that these systems are certified secure, therefore these guys must obviously be wrong. They point out there's never been a proven attack against these systems. The reviewers, they claim, are biased against electronic voting. The academics, they claim, have unrealistic expectations. And our methodology was invalid because we had access to the equipment that we were testing, and an attacker would never have that, and we had source code, which an attacker would never ever be able to get.

Some of the vulnerabilities that we discovered were in fact quite technical, and in fact source code was helpful in locating them in our ten-week project. Apart from buffer overflows, we found some undocumented back-doors that allowed password bypasses that we wouldn't have noticed had we not looked at the code. But there were other vulnerabilities that we were able to find by just looking at the external behaviour of the interfaces, things like the protocol analysis that we did to emulate the personal electronic ballot. Still others like the re-calibration attack were apparent from the manual, or the normal functioning of the machine, and actually in some cases could be triggered at random. So the argument that this was unrealistic as to what the attacker might do, is probably not a very sound argument. But it's hard to argue with the ultimate point that they have, which is that if these machines are so insecure, why aren't they being exploited? Does this mean that we should consider them secure in spite of their vulnerabilities, that the proof is in the past performance?

So I want to talk about the arms race here. We focus as a community on learning about the steady state of the security arms race. There are people who are interested in the question of how do machines get patched, how often do attackers re-attack old vulnerabilities, the effects of viruses and so on, how much impact do countermeasures have. But we know a lot less about what happens before day zero, before the first attack is launched. When will a vulnerability first be exploited by actual malicious attackers? There's very little known about this. Computerised voting appears to be an ideal laboratory for this, these systems have been deployed, they are weak, and they are not being exploited. Perhaps we can learn a broader lesson from this by looking at what happens next and figuring out how it came about. It seems like there are lots of vulnerabilities just waiting for an attacker. So our usual question, the one that we're trained to ask in this community is, how secure is this system? To the extent that we can answer that question, we do it by looking at the intrinsic properties of the system itself. Because this is the question we almost know how to answer, it's the question we usually ask. And our usual conclusion is that the system is insecure, the sky is not only falling, it has already fallen, the only question is how long it will continue to fall. And when we say this about systems that have not been demonstrably attacked, we often sound quite shrill, and that leaves us vulnerable to the charge that we have unrealistic expectations.

A perhaps more interesting, or at least different question is, how long will it be before we would expect this system to be attacked, what's the expected time to day zero? That asks us to model not only intrinsic security, but also something about the motivation of the threat — and the behaviour and capabilities of the threat — not just to carry out attacks, but to discover them in the first place. This question is much harder to answer, but it's the one that people want answered in practice when they have a deployed system and want to know whether to spend money to secure it or to replace it.

So far intrinsic security seems to be a poor predictor. Obviously a system that is truly secure won't be attacked, but no such systems exist, and we don't know how to build such systems reliably. We really only know how to attack old ones. Let me point out that buffer overflows in Internet-facing software existed long before Robert Morris exploited them. And then for some time this was considered a weird anomaly that we didn't really have to worry about as long as we tell Robert Morris to stop doing this. At some point a few years later these attacks just exploded and having Internet facing service with a buffer overflow that can be exploited remotely became something that you could no longer get away with for even an instant. So when should we start worrying about the security of a system? Maybe there are some seismic indicators that we are about to targeted, and therefore have to start applying scrutiny. If so it would be useful to know what they were. It's unfortunate that we don't really have much more than folklore to go on here. The risk analysis community tries very hard to ask this question, and thus far we have relatively little to contribute even though we have the expertise about the intrinsic security of these systems. We have to think a lot like attackers when we analyse them, yet somehow we don't really know how to model actual attackers very well.

Peter Ryan: One underlying issue with voting systems is they can fail in a non manifest way, there's no God-like view of what the correct answer should be.

Reply: That's right, there is certainly a possibility that these insecure systems are being exploited. It's a possibility we should recognise, but it doesn't seem the most likely one because there don't even seem to be failed attacks. One would imagine that if there are successful attackers then there would be some slightly dumber than the successful people getting caught trying to do them, and that's actually not happened in the United States.

One reason we might not have much to contribute is that this may be dominated by non technical aspects, the economic, the social, the political aspects of the motivation for the attacker to attack it, which we can't really model by analysing protocols, we have to know something about the application.

Ross Anderson: I'm not sure that I agree with that. Look at attacks that have been industrialised, phone breaking in the 70s, duplication of ATM cards in the early 90s, and since 2004 the great explosion of the Russian Mafia exploits into online banking, phishing, spam, and so on. In each case there was an industrialisation path for the efforts of a small number of techies who actually construct buffer overflow attacks, or whatever they are. If you're the guy writing buffer overflows in St Petersburg, you're probably selling your codes to the phisher man.

Reply: Right, but that only became possible after this economy got created.

Ross Anderson: Yes, but what on earth is the economy here? If, for example, the Republicans want to steal the presidential election in three months time, that would involve a conspiracy at national level, and expose too many seriously powerful and wealthy people to the prospect of a series of nasty jail sentences.

Reply: Well the thing is, there are lots of people who want to influence the outcome of the election who aren't in fact connected in any way to the candidates.

Ross Anderson: Let's assume that we can go to someone on your team and persuade her for X amount of money to tell us about all these buffer overflows. I then have the organisational task of getting that to, lets say for the sake of argument, 5000 precincts. In the case of these voting machines you can't do it over the Internet, you need some legwork, but relatively little, you need one per county.

Virgil Gligor: Maybe the answer to the question, why haven't you seen this, is because these attacks so far have not scaled. You can launch an attack here, and an attack there, but ultimately you cannot really influence all that much.

Reply: But if you're clever about where you launch the attacks you can have a great deal of influence.

Pekka Nikander: I guess we may learn from motivational models, so maybe the motivation is not to attack the election for a fee, but just destroy the image of fair election, so that nobody trusts the elections anymore.

Reply: Yes, it seems it would be a mistake to underestimate the sophistication of the potential attackers here. But national governments often want to monkey with the elections of other national governments, so modelling the attacker as having the resources of a large government is not unusual here. And, you know, we have the resources of a University.

Richard Claydon: If you're looking an early stage here, so there isn't a market yet, rather than saying, hey, I can sell this to somebody, your average Russian attacker would listen to your talk, and think, hey cool, I could put up a Russian flag on the voting screen for everybody in America.

Reply: Yes, and we haven't yet seen this. Right.

Robert Watson: You need a demo before you can make a sale.

Reply: That's right, well I've got the demo. It's worth noting that no-one has approached us to licence our technology.

Pekka Nikander: You're making the report public, they don't need a licence.

Reply: Well we didn't include the code for the attacks, so we could save you some engineering work for the right price, but nobody has asked.

Steven Murdoch: One difference between these overflows on an Internet connected machine, and exploiting the voting machine, is that the cost of being caught is very large, as we discussed previously. If you get caught stealing an election, then you're probably going to jail.

Reply: That's right, but there's a long history of people being willing to do that, they're not carrying out technically sophisticated attacks historically, but people are willing to go to polling places and commit crimes. In the old ballot stuffing days that was institutionalised, yet we're not seeing it here.

I want to leave with two questions. Why aren't these voting systems being attacked left and right, or are they? And when will this honeymoon be over, and can we use this to learn something about systems that aren't eVoting systems by watching?

George Danezis: I have a complaint that is in the same line, which is that attackers have really let me and my research down. A lot of systems we actually see are vulnerable to trivial attacks, and then when we say, well you know, there are these additional vulnerabilities, and these additional doomsday scenarios, people turn around and say, no-one's going to do those. Basically we need to start understanding better a discipline of attacking, it's not just a negative discipline, because as you said, many governments are now starting to develop this kind of attitude, to do offensive operations against other governments. But we see this strand of know-how being developed behind closed doors, therefore it cannot actually feed back into perfecting systems.

Reply: That's right, one of the advantages we have on the Internet is this very high temperature environment for allowing evolution to take place, this is a much lower temperature world.

Ross Anderson: That leads to another thing that struck me, which is that every election is a one-off. The staff who run the election are not the staff who ran an election before, the volunteers are different volunteers, and so everything is virgin territory, there is no learning process. This is what makes software engineering terribly difficult. This also makes attacks difficult, because unlike in the Internet, you can't attack on Monday, observe the results and attack again on Tuesday, you must wait to attack every two or three years. Are they trying to export these voting machines to other countries? I think a live work environment would increase the temperature.

Reply: Yes, it's worth pointing out that we focused on the machines that are available in the US, all of those companies have aspirations of various degrees.

As a target of information warfare, or information operations, or whatever the current spook buzzword for this is, undermining confidence in an election by demonstrably affecting electronic voting seems like a very profitable target, and I think it will be very interesting to see how this plays out.

Pekka Nikander: What happens in the United States if I manage to launch such an attack, just in such a way that in a couple of counties it becomes clear that the results have been tampered with, and that it might have happened elsewhere?

Reply: It's unclear. Nothing like this has ever really been resolved, except that in the United States, and in most other democracies, a high value is placed on having a deterministic outcome to elections. As we saw in 2000, when there really was a question about who the winner was, there was enormous value placed on coming up with an answer even if it wasn't the pedantically correct, or most accurate, or most satisfying answer, there was kind of a deadline by which a decision has to be made. And if, by the time that deadline has occurred, some of the populace thinks that one candidate won, and other parts of the populace recognise the other winner, that's almost the definition of a political crisis.

Sandy Clark: There's actually been two cases recently, one in 2006 in Florida where the votes didn't match the accepted polls at all, and so a group analysed the electronics specifically to see if it was possible that in that particular election there had been fraud. Their conclusion was that they couldn't find any, but by then whoever had convinced the machines had won. The second case is more recent, it was in 2004 in Ohio, that was the election that actually determined who would be President, and once again, in spite of the fact that everybody was sure there had to be something wrong with the machines, whether it was malicious or accidental, the machines were still trusted, and the results were whatever they had.

Mark Lomas: One of the problems here is that even if you distrust the outcome, the outcome is a possible one. In order to do a proper demonstration you want an impossible one, such as nobody voted Democrat in the entire county.

Reply: A lot of the most powerful attacks are ones that don't actually alter the outcome, but that reduce confidence. If I wanted to disrupt elections using these machines, I probably wouldn't get myself elected governor, I'd probably put up an ad after you've voted: thank you for voting, this election is sponsored by Buzz Cola, or something like that.

Bruce Christianson: Maybe that attack has already been done, and no-one has noticed.

Are You There, Moriarty?
A Victorian Parlour Game

Holmes and Moriarty are holding hands in a darkened room. Both are breathing heavily.

Holmes: Are you there, Moriarty?

Moriarty: Why yes, Holmes, I am actually.

Holmes lashes out at Moriarty's head with the rolled-up newspaper which he is holding in his other hand. Moriarty ducks and Holmes misses.

Moriarty: Are *you* there, Holmes?

Holmes: Yes indeed, Moriarty.

Moriarty strikes with his own newspaper at the point where he believes Holmes' head will be after Holmes dodges. But Holmes remains perfectly still and Moriarty strikes only the air.

Moriarty: Bother.

Holmes biffs Moriarty smartly on the head with his newspaper.

Moriarty: I say Holmes, you're supposed to ask first.

Holmes (a trifle quickly): Sorry old chap, I forgot the protocol.

Moriarty makes no mistake this time.

Holmes: That's a bit thick, the protocol applies to you too you know.

Moriarty says nothing, but hits Holmes over the head again, rather harder this time. Holmes grips his own newspaper like a cavalry sabre and thrusts the tip firmly into Moriarty's solar plexus.

Moriarty, winded, retaliates by lifting his newspaper abruptly between Holmes' legs.

Suddenly a door opens and the room is flooded with light. Holmes and Moriarty, blinking, straighten up slowly, still holding hands. We see that they are in evening dress, although by now looking considerably the worse for wear. Enter Watson.

Watson: Ah, wondered where you two were. We're just about to re-join the ladies.

Holmes: After you, Moriarty. Age before beauty.

Moriarty (over his shoulder): Pearls before swine, Holmes.

(exeunt)

B. Christianson et al. (Eds.): Security Protocols 2008, LNCS 6615, p. 256, 2011.
© Springer-Verlag Berlin Heidelberg 2011

Author Index